Sticky Situations 2

BETSY SCHMITT

Tyndale House Publishers, Inc.

CAROL STREAM, ILLINOIS

Visit Tyndale's website for kids at www.tyndale.com/kids.

TYNDALE is a registered trademark of Tyndale House Publishers, Inc.

The Tyndale Kids logo is a trademark of Tyndale House Publishers, Inc.

Sticky Situations 2

Designed by Melinda Schumacher

Edited by Betty Free

For manufacturing information regarding this product, please call 1-800-323-9400.

Library of Congress Cataloging-in-Publication Data

Schmitt, Betsy.
  Sticky situations 2 / Betsy Schmitt.
    p. cm.
  Includes indexes.
  ISBN 978-0-8423-4232-2 (sc)
  1. Family—Prayer-books and devotions—English. 2. Children—Prayer books and devotions—English.
3. Christian education—Home training. 4. Christian education of children.   I. TItle: Sticky situations two.
II. Title.
BV255.S34 2001
249—dc21   2001027221

Printed in the United States of America

17   16   15   14   13   12   11
15   14   13   12   11   10   9

Contents

Dear Parents,

The *Sticky Situations 2* devotional offers your family a year's worth of situations to explore and discuss together, using circumstances that elementary-aged children encounter daily in the classroom, at home, on the playground, and in church. Through these situations, you and your children will be able to discuss the different choices they might make. You'll want to talk about ways in which God's Word can guide them to make the right choice.

To make it easier for younger children to grasp Bible teachings on a particular subject, each month is devoted to a general topic. For example, January is "Love & Kindness," while February is "Treasures in Heaven." Each monthly topic is presented with a brief introduction that touches on key lessons to be learned throughout the month. A memory verse for the month also is included to help underscore the teachings on that topic. Following each daily scenario and the list of choices are discussion questions to help your family expand on the teaching.

You may use this devotional in a variety of ways. You can read the situation and have your child come up with his or her solution before reading the different choices. Or, after reading the situation, go right to the Bible verse and ask your child how that verse can help in making the right choice.

Talk about the situations with your children. If they have experienced a similar situation, ask how they handled it. What choice did each child make? Did it agree with what the Bible said? Discuss the choices. Some of the choices are obviously humorous, but others may require more thought. Ask why one choice is better than another. Work through the different choices and the consequences of each choice.

Above all, pray with your child following each discussion. Maybe a situation has hit close to home. Pray together for guidance and strength to handle the situation in God's way. Or maybe a situation flags a potential problem area for your child, and you can pray for protection from that problem.

The more you are able to personalize the devotions for your child, the more effective they will be. God bless you and your family as you use each day's material as a springboard for discussing your own sticky situations.

Betsy Schmitt

Love & Kindness

You hear it said all the time. "I just *love* pizza." "You're going to *love* the new video game." "I *love* you, you *love* me." *Love* is a word we say all the time. But what do we really mean when we say the word? Is it what God means when he talks about love?

The Bible has a lot to say about love. In John 13:34 Jesus gave specific directions about it. He told his followers, "Now I am giving you a new commandment: Love each other. Just as I have loved you, you should love each other." The idea of loving others was not a new one. But to love others like Jesus loved them—now that was a very special kind of love!

Jesus' love is not based on warm feelings. It's not being nice only to people who are nice to us. It's loving the person who is hard to love, who isn't so nice to us, or who has hurt us. It's loving someone when you don't feel like it. Jesus' kind of love is an attitude that leads to action! Remember—Jesus loved us so much that he died for us. He couldn't have loved us any more than that.

So how can we love like Jesus loves? As you work through the *Sticky Situations* on Love & Kindness this month, look for ways the Bible says we can love others. Think about how you can show others Jesus' kind of love through your attitudes and actions.

Memory Verse: Now I am giving you a new commandment: Love each other. Just as I have loved you, you should love each other. John 13:34

Tough Love

It's time for Peter's birthday party. After a long discussion, he and his mom decide to go cosmic bowling this year. Peter goes through his list of classmates and puts a star by everyone's name he wants to invite to his party. His mom looks over his list and asks Peter, "Why aren't you inviting Tom this year? He's been to all your other parties." Actually, Peter and Tom had been friends since preschool. But Tom never sits with him at lunch anymore. He doesn't wait to walk home with Peter after school. And last week Tom called Peter "Bunny Boy" because he brought carrots for snack time. Everyone at the lunch table laughed, and Peter felt awful. Peter isn't sure Tom *really* is his friend. What should Peter do?

Should Peter . . .

A. Send Tom an invitation using invisible ink? The words won't show up, so he won't know who it's from.
B. Talk to Tom about what's happened to their friendship? Tell Tom he would like to invite him to the party?
C. Forget Tom—cross him off the list?

 For help in knowing what Peter should do, read Luke 6:27. It's hard to be nice to someone who has not been nice to you. Is there a person who has been unkind to you lately? Think of two things you can do for that person this week to show Jesus' love.

The correct answer is B.

All in the Family

Leslie and her younger sister are invited to Amanda's house after lunch. Amanda moved into the neighborhood last fall. She and Leslie have become good friends. Leslie really likes Amanda. She's funny and always has something cool planned to do. Leslie hurries her sister through lunch. She can't wait to find out what Amanda has going on today—Amanda mentioned a "really cool surprise"! When Leslie and her sister arrive, Amanda announces, "Guess what I made down in the basement? An obstacle course! It's totally awesome—you're going to love it." Leslie hesitates a moment. She knows her sister is afraid of the dark and hates to go down into a basement. But Leslie *really* wants to see Amanda's obstacle course. What should she do with her sister?

Should Leslie . . .

A. Tell her little sister to get lost and find something else to do?
B. Ask Amanda if they could save the obstacle course for another day and do something else today?
C. Tell Amanda that her sister is a scaredy cat and won't go down into the basement with them?

 Read Romans 12:10 to discover what Leslie should do. We're all afraid of *something!* Think of two ways you can be kind to someone who is afraid.

The correct answer is B.

If You Really Loved Me . . .

Natalie *really* wants to go to a sleepover this weekend with her best friend, Tessa. The two planned all week what they were going to do—make some cool crafts they saw in a magazine, eat ice cream, and watch videos. There is only one tiny problem. Natalie's mom said she had to clean her room or she couldn't go. When Natalie gets home from school on Friday, she watches a bit of TV, plays with the dog, and has a snack. By the time Natalie is supposed to leave for Tessa's house, there just isn't time to clean her room. When her mom sees Natalie has not cleaned her room, her mom announces in a calm but firm voice, "Sorry, Natalie, but you can't go to Tessa's house this weekend. You didn't keep your end of the bargain." What do you think Natalie should do?

Should Natalie . . .

- A. Burst into tears and run from the room screaming, "You don't love me"?
- B. Run upstairs, throw everything that's on the floor into the closet, and announce, "It's clean now"?
- C. Accept her mom's decision and tell Tessa she can't come because she didn't clean her room?

 To see what Natalie should do, read Proverbs 13:24. Ask your mom or dad to explain how discipline is really an act of love. Describe a time when you know that your parents disciplined you because they loved you.

The correct answer is C.

The Worst Artist in School

Yesterday Patrick's teacher told the class that each student should work on a map with a partner. Patrick wants his best friend, Tim, to be his partner. Tim is a great artist. Patrick is good at finding facts. Together they'll make a great team! When Patrick gets to school, though, his teacher announces that instead of letting them *choose* partners, she is *assigning* partners. And Patrick is assigned to work with Justin—the worst artist in the class. Justin's art projects are always a mess. He can't even draw a straight line! How is he going to draw a map with lots of squiggly lines? Patrick doesn't want to work with Justin! He is doomed to fail! What should Patrick do?

Should Patrick . . .

- A. Tell the teacher he would rather eat worms than work with Justin?
- B. Do the project himself and put Justin's name on it too?
- C. Try his best and work with Justin?

 Look up 1 John 2:9-11 to find out what Patrick should do. With your mom or dad, read the Bible passage aloud. Now give Patrick advice on how he should work with Justin to do the best project possible.

The correct answer is C.

The Stranger

Angela doesn't know what to do. The new girl in class just asked her over to play after school on Friday and then stay for dinner. Angela doesn't really know the girl that well. She said hi a couple of times, and they played together once or twice on the playground. But the girl is really strange. She comes from a different country. She eats strange food at lunch—with names Angela can't even say! And her English is hard to understand. What if Angela is served some weird food that smells funny for dinner? Worse, what if she can't understand what the new girl is saying? What if everyone at the girl's house speaks a different language at the dinner table? What do you think Angela should do?

Should Angela . . .

A. Go to the girl's house and learn more about this new girl and her family?
B. Go to the girl's house but take her own food, just in case?
C. Tell the girl she only plays with English-speaking children?

 Look up Leviticus 19:33-34 to see what Angela should do. Imagine you are in a foreign country where no one speaks English. What things would be hardest for you?

The correct answer is A.

Nobody Loves Me

It is a horrible day. Nothing is right from the moment Alex gets up. His favorite jeans are in the laundry. He spills his milk at breakfast. He's late for school because he has to finish his homework. Everyone in the carpool is mad at him because no one gets to play on the playground. Then Alex discovers that he did the *wrong* homework. When he asks a classmate what the correct assignment was, he gets in trouble for talking. His friend José is mad at him because he lost José's favorite baseball card. So when Alex gets home, he goes right to his room and locks the door. The way Alex sees it, if he stays in his room he can't possibly mess up anymore, can he? What do you think Alex should do?

Should Alex . . .

- A. Stay in his room until he thinks his luck will change?
- B. Remember that God loves him and always will, no matter how much he messes up?
- C. Pack his bags and join the circus? Maybe he'll make a good human cannonball.

 Check out Matthew 10:29-31 and see who loves Alex (and you!) no matter what happens.
Ever have a day like Alex's day? How do you handle bad days? Why are these Bible verses helpful for you to remember when things get hard?

Great-Aunt Edna

It's the first big snowfall of the season, and to top it off, it happened Friday night! That means Sam has all day Saturday and after church on Sunday to go sledding. He and his friends plan to meet at the sled hill right after breakfast. When he tells his mom about his plans, she shakes her head. Great-Aunt Edna is coming to visit for the weekend, and Sam's mom expects Sam and his sisters to spend time with her. "Oh, Mom," Sam complains, "Great-Aunt Edna always yells at me because I don't speak loud enough, and she's totally bo-r-r-r-ring. All she does is talk about her sick friends. I don't feel like spending my entire weekend with her." Sam's mom doesn't budge. Sam stomps angrily away from the dinner table. What do you think he should do?

Should Sam . . .

    A. Pretend he's come down with "auntitis" and sneak out to meet his friends?
    B. Sit with Great-Aunt Edna, but act totally bored with everything she says?
    C. Entertain Great-Aunt Edna with his sisters and make an effort to get to know her better?

 Read Romans 12:9 to find out what Sam should do. According to the Bible verse, how are you to act toward others, especially people like Great-Aunt Edna, who may not be your favorite people to be with on a Saturday afternoon? Name two ways you can show love to a "Great-Aunt Edna" in your life.

The correct answer is C.

The Waiting Game

Micah stares at the front door, waiting for it to open. No sign of his brother yet. *If Daniel doesn't get out here in five more minutes, we'll be late for school again,* Micah thinks. As Micah watches the minutes tick by on his watch, he gets angrier and angrier. This is the third time this week he has had to wait for his brother. Yesterday the boys had to run the last two blocks to school to make it before the second bell rang. Why can't his brother walk to school by himself? So what if his brother is a bit shy. He can find his way to school. Micah looks at his watch again. If he doesn't leave now, he won't have time to play with Travis before the bell rings. What do you think Micah should do?

Should Micah . . .

- A. Wait for Daniel and play with Travis after school?
- B. Leave a note and a detailed map telling Daniel how to get to school?
- C. Start charging his brother a late fee for walking him to school?

 Check out 1 Corinthians 13:4 to find out what Micah should do.
Rate yourself in the patience scale, with one being a short fuse—no patience at all—and ten the patience to wait forever. Come up with two ways you can improve your rating.

The correct answer is A.

The Sunday School Invitation

Mrs. Jackson challenges the students in her Sunday school class to invite a friend to class during the month. If everyone does, the class can have a pizza party. Marilee is excited! There are so many girls from her class at school that she wants to invite. At lunch she tells her mom about Mrs. Jackson's challenge. "That's a great idea," her mom says. "What about inviting Suzanne?" Marilee looks at her mother as if she has lost her mind. Suzanne lives next door and is not exactly the type of kid you would find in a Sunday school class. For one thing, she *never* goes to church and often makes fun of kids who do. Marilee also knows Suzanne uses swear words a lot and brags about all the R movies she's seen. Marilee's mom has got to be kidding! What should Marilee do?

Should Marilee . . .

A. Ignore her mom's suggestion and invite a more "suitable" friend to church?
B. Ask Suzanne, saying, "You don't really want to come to Sunday school with me, do you?"
C. Tell Suzanne about all the cool things they do in Sunday school and say, "I'd really like you to come with me some-time"?

 To find out what Marilee should do, read Luke 15:3-7. Do you know someone like Suzanne? Think about times you might invite that person to church. Role-play what you would say.
Reminder: Don't forget to work on your memory verse for January. (You'll find it on the page just before January 1.)

The correct answer is C.

Follow My Instructions

Graham is one of eight students chosen to help the kindergartners with their art projects. Graham feels very proud. He loves to draw and is good at art class. This is going to be fun! But when Graham walks into the art room, he can't believe his eyes. He sees paint, glue, and scraps of paper everywhere. About a dozen kids are gathered around the art teacher, asking for help. Mr. Pullman quickly assigns Graham to help a girl repair her project. Graham looks at the lump of gluey paper on the girl's desk. What a mess! How is he going to fix that *thing*? What should Graham do?

Should Graham . . .

- A. Help the girl by giving her careful instructions on how to repair her project?
- B. Trash the project and start over, doing it himself?
- C. Ask the girl, "How can you call that stupid-looking thing art?"

 Read Proverbs 31:26 to find out what Graham should do. Role-play the situation following the advice from the Bible about instructions. Then role-play the situation using angry words. Which would you prefer?

The correct answer is A.

The Lost Necklace

As Tomika is walking to school, something shiny next to the sidewalk catches her eye. She stops to brush away the dirt and discovers a beautiful gold necklace with a lovely ballet slipper charm on it. Tomika smiles with delight. This is exactly the kind of necklace she wants for her birthday. Tomika looks around. No one seems to be looking for it. She shrugs and slips the necklace into her coat pocket. When Tomika gets to school, she notices a girl from another class crying. Several girls are standing around her. As Tomika passes by the girls she hears the words "necklace" and "slipper." What do you think Tomika should do?

Should Tomika . . .

A. Hurry on and pretend she didn't hear anything?
B. Show the girl the necklace and ask if this is the one she lost?
C. Dangle the necklace in front of the girl and tell her, "Finders keepers, losers weepers"?

 To find out the loving, kind, and right thing for Tomika to do, read Deuteronomy 22:1-4.
What does the Bible tell us about the saying, "Finders keepers, losers weepers"? See if your family can come up with a saying that reflects what the Bible says.

The correct answer is B.

Never Enough

Once a month Derek's Sunday school class visits the local nursing home and plays Bingo with the residents there. It's okay, but going to the home makes Derek feel uncomfortable. It smells funny, and the people there are really *old*. Some of them can barely hear, and Derek has to yell the numbers out. Other residents fall asleep before the game is even over. Some get grouchy if they don't win a prize. And if you play the game differently, look out! Someone is going to get mad. Still, Derek goes every month. Today, however, Derek is tired. He watched videos late last night with a friend, and what he really wants to do is hang out at home and watch TV. Besides, other kids in his class *never* go. Why don't *they* take a turn? Derek can hear his dad calling him to get ready to go. What do you think he should do?

Should Derek . . .

    A. Pretend he's asleep and ignore his dad?
    B. Tell his dad he's calling someone else to take his place?
    C. Go to the nursing home and hang out later?

 Check out Romans 13:8 to find out what Derek should do. Discuss with your mom or dad what having a debt means. What does it mean to have a debt related to love? Can you ever pay Jesus back for what he has done for you? Can you keep on loving other people to help pay the debt?

The correct answer is C.

The Plot

Ryan puts another piece of trash into the garbage bag and stretches. It is going to be a long afternoon. He and his friends were caught riding their skateboards on the school playground. Their punishment is to pick up all the trash on the school grounds. While he works, his friend Grant comes up to him and says, "Hey, Ryan, I know who told on us. It was that old lady who lives in the house on the corner. I know because she stands by the window and watches everything. I have a great plan. Tonight we'll go back in the dark and egg her house. It'll be fun. She deserves it!" Ryan isn't as excited about the plan as his friend is, but he doesn't want to seem like a wimp. What do you think Ryan should do?

Should Ryan . . .

 A. Order up some scrambled eggs "to go" so the egging won't be so messy, and join his friends?
 B. Go along with his friends, but only carry the eggs?
 C. Tell his friend he doesn't want to be part of their plot?

 Look up Zechariah 7:9-10 to find out what Ryan should do. Ask your mom or dad to share a time when they wanted to get back at someone. What did they do? What happened as a result of what they did?

The correct answer is C.

Opportunity Knocks

During recess Betsy and her friends make plans for after school.
It is a beautiful winter day, and they decide to go ice skating.
So far, Betsy doesn't have much homework so she should be
able to go with her friends. Before school lets out, the teacher
makes a brief announcement. One of the girls in Betsy's class
has been in the hospital and came home yesterday. The
teacher asks for a volunteer to take the girl some get-well cards
that the class has made. Betsy looks around the room. No one
has raised a hand. Betsy walks by the girl's house on her way
home. But if she stops, she won't have time to do her homework and go ice skating with her friends. Still, no one else has
volunteered. What do you think Betsy should do?

Should Betsy . . .

- A. Take the cards and visit with the girl?
- B. Throw the cards on the driveway as she walks home?
- C. Pray someone else will volunteer?

 To find out what Betsy should do, read Galatians 6:10.
Name three opportunities you have to do good today. Do
one!

All about Love

1 Corinthians 13 is sometimes called the *Love Chapter.* It helps us understand what godly love should look like. In the opening verses of Chapter 13, Paul shows what a person is like who believes in God and does great things for him, but who does not act kind or loving.

Connect the dots to discover what this person is like.

Read 1 Corinthians 13:1 to see what Paul says this kind of person does.

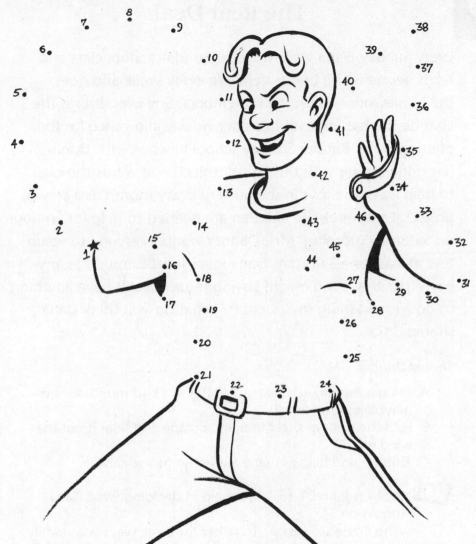

*There are three things that will endure—faith, hope, and love—
and the greatest of these is love.*

1 Corinthians 13:13

The Real Deal

Every Sunday Dana walks into her Sunday school class and takes her seat. She brings her Bible every week and does the homework—when she remembers! She even brings the change she has left over from her weekly allowance for the offering plate. But her Sunday school teacher, Mrs. Danner, has gone too far with this latest project. She wants the class to help wash the toys in the nursery every month as a service project. Each week five children are needed to help for an hour on Saturday morning. Mrs. Danner wants everyone to volunteer at least one Saturday. Dana loves Jesus as much as anybody, but this is too much! Loving Jesus doesn't have anything to do with washing toys, does it? What do you think Dana should do?

Should Dana . . .

    A. Tell her Sunday school teacher this is a bad month for her—maybe another time?
    B. Fold the sign-up sheet into an airplane and float it out the window?
    C. Sign up and help as many Saturdays as she can?

 Look up John 21:15-17 for help in deciding what Dana should do.
Who are Jesus' sheep? Together list three ways your family can show that you love Jesus by caring for the people in his family—his "sheep."

My Enemy

The closer Eric gets to the school playground, the slower he walks. He doesn't want to tell his mom and dad, but going to school is a real struggle. Every day a much bigger kid waits by the playground for Eric to come by. And he isn't waiting there to play with Eric. No, he is waiting to pick on Eric. This boy calls him names and makes fun of what he wears. Today, when Eric arrives at the playground, he is amazed to see that the older kid is not around. Then Eric spots him over by a group of even bigger kids. Eric can see that the boy's nose is bleeding— a lot! What do you think Eric should do?

Should Eric . . .

- A. Do a victory dance around the big kid?
- B. Offer to take the big kid to the nurse?
- C. Keep on walking past the boy?

 To find out what Eric should do, read Matthew 5:43-44. Have your mom or dad tell you about a time when they had an enemy at school or in the neighborhood. Ask them to tell you how they handled that person. How would they handle that situation differently now?

The correct answer is B.

Payback Time

Stacy hurries to the lunch table and grabs a chair. She isn't going to be the last one at the table today if she can help it. Yesterday she had to wait in line for milk. When she got to the table, there was only one seat left. She was going to sit down when a bossy girl announced loudly that she was saving that seat for another girl. Stacy ended up sitting with a bunch of older boys who made fun of her all through lunch. Today as Stacy begins eating she notices the bossy girl coming toward the table. There is only one seat left, and this girl is heading straight toward it. As the girl gets to the table she asks, "Is anyone sitting here?" Stacy looks around. Now is her chance to pay the girl back. What do you think Stacy should do?

Should Stacy . . .

    A. Ask the girl if she has reserved a place at that table?
    B. Invite the girl to sit down and eat lunch with her?
    C. Tell the girl she knows some older boys who would love to eat lunch with her?

 Read 1 Thessalonians 5:15 to see how Stacy should react. Have you heard the expression, "Don't get mad—get even"? Role-play a situation in which you want to get even with someone. Act out two different ways to handle the situation.

The correct answer is B.

Fighting Words

Carly is one of the biggest know-it-alls in her class. She thinks she knows *everything!* She even corrected the teacher once. Carly is always right. Today on the playground Keisha and her friends are talking about the newest movie coming out starring the Watson twins. The girls are making plans to see it on Saturday. Carly overhears the conversation and jumps right in. "Well, for your info, the movie doesn't start for another week. You can meet at the movie theater this Saturday, but you'll have to see something else," she says and starts laughing at them. "Boy are you dumb! You don't know anything." Keisha read about the movie in the newspaper last night, and she knows that Carly is wrong this time. What do you think Keisha should do?

Should Keisha . . .

   A. Keep quiet and call her friends later to set up the time?
   B. Tell Carly that for a know-it-all, she is pretty clueless?
   C. Bring in the newspaper ad the next day to prove beyond a doubt that Carly is wrong?

 To find out what Joan should do, check out 2 Timothy 2:24. Think about the know-it-alls in your life. Plan ways to avoid fighting with that type of person.

The correct answer is A.

The Class Party

Everyone in Mrs. Kenneth's third-grade class is excited. Because they have worked so hard during the past month, Mrs. Kenneth is letting them have a class party. The students are planning for the party in groups. One group is in charge of decorations; another group is going to plan some games to play. Dean's group is in charge of food. One of Dean's class-mates offers to supply all the cold drinks. Another student will bring in the napkins, cups, and plates. A third student offers to bring in bags of chips and pretzels. As Dean writes this down, he notices that one member of the group is very quiet. It's his neighbor Keith. Keith's family isn't exactly well-off. Dean feels bad for Keith, but everyone is supposed to bring something. What do you think Dean should do?

Should Dean . . .

A. Suggest that Keith join another group, such as games, where he doesn't have to bring something in?
B. Complain to the teacher that Keith isn't bringing anything?
C. Ask Keith if he wants to come over to his house and help bake cookies for the party?

 Check out Proverbs 14:21 to see how Dean should handle this situation.
As a family have a "clean-out-your-closet" day. Donate any old clothes or toys you find to the Salvation Army or a shelter near your neighborhood.

The correct answer is C.

Love in Action

Jeremy drops his backpack on the kitchen floor with a thud. He has *tons* of homework. Of course, if he hadn't been goofing around, he could have gotten some of it done in school. But now he has to do it all tonight. He grabs a couple of cookies and heads to his room. If he gets started now, he probably still can watch his favorite show on TV after dinner. As he passes his mom's bedroom, he notices she is lying down on the bed with a washcloth over her head.

"What's the matter, Mom?" Jeremy asks.

"I'm not feeling very good," she says. "Can you keep track of your little brother until your dad gets home?"

Jeremy wants to scream. How can he get all his work done now? What do you think Jeremy should do?

Should Jeremy . . .

    A. Tell his mom he's sorry, but he has too much homework?
    B. Tell his brother to sit quietly in the corner in his room while he works, and he'll buy his brother an ice cream cone later?
    C. Take his brother out to play and plan on getting his work done after his dad gets home?

 To find out what Jeremy should do, read 1 John 3:18. Think of someone in your family who could use a little extra love this week. Think of at least one thing you can do for that person to put your love for them into action.

Grudge Match

It has been a week, and Alexa still feels hurt. Her best friend, Madison, has been playing a lot with another girl from her class. One afternoon the two girls were playing outside, but when Alexa came over to see what was going on, the two girls ran inside. Madison hasn't talked to her since, and Alexa has been avoiding her as well. Alexa eats lunch at another table, plays with other girls on the playground, and invites other friends over to her house. But she misses her best friend terribly even though it's really Madison's fault. Today after school the phone rings. It's Madison. She wants to know if Alexa can come over and play. What do you think Alexa should do?

Should Alexa . . .

A. Demand an apology first before she accepts?
B. Go play and apologize for ignoring Madison during the past week?
C. Use a fake voice and say Alexa isn't taking calls from people whose names begin with *M*?

 Check out Leviticus 19:18 to see what Alexa should do. Have your mom or dad tell about a time when someone they knew held a grudge against them. How did they resolve that situation?
Reminder: Don't forget to say your memory verse for January. (See the page just before January 1.)

The correct answer is B.

Leading Lady

This month Danisha's school is ten years old. For the special party the school is going to have, Danisha's class will perform a short skit. It will be about the woman the school was named after, Rosa Parks. Danisha tried out for one of the major parts in the story but didn't even get a small part. Instead, she was asked to help out behind the scenes. Danisha feels bad, especially after finding out that the girl who recently moved in next door is going to play the part of Rosa Parks. Danisha thinks her teacher ought to give the big part to someone who has been in class all year. While Danisha is out walking her dog, she notices the new girl playing in her front yard. She has to walk by the girl to get home. What do you think Danisha should do?

Should Danisha . . .

    A. Tell the girl how great it is that she got the part and offer to help her learn her lines?
    B. Pretend her dog is running away and run by without saying anything?
    C. Say, "Boy, did you get lucky. I can't believe you got that part"?

 Read Romans 15:2 to see what Danisha should do. Talk about three ways you can "build someone up" at school.

Share the Load

Karl knows his best friend, Jon, is going through a bad time. Jon's mom has been ill for a long time and has just come home from the hospital. Jon has to help around the house a lot and can't play after school as much. Karl tries to be understanding. But every time he wants to do something, Jon always has to be at home. It has gotten to the point where Karl doesn't even call Jon anymore. In school today Karl notices that Jon isn't there. The teacher gives the class a project to do. There are a lot of directions, so Karl is glad he is there to hear them. Karl is looking over the project at home when the phone rings. It's Jon, and he wants to know the directions. This is going to take some major time. What do you think Karl should do?

Should Karl . . .

A. Tell Jon to get the teacher to explain the directions to him tomorrow?
B. Read the directions to Jon as fast as he can?
C. Offer to come over and explain the project to Jon because it's too hard to explain on the phone?

 To find out what Karl should do, read Galatians 6:2-3. Talk about a time when your family needed someone to share your troubles and problems. How did people help you? How did you feel about the help you received?

The correct answer is C.

The New Kid

Zachary didn't want to move. But here he is in a new house, a new neighborhood, a new school, a new everything. Now it's Sunday, and he has to go to a new Sunday school. The knot in the pit of his stomach grows larger with every step he takes toward the church. He loved his old Sunday school class with the funny posters and the neat crafts his teacher planned every week. It can't possibly be the same in this Sunday school. As he enters the door, all eyes are on him. The teacher walks over and greets him with a warm smile. She asks one of the boys to sit with Zachary. The boy seems nice enough. As they sit down, the boy asks Zachary, "So how do you like it here so far?" What do you think Zachary should say?

Should Zachary . . .

   A. Scream, "I hate it here—I can't wait to go back to my real home"?
   B. Say it was hard to leave his old home, but he's looking forward to getting to know everyone?
   C. Start telling the boy all about the cool things that they did in his old Sunday school?

 Check out Hebrews 13:1 to see what Zachary's attitude should be toward his new friend.
Moving to a new place is a hard thing to do. Think of someone who is new in your church or school. What can you do to help make that person's move a bit easier?

It's My Turn!

Demi can tell it must be a bad day for her mom by the way she hustles Demi and her sister out of the library. Usually her mom lets them get a drink of water from the fountain, but not today. As they walk to the car her mom tells Demi and her younger sister, "When we get home, I need you to pick up the toys in the family room because I'm having some people over for a Sunday school meeting." *Oh, so that's it,* Demi thinks. Meetings usually mean a stressed-out mom! When they get to the car, Demi opens the door to the front seat. Her sister begins whining, "It's *my* turn to sit in the front!" Demi is certain that it's *her* turn. As she begins to answer, Demi catches her mother's face in the side mirror. She looks ready to explode! What do you think Demi should do?

Should Demi . . .

    A. Yell at her sister, "Stop whining! Can't you see you're bothering Mom"?
    B. Politely, but firmly, explain to her sister that she, in fact, rode in the front yesterday to the dentist?
    C. Let her sister have the front seat?

 To find out how Demi should handle this, read Luke 6:29. Think of a time when someone gave up something for you, like the last piece of cake or a seat on the sofa. Talk about how that made you feel.

The correct answer is C.

Time to Sing

The alarm wakes Raúl up with a jolt. He hits the snooze alarm and rolls back over. A few minutes later his mom knocks on his door. "Raúl, come on. You have to get up now or you'll be late for church. Remember, the choir is singing this morning." Raúl throws off his covers. He grumbles to himself as he gets dressed. "Why do I have to sing today? I don't feel like it. The lights in church are too bright and they make my eyes water. I hate wearing a tie. Do I have to do this?" All the way to church, Raúl looks angry. When he joins the choir in the front of the church, the choir director gives them some last-minute directions and ends as she usually does: "And remember children, we are here to worship God. I want you to sing your best." Raúl *still* doesn't feel like singing. What do you think Raúl should do?

Should Raúl . . .

- A. Move his lips as if he is singing? No one will know the difference.
- B. Decide to do his best, even though he doesn't feel like it?
- C. Ask the choir director if he can give his voice a much-needed rest today?

 Take a look at Deuteronomy 10:12 to see what Raúl should do.
Ask your mom or dad to name a time when they had to do something that they didn't especially want to do. Talk about what they did in that situation. What were the results?

The Welcome Mat

Melina is a bit nervous. Her Sunday school class is expecting a busload of kids from another church in the city. She has never been to the church before, but she has heard that many of the people attending that church are poor. Their class has planned a lunch for the visiting children and a short play to perform. Her teacher also wants them to pair up with one of the visitors. Melina isn't real good at meeting new people; in fact, the thought of it makes her mouth dry. She looks again at the slip of paper that has the name of the girl she is paired with. What is she going to say to this girl? What if the girl doesn't like her? Melina watches as the bus pulls into the church parking lot and the kids all get off. What do you think Melina should do?

Should Melina . . .

A. Ask the girl a lot of questions about herself to get to know her?
B. Run and hide in the supply closet?
C. Keep busy by helping in the kitchen with the parents cooking the lunch?

 Read Acts 28:2 for an example of how Melina should act in this situation.
Think of a time when you walked into a room and didn't know anybody. Talk about how you felt and what helped you in that situation.

The Ball Hog

Marcus runs in the house and asks his mom if he got any mail. He is expecting the soccer team list. He wants to be on Barry's team this year. His mom hands him an envelope. It's the list! Marcus rips open the envelope and scans the list. No Barry. But there is Andrew. "Oh, no!" Marcus yells, throwing down the list.

"What's the matter?" Mom asks.

"I'm on the team with Andrew again. He's such a ball hog. I can't stand him." Marcus goes on and on.

His mom sits down by him. "You know, Marcus, Andrew's mom and dad just got a divorce. He needs a friend like you."

The first day of practice, Marcus is kicking the ball around with some of his friends when he sees Andrew approaching the group. What do you think Marcus should do?

Should Marcus . . .

    A. Invite Andrew to kick the ball around with him?
    B. Sound the "Andrew alarm" and scatter at the count of three?
    C. Ignore Andrew and hope he goes away?

 To see what Marcus should do, check out 2 Peter 1:7. Think of a person in your school, neighborhood, or church who needs a friend. Challenge yourself to take the first step in getting to know that person.

My Way—or Else!

Karyn and her friend Meredith are hanging out after school at Karyn's house. She's got a brand new computer game that she wants to show her friend. After a quick snack, she suggests that she and Meredith try out the new game. "You can create your own model on the screen, and then give her all sorts of hair styles and stuff. It's really cool," she explains to her.

Meredith doesn't act very interested in Karyn's computer game. "I've already seen that computer game," she says. "I really want to play outside instead of staying in the house. Why don't we go out and play in the snow?"

Karyn thinks her friend is being stubborn. What do you think Karyn should do?

Should Karyn . . .

> A. Insist that they do what she wants to do because it's her house?
> B. Go outside and play the computer game later?
> C. Find another friend who *wants* to see her computer game?

 Take a look at 1 Corinthians 13:5 to help you know what Karyn should do.
Talk with your family about times when some of you have tried to make sure things were done *your* way. What happened?

The correct answer is B.

Review Time!

List three things you have learned about Jesus' kind of love this month.

1.

2.

3.

Bonus

List three ways you can show love to others.

1.

2.

3.

Say your memory verse to a family member. (The verse is printed on the page just before January 1.) Tell her or him how Jesus showed he loved us.

Treasures in Heaven

What things are most important to you? Playing soccer? Spending time with your family and friends? Going to church? The Bible tells us there should never be anything more important to us than living for God. He should be at the top of our list each day. But what does that mean? It means thinking about God and what he wants for us before we think about ourselves and what we want to do. It means obeying God and "treasuring" the things that God treasures. When we do this, God promises that everything else will be taken care of—and that's a promise you can count on!

When we put God first and obey him, we are storing up "treasures in heaven." These treasures are not like the treasures on earth—things like jewels, money, gold, and other stuff we like to collect. The Bible tells us that those kinds of treasures fade away, break down, or can be stolen. But treasures in heaven will last forever.

What kinds of treasures are you storing up? As you work through this month's *Sticky Situations,* look for the things in your life that can crowd God out of first place. Make sure you're making God Number One!

Memory Verse: Don't store up treasures here on earth, where they can be eaten by moths and get rusty, and where thieves break in and steal. Store your treasures in heaven, where they will never become moth-eaten or rusty and where they will be safe from thieves. Wherever your treasure is, there your heart and thoughts will also be. Matthew 6:19-21

The What-Ifs . . .

Next week Lauren's family is leaving on a two-week vacation to Florida! Lauren is so excited. Her family is going to Disney World and the Kennedy Space Center. It will be her first time on an airplane and her first real vacation. But as the departure day approaches, Lauren has to confess she is more than a bit nervous. At night she thinks about the trip and worries. What if she isn't ready when it's time to go to the airport? Even worse, what if she gets lost at the airport or at the Magic Kingdom? *What if* . . . The what-ifs float through her mind over and over. How is she ever going to get through the next couple days without going completely bonkers? What do you think Lauren should do?

Should Lauren . . .

    A. Remember that God is in control and take her fears to him?
    B. Gather all the good luck charms she can find and keep her fingers crossed?
    C. Tell her mom and dad thanks for the trip, but maybe next year?

 Check out Matthew 6:31-33 to find out how putting God first can help Lauren.
Imagine you are in Lauren's shoes. Role-play with your parents what you would say as Lauren; then role-play what you would say as Lauren's mom or dad.

The correct answer is A.

Make a Choice

Nathaniel watches the clock tick off the minutes of the school day. He can't concentrate on his schoolwork. He is itching to finish the video game his parents just bought for him. He started a game last night, and if he gets enough points, he can move up a level in the game! At lunch one of his friends told him a secret to getting there, and Nathaniel can't wait to try it. Finally the bell rings. As Nathaniel heads out the door, Joseph stops him and asks, "Hey, Nathaniel, would you like to stop by after school today and shoot some hoops?" Nathaniel hesitates. Joseph is the new kid in school and pretty shy. Nathaniel is surprised that Joseph would ask him to come over. What about his video game? He *really* wants to finish that game! What do you think Nathaniel should do?

Should Nathaniel . . .

A. Pretend he doesn't hear Joseph and dash out the door?
B. Tell Joseph that he'd love to but he has a blister on his shooting thumb; maybe another time?
C. Tell Joseph he would love to come but needs to check with his mom first?

 To find out what Nathaniel should do, read Mark 12:31. Get a piece of scrap paper and fold it in half. Put *video game* at the top of one column and *friend* at the top of the other column. With your mom or dad, write down the pluses and minuses of putting each one first. What do you think God would tell you to put first in a choice like this?

The correct answer is C.

A Pack of Trouble

Brent is in real trouble. The other day he found a pack of cool new gel pens on the school playground. It didn't appear that anyone was looking for them, so he put them in his backpack. When class begins today, his teacher announces that Michelle lost a pack of gel pens on the playground. She asks the class to look for them. Brent knows he should return them, but he doesn't. As he's getting his homework out of his backpack, Luis sees the pens in his backpack. "Aren't those Michelle's pens?" Luis asks.

Brent quickly stuffs his backpack under his chair. "No, these are mine," he says. When school gets out, he sees Luis hurry over to Michelle and point to him. What do you think he should do?

Should Brent . . .

- A. Run home as fast as he can and ditch the pens in a trash can?
- B. Confess that he picked up the pens and accept whatever will happen to him?
- C. Look in his backpack and exclaim, "Wow! How did they get here?"

 Read Judges 4:1-3 to see what happened to the Israelites when they forgot about God and did the wrong thing. Ask your family to think about a time when you tried to handle a big problem by yourselves and it only got worse. (Can you think of one yourself?) What should be the first step you take when facing a hard problem?

The correct answer is B.

Is That Your Best?

Brittany hangs up the phone. "Mom," she yells, searching for her mother throughout the house. "Where are you?" She finally finds her mom outside pulling weeds. "Ashley just called and asked if I could sleep over Saturday night. Her parents will get me to church on time," she hurriedly adds, knowing that will be the first thing her mother will ask about.

Her mom answers, "It's okay with me, but check the calendar first to make sure nothing else is going on Sunday morning." When she looks at the calendar, her heart sinks. The choir is singing on Sunday. Brittany knows that she will be tired from the sleepover. And when she's tired, she doesn't sing very well. What do you think Brittany should do?

Should Brittany . . .

A. Tell her mom about choir, but convince her she can sing on three hours of sleep?
B. Tell her mom she'll have to reschedule the sleepover for another weekend because of choir?
C. Erase "choir" from the calendar, go to the sleepover, and act surprised when she sees the choir lining up?

 For help in knowing what Brittany should do, take a look at Deuteronomy 17:1 to see what God desires from each of us. Talk with your mom or dad about something each of you does really well. What are some things that keep you from doing your best? What are some things that help you perform at your top level?

The correct answer is B.

Attitude Check

Greg almost jumps out of his chair when he is named one of the five hall monitors for the school year. Ever since Greg was a little kid, he has wanted to be one of those cool older kids who tells everyone not to run in the halls, or to get a pass, or to be quiet. Now it's his turn! On his first day as hall monitor, Greg stands nearly at attention at the end of the hall. He watches the younger kids go by on their way to recess, giving a slight nod to some of his friends' younger brothers and sisters. From the corner of his eye, he sees some older kids coming down the hall. Among the group is the meanest boy in school. The kids aren't doing anything wrong, but Greg thinks this is a great chance to give that boy a hard time. What do you think Greg should do?

Should Greg . . .

- A. Use his full authority to bust the kid for goofing around in the hall?
- B. Pretend to write down the kid's name so the boy thinks Greg is going to report him to the principal?
- C. Let the kids pass by and not say anything?

 Take a look at Judges 9:16 for some good advice on how to treat others.

Discuss with your mom or dad what it means to act honorably and to treat others with respect. Think of a time you were put in charge of something. Why did you like being in charge? Why do you think Greg likes being the hall monitor?

The correct answer is C.

Pray for What?

Today was a bad day. Yoshi got into a big fight with the group he is working with on a social studies project. They have been working together on the big project for the past three weeks. Yoshi had a really good idea about how to present the information they have collected, but the other kids in the group thought it would mean too much work. One kid even called Yoshi a stuck-up bully!

Tonight as he and his dad are saying prayers, Yoshi tells his dad about what happened with his social studies group. After hearing the whole story, Yoshi's dad suggests that they pray about the situation. That sounds like good advice to Yoshi, but what should he pray for? What do you think Yoshi should say?

Should Yoshi . . .

    A. Pray that God gives him wisdom to know how to best help the group?
    B. Pray that the teacher would move him to another group?
    C. Pray that the other kids would wise up and listen to him?

 Read 2 Chronicles 1:11-12 for an example of the right things to pray for from God.
Think of a situation you are experiencing now. Write down or say a prayer in which you ask God for wisdom. He will help you think of ways to put him first in this situation.

First Things First

Alyssa has promised to help out once a month with the toddlers during her church's midweek program. It isn't a big job—getting diapers for the adult helpers, playing with the children, and cleaning up afterward. Still, it helps Alyssa get some good experience in learning how to baby-sit when she gets old enough. The only trouble is that every time it's her turn to help, she either forgets about it or finds something else she would rather do. Last month she canceled because she had too much homework. The midweek program director calls tonight and tells Alyssa if she misses again, she will be dropped from the program. Alyssa needs to make a decision about the program. What do you think Alyssa should do?

Should Alyssa . . .

A. Tell the director she'll do her best to make it—unless, of course, something else comes up again?
B. Apologize to the director for not helping as she had promised and say she is making the program a priority in her schedule?
C. Tell the director it's her mom's fault that she doesn't make it?

 Check out Haggai 1:7-9 to find out what Alyssa's priorities should be.
With your mom or dad, go over your weekly and monthly schedule. What keeps you the busiest? What do you do for God? What do you do for others? What do you do for your-self? What changes, if any, do you need to make in your schedule?

The correct answer is B.

That's a Good Joke?

Brian joins the group of boys gathered around Dave. Dave always has the funniest jokes. Dave has a couple of older brothers, and they tell him all the latest jokes going around the high school. Brian has to admit that sometimes he doesn't understand the jokes and sometimes the jokes include bad words. Most of the time, though, Dave's jokes are very funny. Brian listens to Dave's latest joke. He laughs along with the others when Dave gets to the punch line, but he doesn't feel good about it because Dave's joke used God's name in a bad way. As he is leaving the group to play on the monkey bars, another friend grabs him and says, "Hey, did you hear Dave's joke? Tell me!" What do you think Brian should do?

Should Brian . . .

    A. Tell his friend he has forgotten the joke already?
    B. Tell him the joke like Dave did—after all, it isn't *his* joke?
    C. Tell his friend he'd rather not repeat the joke?

 Look up Malachi 2:1-2 for help in knowing what Brian should do.
Discuss with your mom or dad why you think God cares so much about his name. What are some other ways we might dishonor God's name? Come up with some other ways to handle a situation like Brian's.

The correct answer is C.

Time to Pray

Paige's Sunday school class has been learning about prayer. Her teacher suggests that each student find a special time to pray every day. The first day Paige gets up early to pray, but she discovers that the birds are up early too. By the time she is through watching them, it's time for breakfast. The next day is no better. She decides to set up a corner in her room where she can best sit and pray. By the time she has it ready, it's time to practice piano. No matter what time of day Paige sets aside for praying, something always seems to come up. Paige is upset. Maybe praying every day isn't such a good idea after all. What do you think Paige should do?

Should Paige . . .

    A. Forget about trying to find a time to pray?
    B. Ask her mom to help her come up with a time that will work most days?
    C. Promise herself that she is really going to get down to business tomorrow—right after she arranges the shoes in her closet?

For help in knowing what Paige should do, look up Luke 10:38-42.
Have your family name activities that keep you from either reading the Bible or praying. Name some things you can do so these things won't stop you from putting God first.

The Wrong Path

Travis and his younger brother are going with some friends to the winter carnival. Each year Travis's town holds an indoor carnival with pie-eating contests, games, and other stuff. This is the first year his parents are letting him and his brother go with friends for the afternoon. When the boys get to the carnival, they see a long line for tickets. It probably will take them a half hour just to get inside. Then they will have less than an hour to have fun. They are about to turn around and go home when Michael suggests, "Hey, look. We can sneak in the back way. No one is watching." All the boys think Michael's idea is great. Travis is not so sure. What do you think he should do?

Should Travis . . .

    A. Go along with the crowd and hope no one catches them?
    B. Suggest they cut in the ticket line instead?
    C. Tell the boys he is going to wait in the line with his brother, and they'll meet the rest of them later?

 Check out Psalm 119:127-128 to know which path Travis should take.
Think about some times when you might feel like choosing the wrong way. What could happen as a result of that? What should you do?
Reminder: Don't forget to work on your memory verse for February. (You'll find it on the page just before February 1.)

Stylin'

Sarah checks out the two girls walking by her on the way home from school. Each has on the latest shoes, and they are talking rather loudly about "those dorky kids" who don't have these "stylin' shoes"—kids like Sarah and her sister. Unfortunately for Sarah, the shoes cost about $120. There is no way her parents are going to buy them for her. Her dad just lost his job, and there hardly is enough money from her mom's part-time job to pay for food. *It isn't fair*, Sarah thinks angrily as she turns into her driveway. It seems like she and her sister are the only ones in the entire school who don't have a pair of those shoes. There has to be some way to get a pair. What do you think Sarah should do?

Should Sarah . . .

    A. Paint the logo of the stylin' shoes on her old pair of shoes?
    B. Beg her parents to get the shoes, saying that she really, really, really, *really* needs those shoes?
    C. Forget about the shoes, and remember all the things she has to be thankful for, including the pair of shoes she has?

 To find out what Sarah should do, read 1 Timothy 6:17. Have your mom and dad tell about a few of the fads from their school days. Share some of the fads from today. Talk about what a fad is. What are some things that will never go out of style?

The correct answer is C.

Ready, Set, Go!

Although it has been snowing for several hours, Neil and his family are thinking about summer. Specifically, summer camp. One of Neil's friends is going to a cool soccer camp for the summer and wants Neil to go with him. But his mom and dad are leaning toward a church camp. Sure, some of his friends from Sunday school are going. But church camp? C'mon. All you do there is read the Bible, sing songs, and make some stuff. His mom and dad say the church camp will help him serve God, but hey, he is only a kid! There will be plenty of time later to serve God. What Neil really wants to do is prepare for getting on the top soccer team in the fall with his friends. What do you think Neil should do?

Should Neil . . .

A. Go along with his parents and plan to go to the church camp?
B. Make a deal with his parents that if he can go to the soccer camp this year, he'll go to the church camp . . . later?
C. Go to the church camp, but make sure to pack a soccer ball and skip the camp activities to practice soccer?

 Read 2 Timothy 2:21 to find out the importance of being ready to serve God whenever and wherever he calls you. Have your mom or dad share how something they learned in Sunday school or at a camp helped them prepare for serving God. Talk about different ways you can "be ready for the Master to use you for every good work."

The correct answer is A.

Just Do It!

It's the final day of school before midwinter break, and DeWayne's class has a substitute. All day the class has made things hard for the sub. Several kids pretend to be other students. When the sub asks them to turn in their homework, a bunch of kids tell the sub they don't have any homework. Other kids keep asking silly questions. At recess some of DeWayne's friends ask him to help play a prank on the sub. When DeWayne doesn't seem sure about it, his friends jump in: "C'mon, DeWayne. It's just a prank. And nobody will ever know who did it. It'll be fun!" What do you think DeWayne should do?

Should DeWayne . . .

A. Go along with his friends, but be prepared to blame them for coming up with the idea?
B. Tell his friends no thanks and walk away?
C. Go to the nurse and say he doesn't feel well so he can go home early?

 Check out Titus 2:11 to know what DeWayne should do. Make a list together with your mom or dad of times when you need self-control so you don't do the wrong things that those around you want to do. Then give yourself a grade for self-control in each of those areas. For those areas with lower grades, pray for God's help to show self-control.

The correct answer is B.

God Power!

Juanita is the last child to leave choir practice. "What took you so long?" her mom asks as they walk to the car.

"Oh, I just had to stay after," Juanita explains, then quickly changes the subject. "What's for dinner?"

Later that evening as Juanita is getting ready for bed, her mom sits on her bed. "What's wrong, my Juanita? You've been so quiet ever since choir practice. You always tell me what's going on. This isn't like you."

Juanita bursts into tears. "Oh, Mom, Mrs. Applebee gave me a part in the Easter musical, and I just can't get it right. She makes me go over and over the lines, but I can't remember them! What am I going to do?" Her mom prays with her, but Juanita still is worried. What do you think she should do?

Should Juanita . . .

    A. Pretend she loses her voice the night of the musical?
    B. Keep working at it, trusting that God will help her do her best to tell the Easter story through her part in the musical?
    C. Tell Mrs. Applebee she can't do it and ask her to find someone else to take the part?

Look up Hebrews 13:20-21 for verses that will help Juanita get through the play.

Practice using the above verses as a prayer, putting in specifics about times when you need help to serve God. (For example, *And now, may the God of peace . . . equip me to do my best when I talk to the woman next door about him. . . .*)

The correct answer is B.

Digging for Heavenly Treasure

Unscramble the words found in the treasure chest to discover some of the "heavenly treasures" that we have in Jesus. For the first four words you'll see that the first letter has been filled in for you.

H _ _ _ _ _

F _ _ _ _ _ _ _ _ _

P _ _ _ _ _

F _ _ _ _ _ _ _ _ _ _ _

_ _ _

_ _ _ _

Wherever your treasure is, there your heart and thoughts will also be.

Matthew 6:21

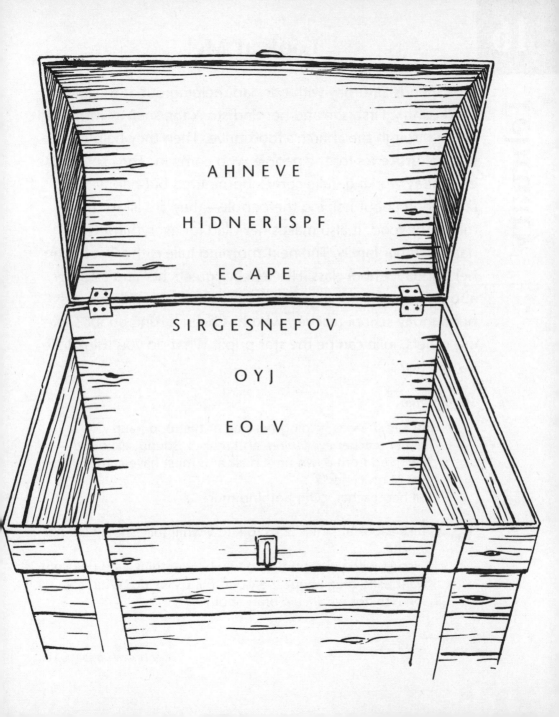

Look at Me!

Julie spends Saturday with her dad, helping out at the local food pantry. First, she and her dad stock the shelves with food given through the church's food drive. Then they help carry bags of groceries for the people who come in. They spend the entire day working. Julie comes home tired but happy. She feels good about helping the people—they are all so thankful for the food. It also makes her glad for everything God has given her family. The next morning Julie is the first one in her Sunday school class. Her teacher greets her and asks her about her weekend. Boy, here's her chance to really impress her Sunday school teacher, who has been talking about serving others. Julie can be the star pupil! What do you think Julie should do?

Should Julie . . .

- A. Just say she was helping her dad at the food pantry?
- B. Tell her teacher *everything,* and make it sound real good— "I worked from dawn until dusk and must have carried three tons of groceries"?
- C. Tell her teacher, "Oh, nothing much"?

 Take a look at James 3:13 to know what Julie should tell her teacher.
Discuss with your mom or dad why you think God does not want us to brag about the good things we do. What are some things we *should* brag about?

The correct answer is A.

Behind the Scenes

Tonight is the Black History Month play at Isaiah's school. Isaiah doesn't have a speaking part, and he isn't part of the chorus. But along with several other students, Isaiah has worked hard with the art teacher putting up the scenery. They have spent many afternoons after school painting and putting together the props for the show. As Isaiah watches the curtain go up, he smiles when he hears the whispered comments, "Boy, doesn't that look great!" When he opens his program, however, his mouth falls open. His name isn't listed along with the others as helping with the scenery. He can't believe it! What do you think Isaiah should do?

Should Isaiah . . .

A. Run down to the rows where the people are sitting and write his name in all the programs?

B. Say loudly in his seat, "Wow! That scenery *I, Isaiah Tanner, worked on* really looks great"?

C. Realize that the people most important to him—his parents, his art teacher, and his classroom teacher—know what a good job he did?

 Read Hebrews 6:10 to know what Isaiah should do. Talk with your mom or dad about a time when you worked hard on a project. Who knew about it and who didn't? How did that make you feel? Who will always know what you do for him?

The correct answer is C.

I've Got It All!

Conner is having a great school year. His best friend is in his class, he just made it into the advanced math program, and his teacher is the best in the entire school. Not only that, but he also is doing well on his basketball team and scored the winning basket in last week's game! *Things couldn't get much better*, Conner thinks. Everything is definitely going his way! At dinner one night, Conner's mom mentions the library is having a reading buddy program for kids from needy families. She asks if Conner would like to be a buddy. Conner doesn't answer at first. Why should he waste his time with these kids? He has a lot going on already, and a lot better things to do. What do you think Conner should do?

Should Conner . . .

A. Tell his mom to check back with him when his schedule is a bit freer?
B. Tell his mom no way does he want to spend time with a bunch of kids who can't read?
C. Agree to give it a try?

 Check out Revelation 3:17-19 to know what Conner should do.
As a family, discuss how things are going for you right now. Are you on top of the world, like Conner, or is life a bit hard for you right now? Talk about ways to put God first in the good times and the bad times.

The correct answer is C.

Join the Club

Tina has been spending time with Erin and Samantha, who live down the street from her. They are a year older than she is, and Tina enjoys being part of their group. It makes her feel really cool. She wants her school friends to meet her new older (and cooler) friends. As they sit around one afternoon, Samantha suggests that the girls form a club. The three girls spend the rest of the afternoon making up the name, what kinds of things they will do, who will be president (Samantha, of course—it was her idea!), and what the rules will be. Erin says, "The most important rule is that no one younger than us can be in the club—except Tina because she's already in." What do you think Tina should do?

Should Tina . . .

    A. Tell the other girls, "Sorry, but I can't go along with that rule"?
    B. Tell her friends at school, "Sorry, but you can't join the club because you're too young"?
    C. Join the club but secretly play with her other friends too?

 Read Acts 5:27-29 for help in knowing what Tina should do. If you want to put God first in your life, name some club rules that would be okay. Name other rules that would not be okay. Think about ways that God wants you to treat people.
Reminder: Don't forget to work on your memory verse for February. (You'll find it on the page just before February 1.)

The correct answer is A.

A Good Place to Be

At lunch Kyle hears his friends talking about the hottest new cartoon on TV, *Squiggy the Squid*. "Hey, did you see the episode where Squiggy gets attacked by the man-eating ray? It was so cool," one boy says.

"Well, my favorite episode is when Squiggy gets caught in the net and almost gets hauled out of the water," says another kid.

Kyle has never seen the show because it's on Sunday mornings when his family is at church. "Hey, Kyle, what's your favorite Squiggy episode?" one of the boys asks him. Kyle has been hoping the boys would ignore him. If he tells his friends he's never seen the show because of Sunday school, they will never stop teasing him! What do you think Kyle should do?

Should Kyle . . .

   A. Make up a story and tell the boys that it was the first episode that not many people saw?
   B. Tell the boys that he's at church when the show is on and hasn't seen any episodes?
   C. Tell the boys his family won't let him watch any shows about sea creatures because he gets sick when he's around fish?

 Look up Psalm 84:10 to know what Kyle should do. Make a list of all the things you enjoy about going to Sunday school and church. What would you say to a friend who made fun of you because you go to church?

My Heroes!

For the past week the entire school has been buzzing about the news—the Dirty Dogs are coming to town for a concert. The Dogs are the hottest new band to hit the music scene. Everyone has their newest CD. Stephanie's best friend Mia has an older sister who is into the Dogs. Stephanie hears the music every time she goes to Mia's house. Stephanie doesn't really like the Dogs. To be truthful, she would rather listen to Christian singers. They are her heroes. Now, Stephanie has a problem. Mia's parents are taking her and her big sister to the Dirty Dogs concert, and Mia wants Stephanie to go with them. What do you think Stephanie should do?

Should Stephanie . . .

    A. Go, but wear earplugs and dark sunglasses?
    B. Tell Mia that her long-lost great-uncle is coming into town that night and she'd better stay home to see him because he may get lost again?
    C. Tell her friend that she doesn't really like the music and would rather not go?

 For help in knowing what Stephanie should do, read Psalm 16:3.
Make a list of the people you consider to be your heroes. What is it about these people that you most admire? Would your list be the same as that of your friends?

The correct answer is C.

Make a Decision

At age 7, Rebeka has been asked to join the intermediate level ballet classes at her dance school. This is quite an honor for Rebeka. Usually girls don't enter the intermediate classes until they are 9 or 10. But her instructor feels Rebeka will fit in. Rebeka is not totally sure this is right for her. If she moves to the higher-level class, she won't be with her best friend any-more. Her mother also told her she'll probably need more practice time to keep up with the other girls. And that will mean less time with all her friends! How is she going to make this decision? What do you think Rebeka should do?

Should Rebeka . . .

A. Pray about it and tell her concerns to the people she trusts the most—her parents and her dance instructor?
B. Toss a coin—heads, she moves up; tails, she stays where she is?
C. Look for a Bible verse that says, "You shall go to the interme-diate dance class"?

 Check out Proverbs 3:5-6 to know where Rebeka should go for help in making her decision.
Ask your mom and dad to share a time when they had an important decision to make. Talk about how they made that decision. How can you put God first when you have impor-tant decisions to make? Can you ask for his help to make the best decision?

I'm on Vacation

David wriggles his toes underneath the sheets. He is enjoying a nice, long weekend, with no school until Tuesday. David stretches, enjoying the chance to stay in bed as long as he wants without having to get up and rush around getting ready for *anything!* What will he do today? Go sledding with his buddies? Play computer games? Maybe catch a video? Suddenly he hears his mom's voice calling him. "David, it's time to get ready for church! Better get up now!"

What's this? Church? That is definitely not part of David's plans for today! Why does David need to go to church on his long weekend off from school? Shouldn't he get some time off from Sunday school, too? What do you think David should do?

Should David . . .

- A. Pretend that he's sleeping and ignore his mom?
- B. Tell his mom he's taking a vacation from church today?
- C. Get with it—get out of bed and go to church because God doesn't take a vacation from caring for David, and neither should David take a vacation from worshiping God?

Read 1 Peter 1:15-16 to see what God desires for David—and for you.
Read the Bible passage aloud. What do you think it means to be holy in everything you do? Make a list with your mom or dad of things you can do to be holy.

The correct answer is C.

Top This!

Eric and Joel are walking to school. As they near the corner, they are joined by Hanson, the biggest bragger in the entire school. Sure enough, as soon as they join him, Hanson says, "My parents just bought the biggest TV set you've ever seen. It covers the entire wall in our family room. It's just like going to the movies."

Joel answers, "Oh yeah? Well, we've got a big-screen TV in our family room *and* down in the rec room so my brothers and I can play video games. It's awesome!"

The two boys look at Eric. Eric doesn't know what to say. His family only owns one regular-sized TV set. And besides that, he and his sisters aren't allowed to watch much TV anyway. What do you think Eric should do?

Should Eric . . .

    A. Tell the boys, "My mom and dad are letting me have the biggest TV you've ever seen for my own room"?
    B. Say, "That's great, you guys," and change the subject: "Did you get the math homework?"
    C. Tell his friends that watching too much TV on a big screen causes your eyes to pop out?

 Check out Jeremiah 9:23-24 to know what really is worth bragging about.
With your family, make a list of the things you have as a believer in Jesus to brag about.

The correct answer is B.

It's Movie Time

Cameron opens the note and sees that his friend Casey is asking him to come to a movie party. Cameron knows if he wants to go he has to find out what movie they are going to see before his parents give the okay. Cameron calls up his friend and knows that it's hopeless. Casey plans to take his friends to see a movie that's not only PG-13, but it also is superviolent. That's why most of the boys in his class like the movie—there is lots of action and lots of blood. Cameron knows his parents won't let him see that movie, but he really wants to go to Casey's party. All the guys in his class are going. He doesn't want to be left out. What do you think Cameron should do?

Should Cameron . . .

A. Tell his mom and dad that they are going to see *Bambi Returns*?
B. Tell his mom and dad that he if he goes, he'll go get popcorn during the violent parts?
C. Tell Casey that he's sorry, but he can't come to the party?

 Take a look at Psalm 97:10 for help in knowing what Cameron should do.
The Bible passage says you should love the things that God loves. With your mom or dad, make a list of things that God loves. Then make a list of things that God hates. How does knowing this help you make good choices?

When I Grow Up . . .

Abby is at her friend Mallory's house for a sleepover party. As the girls get into bed and turn out the light, they keep talking about what they want to be when they get older. "That's easy," says Mallory. "I want to be a lawyer, just like my dad. Then I'll be able to have a big house, drive a cool car, and have lots of money."

"Well," says Jenna, "I want to be on stage. Everyone says I have a good voice, and I love to act. I want to see my picture in all the magazines someday."

Abby doesn't know what to say. She loves helping her mom with the preschool Sunday school class, and she's thinking about being a teacher. Abby also knows that God is part of her future plans. But that doesn't sound as exciting as being famous or rich. What do you think Abby should say to her friends?

Should Abby . . .

A. Tell her friends she hasn't decided but it's between being president and being a race car driver?
B. Tell her friends she is thinking about being a teacher, but it depends on what God wants her to do?
C. Tell her friends she plans to buy a Magic 8-Ball to help her decide what to do?

 Read James 4:15-16 to know how Abby should handle this situation.
What do you want to be when you grow up? Discuss with your mom or dad how you can make God a part of your future plans.

The correct answer is B.

The Collection

Miles has a cool collection of miniature cars. He never really *plays* with his cars. Sometimes he'll take out one box and look at the cars, but he doesn't race them around his room or roll them down the driveway. What Miles *does* like is collecting them! Whenever he has some money, he begs his mom to take him to the hobby shop so he can get one more car. Today his Sunday school teacher is talking about "stuff" that can become more important than God. Miles thinks about his car collection. He knows it's not more important than God, but he doesn't want anyone messing with it! Then his teacher says there will be a used-toy drive for poor kids. She suggests this might be a good time to get rid of some "stuff." What do you think Miles should do?

Should Miles . . .

    A. Bring in one car as a donation?
    B. See what's in his sister's closet that they could donate to the toy drive?
    C. Decide there probably are lots of kids who would enjoy playing with those cars and donate most of his collection?

 Look up Luke 12:33 for help in knowing what Miles should do.
What is the "stuff" that's important in your life? (If you're not sure, take a look in your closet or under your bed!) Arrange an early spring cleaning and look for items you might be able to give away.

Review Time!

Think of three things you learned about storing "heavenly treasures" during this month.

1.

2.

3.

Bonus

List three treasures you plan to store.

1.

2.

3.

Repeat your memory verse to someone you admire today. (The verse is printed on the page just before February 1.)

Faithfulness

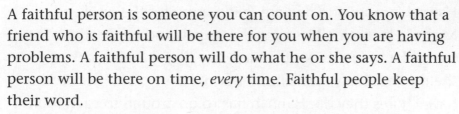

A faithful person is someone you can count on. You know that a friend who is faithful will be there for you when you are having problems. A faithful person will do what he or she says. A faithful person will be there on time, *every* time. Faithful people keep their word.

When you think of someone who is faithful, who comes to mind? Is it your pet dog who greets you with a big, sloppy, wet kiss every day after school—no matter what? Is it your mom or dad who are there to comfort you when you wake up in the middle of the night with a bad dream? Do you think of God, who promises he will never leave you or forget about you (Hebrews 13:5)?

God calls us to be faithful people. We need to be faithful in our words, our work, our friendships, our family, and our relationship with God. Being faithful is not always easy. We may not always feel like going to choir practice or saying our prayers. Or maybe we would rather watch TV than do chores or help a friend. Our situation or circumstances may make it difficult to be faithful. But God can help us be faithful because he is always faithful to *us*.

As you work through this month's *Sticky Situations*, think about the different times when God calls you to be faithful. Look for opportunities to be faithful at home, school, or in the neighborhood.

Memory Verse: Unless you are faithful in small matters, you won't be faithful in large ones. If you cheat even a little, you won't be honest with greater responsibilities. Luke 16:10

Weekend Chores

Hannah's mom and dad are going away for the weekend. Michelle is coming to stay with Hannah and her brother. They have a lot of fun things planned, like going to the park and the movies. Every weekend, though, Hannah and her brother have chores they do. Hannah has to go around to each room and empty the wastebaskets. Her brother has to pick up all the toys in the basement. And they both have to take the sheets off their beds and pick up their rooms. When Hannah and her brother come downstairs Saturday morning, Michelle tells them as soon as they get done with breakfast, they can get ready to go to the park. Hannah and her brother look at each other. Michelle didn't say a word about their chores! What do you think Hannah should do?

Should Hannah . . .

> A. Give her brother a high five and eat breakfast so they can get out of the house fast?
> B. Say nothing about the chores and tell her parents that Michelle said they didn't have to do any chores?
> C. Tell Michelle that they really need to do their chores first before they go out?

 Check out Matthew 24:45-51 for help in knowing what Hannah should do.
Being faithful about doing your chores is a challenge, especially if no one is there to tell you to do them! Talk with your mom and dad about a time when they didn't do their chores. Ask what happened.

The correct answer is C.

The Paper Boys

The Paper Boys, one of the hottest Christian bands, are coming to Jared's church for a concert. It seems that the pastor's son knows the drummer, so the group is stopping here as a favor. Jared's mom and dad bought some tickets and told him that he could invite a friend. Jared wants to invite his best friend, Mason. His friend doesn't go in for much church stuff. But the boys like the same kind of music, and Jared knows Mason will enjoy the concert. When Jared asks him, though, Mason says, "They aren't going to talk about all that God stuff, are they?" Jared doesn't know for sure, but he thinks they probably will talk about what they believe. What do you think Jared should tell his friend?

Should Jared . . .

A. Tell Mason he doesn't know; he can bring along some cotton balls just in case?
B. Tell Mason what he knows—that the group usually talks about their beliefs and they probably will share their stories at the concert?
C. Tell Mason no, then act surprised when the "God stuff" comes up?

 Look up 2 Corinthians 4:2 for some help in knowing what Jared should do.
Faithful friends are honest with one another. Think of a time when someone was not totally honest with you. How did you feel? What did you do?

Treats for Everyone

Nicole's class has worked hard to earn points for a party. Not only did they earn the number of points needed, they doubled the number! Her teacher has prepared a bag of treats for everyone. Each bag has candy, a cool pencil and notepad, and some awesome stickers. As the student who did the most outstanding job, Nicole gets to hand out the treats. When she is done, she has one bag left over. It's Jason's bag, but he had to leave early. Nicole can easily slip the extra bag in her desk. Jason is always making trouble anyway and really didn't help the class earn points. Nicole *really* worked hard. What do you think Nicole should do?

Should Nicole . . .

A. Return the bag for her teacher to give Jason—even if Jason doesn't deserve it?
B. Take just the notepad and stickers from Jason's bag and give the rest back to the teacher?
C. Hide the bag in her desk and hope the teacher doesn't remember that Jason left?

 Find out what Nicole should do by reading 2 Chronicles 31:14-15.
Talk with your mom or dad about what might happen if the teacher found out that Nicole took a treat bag. Why do you think it is important to be faithful in carrying out tasks?

The correct answer is A.

The Missionary Kid

Coretta's church has had a missions conference this weekend. It has been a fun conference. There were craft booths and games from other countries for the kids to try out. There was a puppet show about being a missionary. And a missionary family from South America spoke at the Sunday night program. They are missionaries to a tribe that lives in the rain forest. Coretta loved to hear their stories. She is helping to put out pieces of cake when she sees the missionaries' daughter standing by herself. *Someone ought to go over to talk with her,* Coretta thinks, *but everyone is busy.* What do you think Coretta should do?

Should Coretta . . .

    A. Wildly signal to one of her friends to go over and talk with the girl?
    B. Look busy and hope someone else notices the girl standing there?
    C. Go over and ask the girl if she would like to help her with the cake?

 Take a look at 3 John 1:5 for help in knowing what Coretta should do.
Talk with your mom or dad about ways that you can be faithful to missionary families, such as by sending cards, writing letters, and praying for them. Plan something you can do this week.

The correct answer is C.

The Solo

Emily and her friend Kim wait for the music room door to open. They are trying out for a role in the school's spring play. When it's time to go in, Emily goes first. Then she waits outside the room for Kim. She can hear Kim saying her lines. Then she hears her singing as she tries out for a solo. Everyone else hears her too. Soon all the kids behind Emily are giggling. Kim is great at playing basketball, and she is a good reader, but she can't sing. Everyone but Kim knows it. As she and Emily walk home Kim says, "I can't wait to see if I got the solo part. I think I did really well, don't you? This is so exciting!" Emily doesn't know what to say. Emily is doubtful *she* will get the part, and she sang better than Kim. What do you think Emily should tell her friend?

Should Emily . . .

    A. Let Kim see for herself when the list goes up?
    B. Tell Kim that she isn't a good singer, and a lot of other kids sing better than she does?
    C. Agree with Kim that she did her best, but gently remind her that a lot of kids with good voices tried out, so she shouldn't get her hopes up too high?

 Look up Proverbs 27:6 for advice on what Emily should do. It's not easy telling someone news the person doesn't want to hear—especially a friend! Role-play the situation with your mom or dad. How does a faithful friend give bad news?

The "Morning Club"

Early in the school year Miss Kelty asked her students if they would like to take turns being part of her "morning club." These students come in before school starts and help Miss Kelty get things ready for the day. Eric is part of the club for the month of March. He enjoys helping around the classroom, and Miss Kelty always has donuts! It is hard getting up sometimes, but Eric has been faithful in making every single "club" so far. Last night Eric and his family were out late for his older sister's band concert. Before going to bed, Eric wonders if it would be okay to sleep in and miss the "morning club." What do you think Eric should do?

Should Eric . . .

A. Wait until the morning and see if he gets up in time to make the club?
B. Tell his mom to wake him up—he doesn't want to miss club and let Miss Kelty down?
C. Try to make the last five minutes, so he can keep his perfect attendance record going and grab a donut, too?

 Look at Proverbs 25:13 for some good advice on what Eric should do.
What makes a person a faithful member of a group? Why do you think that's important to the leader of that group? How would you rate yourself as a faithful or trustworthy messenger?

Practice Time

Kayla looks at the clock. Only five minutes have gone by! Why is practice time the slowest time on earth? It seems like hours that she has been playing the same piano scale over and over again. But she still has ten more minutes to go! Her mom always sets the timer in the kitchen so they both know when practice time is over. Her fingers go over the scale for the hundredth time. Where is her mother? Kayla stops and calls out, "Mom! Hey, Mom!" No answer. If her mom can't hear her maybe she is in the basement laundry room. Kayla glances again at the clock. Only one minute has gone by. All she has to do is quietly tiptoe into the kitchen and move the timer ahead. Then she will be free to go outside and play before dinner! What do you think Kayla should do?

Should Kayla . . .

A. Move the timer ahead and tell her mom she finished as she runs outside?
B. Stay and finish practicing—her mom probably would figure it out anyway?
C. Throw the timer out the window and tell her mom her practice time really flew by?

 Proverbs 12:19 should help you know what Kayla should do. What happens at your house if someone cheated a little? Plan as a family what will happen if someone tells a lie this week. Plan a fun activity for your family if everyone tells the truth all week.

The correct answer is B.

New Friends and Old

Valerie races to catch up with Caitlin. "Hey, Caitlin, how ya doing?"

Caitlin turns and gives Valerie a big smile. "Where have you been? I haven't seen you in ages," she says. It's true. Valerie hasn't been around much lately. She and Caitlin have been good friends since kindergarten. Now, though, Valerie has been spending more time with Jill, who has an amazing house and even more amazing toys. She has a trampoline in the backyard, too. Valerie almost lives over at Jill's house. Before Valerie can answer, Caitlin asks her to come over to bake brownies with her and her dad on Saturday morning. Valerie doesn't have any plans made yet, but she is hoping that Jill will call and ask her over. What do you think Valerie should do?

Should Valerie . . .

   A. Tell Caitlin she's developed a "brownie allergy" and she better not chance it by coming over?

   B. Call Caitlin later, after she sees if Jill is going to ask her to come over?

   C. Tell Caitlin sure, she'll be over on Saturday?

 Check out Proverbs 20:6 to know what Valerie should do. What kind of friend are you? Together with your mom or dad, come up with five words that describe a good friend. How many of these words would you use to describe yourself?

The correct answer is C.

It's All Make-Believe

Andrew and his best friend, Jacob, are goofing around at Andrew's house after school. The two boys are building a bridge out of connector blocks and are a few short to make the bridge balance. Jacob grabs a book off of Andrew's desk to help prop up the bridge. "Hey, what's this?" he asks. The book Jacob grabbed is Andrew's new Bible. Jacob flips through the pages and starts to read about Moses and the Red Sea. "Hoo boy! You don't believe this stuff, do you? This is just make-believe," Jacob says, shaking his head at Andrew. "They make cartoons out of this stuff!" Andrew doesn't know what to say. He's never really thought about the fact that some people would think the Bible is not true. What do you think Andrew should do?

Should Andrew . . .

    A. Kick Jacob out of his room for saying that stuff about his Bible?

    B. Toss the Bible under his bed and say, "Oh, I don't really believe it"?

    C. Explain to Jacob that he believes that the Bible is true because it is God's Word?

 Check out what Andrew should do by reading Psalm 33:4. Do you have friends who question things about the Bible? How can you remain faithful to what you believe in the face of those questions? Share your thoughts with your mom or dad.

The correct answer is C.

The Young Artist

Kevin is very good at drawing. His art teacher says nice things about his work and always hangs it up where everyone can see it. At church his Sunday school teachers see how good he is at art and crafts, too. When it comes time for making decorations for the church's ham dinner, Kevin's Sunday school teacher calls him and asks if he would help. A group is getting together on Sunday afternoon. Kevin knows that the stuff he will be asked to do won't be very hard for him. In fact, Kevin thinks anyone could do it. Besides, he would rather spend the afternoon working on his art project for the school's art fair. What do you think Kevin should do?

Should Kevin . . .

    A. Go and help out with whatever is needed?
    B. Give the group a list of other possible helpers who can do the job just as well as he can?
    C. Tell the group that someone who is as good at art as he is doesn't "do" decorations?

 Read Luke 19:26 to see what Kevin should do.
Make a list of your abilities and talents. How faithful are you in using those gifts to help other people? What are some more ways you can use your gifts?
Reminder: Don't forget to work on your memory verse for March. (You'll find it on the page just before March 1.)

The correct answer is A.

Take That First Step

Vickie's dance class meets on Saturday mornings right after the very youngest girls have their class. Vickie is one of the best dancers in the class. Often she and a friend come a little bit early to stretch and warm up. Sometimes they stand around and watch the little girls practice their dance steps. There is one little girl who tries very hard but doesn't seem to get the hang of it. She's always a beat or two behind the other girls. Today is a very bad day for this girl. Not only does she do the steps wrong, but she also falls down trying to do the steps! The class breaks out laughing, and even Vickie's friend starts to laugh. Vickie feels sorry for the little girl. What do you think Vickie should do?

Should Vickie . . .

    A. Not worry about helping the girl because it's the teacher's problem?
    B. Offer to help the little girl practice her steps after class?
    C. Tell the little girl to try something that's easy to do, like walking?

 For help in knowing what Vickie should do, read 2 Chronicles 34:12-13.
Ask your mom or dad to share a time when they were faithful in using their skills to teach someone else. What are some skills you can help others to learn?

The correct answer is B.

Get Rid of Those Doubts

Nate hears his dad walk into the house. He runs up and asks him, "Did you get it? Did you get it?"

His dad gives him a tired smile and shakes his head no. "Sorry, Son, but it looks like they are going to hire someone else," he says.

Nate runs to his room so his dad won't see him cry. It has been nearly nine months since his dad lost his job. Every time his dad goes on an interview Nate prays to God like crazy, "Please, God, let this be the job." And every time his dad comes home with no job. Nate is beginning to think that God just doesn't hear him. Nate hits his pillow in anger. What is the point of all these prayers if God doesn't hear him? What do you think Nate should do?

Should Nate . . .

    A. Get his pastor to pray instead; maybe he has a better connection to God?
    B. Forget about praying and start looking for a four-leaf clover?
    C. Keep on praying and believing that God hears our prayers and will answer them?

 Check out James 1:6-7 for help in knowing what Nate should do.
Ask your mom or dad to share a time when they had to keep praying faithfully and wait a long time for an answer. Ask them to share what kept them going.

The correct answer is C.

The Blame Game

Every day after school Karla and Ryan fix themselves a snack before watching TV and then starting their homework. Every evening their mom comes into the family room and tells them to clean up their snack dishes. Karla remembers sometimes, but her brother *always* forgets! Today Karla gets home from school late. Her brother already has had his snack and has gone to a friend's house. It's hard to believe, but Ryan put his snack dishes in the dishwasher! Karla makes her snack and hurries to watch the last half of her TV show. As she is watching TV, Karla hears her mom come into the kitchen. "I have told Ryan a thousand times to put away his dishes," she hears her mom saying. Karla knows that those dishes are *her* dishes. What do you think Karla should do?

Should Karla . . .

> A. Keep quiet and hope that her mom forgets about the dishes by the time her brother comes home?
> B. Run in and offer to clean it up, saying, "You would think Ryan would learn how to do this by now"?
> C. Tell her mom, "Sorry, Mom, but those are my dishes"?

For help in knowing what Karla should do, read Proverbs 14:5.
Think of a time when it was difficult for you to faithfully tell the truth. How did you handle that situation?

The Math Test

Brooke is having a hard time with math. Her teacher might as well be speaking another language whenever it is time for math. The problems she has to work for tomorrow are even harder than usual. Her dad tries to help her, but Brooke simply doesn't get it. Finally Brooke runs crying from the family room. Her dad follows her up to her room and waits for her to calm down. "You know, Brooke, I had trouble in math too, when I was your age," he tells her. "But somehow with a lot of hard work *and* with a lot of prayers, I got through it. I'll be praying for you, but you should pray too." After her dad leaves, she thinks about what her dad said. She never thought to pray about math before. What do you think Brooke should do?

Should Brooke . . .

   A. Begin to pray and see what happens?
   B. Tell her dad she "prayed" about it and is going to give up math?
   C. Leave the praying up to her dad?

 Read Colossians 4:2 to see what Brooke should do.
Talk with your family about school situations that you should be praying for. How can being faithful in praying about the non-emergency situations help you later?

A Faithful Friend

There are many examples in the Bible of people being faithful—to their families, to their friends, to their country, and most of all, to God. One of those examples of faithfulness is Ruth. She promised her mother-in-law, Naomi, that she would not leave her but would go wherever Naomi went. For Ruth, that meant leaving her country and going to a strange place. Ruth did what she promised—she was faithful. You can read about her story in Ruth 1:1-22.

Help Ruth follow Naomi's path to their new home in Bethlehem.

Ruth replied, "Don't ask me to leave you and turn back. I will go wherever you go and live wherever you live. Your people will be my people, and your God will be my God."

Ruth 1:16

The Birthday Surprise

Ben and his mom are going out shopping tonight for his little brother's birthday. It's next Wednesday, and his brother has been begging for a Teddy Train Set. It's all he ever talks about! Ben and his mom go to four stores before they find the train set. Actually, it's a much bigger set than the one his brother has asked for, and Ben knows his brother will go bonkers once he sees it. Ben's mom makes him promise he won't tell his brother about the gift. Right after Ben and his mom get home, Ben's younger brother begins begging Ben to tell him what they bought for him. At first Ben doesn't answer his brother's questions. But after an hour or so of begging, Ben can't take it anymore! What do you think Ben should do?

Should he . . .

A. Tell his brother what they bought and spoil the surprise because his brother is being such a pain?
B. Tell his brother they bought him a year's supply of underwear and brussels sprouts?
C. Tell his brother he'll have to wait until next Wednesday to find out what the surprise is?

 Look up Proverbs 11:13 for help in knowing what Ben should do.
How good are you at keeping secrets? Plan a surprise for a family member and keep it a secret!

The correct answer is C.

Show a Little Faith

Stephen's Sunday school teacher is trying to get some students from class to help pick up the grounds at the local homeless shelter once a month. Stephen thinks it's probably a wonderful way to help people, but quite honestly, he is really busy. He plays on a basketball team twice a week, he takes piano lessons, and he's involved in scouts. The scouts do community service projects, too, so Stephen believes he's got things covered in the good deeds department. Besides, he goes to Sunday school every week, and he even takes time to learn the Bible memory verse each month. Isn't that enough? What do you think Stephen should do when the sign-up sheet comes around?

Should he . . .

    A. Agree to go and help out at least once?
    B. Tell his Sunday school teacher that he already is "covered" in the good deeds department?
    C. Go over his schedule with his Sunday school teacher and prove to him that he really doesn't have time for one more good deed?

 Take a look at James 2:17-18 to see how Stephen should respond.
Discuss with your mom or dad why you think it's important to do good deeds as a Christian. What do you think your good deeds show to other people? Can you ever do enough good deeds?

Take a Message

Karina is watching TV when the telephone rings. Naturally, it's for her older sister, Jackie, who is in high school. She is never at home, and Karina ends up being her chief message-taker. Usually it's one of Jackie's friends, so it's no big deal. But today it's Mrs. Jefferson, who wants to know if Jackie can baby-sit on Saturday. She asks Karina to have Jackie call her back that evening. Karina knows that Jackie is taking all the jobs she can because she is earning money for a band trip to Florida. Karina promises Mrs. Jefferson she'll get the message to Jackie. When she hangs up the phone, Karina thinks to herself that this would be a good time to get back at Jackie. Karina still is angry because Jackie wouldn't let her listen to her new CD the other day. What do you think Karina should do?

Should Karina . . .

A. "Accidentally" drop the message in the garbage can and later claim that she lost it somewhere?
B. Make sure Jackie gets the message as soon as she gets home?
C. Give Jackie the message the following day—when it's too late for her to reply to Mrs. Jefferson?

 Check out Proverbs 13:17 to see what Karina should do. When have you had to be a reliable messenger? Talk with your family about why being faithful to pass along messages is important in a family, at school, and with your friends.

The correct answer is B.

Neighborhood Nerd

Isabella is really upset with her neighbor, Garret. She wonders why this always has to happen. It's so typical. She and her friends will be playing a game, and Garret asks to join them. When he does, he always causes a big fuss. Just like now. Isabella usually feels sorry for Garret and tries to stick up for him. He's short, wears thick glasses, and just doesn't know how to get along with the other kids. He always seems to know exactly what to do to bother everyone. Today he has even upset Isabella. As he picks up his stuff to go home, a couple of the kids begin to shout, "Garret is a nerd ball! Garret is a nerd ball!" Isabella is angry enough with Garret to join in too. What do you think Isabella should do?

Should Isabella . . .

    A. Yell the loudest because she is the most upset?
    B. Walk home with Garret and try to explain how to get along with the others?
    C. Agree with the other kids that they will never allow Garret to play with them again?

 Look up 1 Peter 2:12 for some good advice on what Isabella should do.
Talk with your mom or dad about times when it's important to stand up to the "crowd" and not follow what they are doing. Have you ever done this?

The correct answer is B.

The Panic Button

It has been a busy week for Bradley. His grandma came for a visit, so before she came he was busy getting the house ready. After she came he spent a lot of time with her. Plus, it has been a busy week at school. Now Grandma has gone home, and he has the rest of the afternoon to chill out before school tomorrow. Bradley is kicking back, surfing through the TV channels, when he sees there is a show on the Loch Ness monster. He hears these words: "Let's visit this small village in Scotland . . ." Bradley sits up with a jolt. Scotland! His report for school on Scotland is due tomorrow! He forgot all about it during the week! The library closes in another thirty minutes. What do you think Bradley should do?

Should Bradley . . .

- A. Go into panic mode and run through the house screaming, "Tell me everything you know about Scotland"?
- B. Tell his teacher that the Loch Ness monster, er, his dog ate his report?
- C. Tell his mom or dad about it and come up with a plan for doing as much as he can before school?

 Take a look at 2 Timothy 4:5 to see how Bradley should respond in that situation.
Ask your mom or dad to tell about a time when they had a tough job to complete at work, home, or church. What helped them to be faithful and complete it?

The correct answer is C.

Sing Your Heart Out!

Mika hates to sing. It's not because he doesn't enjoy music. He likes to listen to *other* people sing. But he doesn't think his own voice sounds very good. When Mika sings by himself in his room, his dog hides under the bed and his parakeet starts to screech. At church his Sunday school recently started a worship time just for kids. Mika usually sits in the back of the room with the other boys his age. Before going to the worship time today, his Sunday school teacher pulls him aside. "You know, Mika, the other boys really look up to you and follow you. You could help us out in getting the others to sing if you would join the singing." That's the last thing Mika wants to do! What do you think Mika should do?

Should Mika . . .

  A. Explain to his teacher that having a group of howling dogs would be better than him singing?
  B. Be a good example and sing, no matter what sound comes out?
  C. Tell his teacher he'll mention it to the other boys?

 Read Nehemiah 5:16 to see how Nehemiah worked along with all of the others, leading them in rebuilding the wall around Jerusalem.
Think of some areas at school or at home where you could show leadership. How can you be a faithful leader in those situations?

Show Some Respect

Amanda really doesn't like going to Sunday school anymore. She still enjoys seeing her friends at church, and she really likes learning about Jesus. But she doesn't like her Sunday school teacher at all! Mr. Martin has no sense of humor. He tells the kids where to sit, but worst of all, he seems to like the boys more than the girls. Whenever he has a question, he never calls on a girl. Amanda has to admit that Mr. Martin knows a lot about the Bible. Still, she thinks he is totally unfair, especially to her and her friends. Today in class Amanda has raised her hand three times to answer a question, but Mr. Martin never calls on her. Amanda is totally upset. What do you think she should do?

Should Amanda . . .

    A. Ask her parents if they can go to another church?
    B. Start acting up in class. Maybe Mr. Martin will notice her then?
    C. Keep trying and do her best in class no matter how she feels she is treated?

 Take a look at 1 Timothy 6:1-2 for help in knowing what Amanda should do.
Is there a "Mr. Martin" in your life? Talk with your mom or dad about how you can be a faithful member of that class, troop, or activity.

The Perfect Opportunity

David and his friend Cade are going to play together after school at David's house. Cade just moved into the neighborhood, but he and David have already become good friends. After having a quick snack, the boys head up to David's room to find a game to play. As David is looking for a game in the closet, Cade looks at all the other stuff in his room. "Hey, you have a lot of stuff about the Bible and God in your room. How come?" Cade asks. David gets a twinge in his stomach! This is exactly what they have been talking about in Sunday school—being faithful witnesses when opportunities come up to talk about what they believe! And this is the perfect opportunity! What do you think David should do?

Should he . . .

  A. Shrug his shoulders and say, "My mom likes to put that stuff in here—I don't know why"?
  B. Explain that he and his family believe in God and like to read about him in the Bible?
  C. Change the subject quickly and say, "Why don't we go outside to play?"

 Look up 1 Peter 3:15-16 for help in knowing how David should respond.
Role-play the situation above with your mom or dad. What would you say to David's friend to explain what you believe? What opportunities have you had to be a faithful witness?

The correct answer is B.

The Zoo Trip

Trisha is going to the zoo with her aunt this morning. Trisha's older sisters are away on a church retreat, so this is a big treat for Trisha to be with her aunt all by herself. Her aunt lives in the city, has a really cool apartment, and shops in lots of fun stores. Trisha's mom has given her some money so she can get something for herself when they go shopping later. Trisha is sure it's going to be a great day! The first thing on their list of things to do is go to the zoo. When they get there, Trisha's aunt studies the admission prices. She decides since Trisha is on the short side, she can pass for "Under Six" even though Trisha is almost seven. Trisha knows her parents always pay regular admission for her. What do you think Trisha should do?

Should Trisha . . .

A. Tell her aunt that her mom gave her some extra money to spend and buy her own admission ticket?
B. Let her aunt make the decision?
C. Make sure to act like a six-year-old so when she gets up to the ticket booth they won't question her?

 2 Timothy 3:14 should help you decide what Trisha should do.
Talk with your mom or dad about why it is important to be faithful in doing the right thing even when others don't choose the right way.

The correct answer is A.

The Kid Next Door

Even without answering the door, Dominick can tell who's there. Only one person keeps ringing the doorbell that way—Wayne, his little next-door neighbor. Wayne tags after Dominick every chance he gets. If Dominick is outside shooting hoops, Wayne runs and gets his ball, even if he can't hit the rim with the basketball. When Dominick is outside pulling weeds for his mom, Wayne is right beside him, asking him all sorts of questions. As soon as Dominick gets home from school—like today—Wayne is ringing the doorbell, wanting to know if Dominick can play. Dominick wants to hang around the yard or shoot some hoops by himself today. The doorbell has rung about twenty times. What do you think Dominick should do?

Should Dominick . . .

A. Shout out the window, "There's nobody here but us chickens"?
B. Tell Wayne he can play as long as he chases all the basketballs that roll away?
C. Invite Wayne to shoot some hoops with him and lower the basket so Wayne can make some shots too?

 Check out Joshua 22:5 to know what Dominick should do. Think of expressing love to others as a way to know how faithful you are to God. Are you faithful to him even when it's hard to love someone?

The correct answer is C.

Family Devotions

Sydney's parents told the family that every night after dinner they will do a family devotion. They explain that they will just read a few verses from the Bible and talk about them. Sydney's brother says he needs to practice his saxophone after dinner. Sydney has math homework almost every night, and now it will take her longer to get it done. Sydney's dad says devotions need to come first, so he begins to read from the Bible. As her dad reads several verses, Sydney realizes that they talk about how to act in a situation that occurred at school today! She can't believe that anything that happened so long ago (to people who didn't even have microwaves or VCRs) could be so similar to her world today. What do you think Sydney should do?

Should Sydney . . .

    A. Listen and try to get something out of the family devotional time?
    B. Share what happened today and talk about how it relates to what it says in the Bible?
    C. Roll her eyes, slump in her chair, and tune her dad out?

 Take a look at Psalm 31:23-24 for help in knowing what Sydney should do.
In what ways can you be faithful in loving God? With your mom or dad, make a list of things you can do as a family and by yourself.

Fish Food

Jasmine has been chosen by her teacher to take care of the class pet fish over the long holiday weekend. It's quite an honor to be chosen. Only students who have turned in all their homework and who have been good workers are selected. Jasmine proudly carries the goldfish home on Friday afternoon. She and her mom find a good place to put the fishbowl so they'll remember to feed it each day. When her dad gets home—before Jasmine can even show him the fish—he says that he just got a great deal for a family getaway trip in a nearby city. Jasmine has always wanted to visit this city, and she is really excited. Then she sees the class fish on the kitchen counter. What is she going to do about the fish!? What do you think Jasmine should do?

Should Jasmine . . .

    A. Start calling some of her friends to see if they can take care of the fish while she is away?
    B. Dump some fish food in the bowl before they leave and let the fish eat that over the weekend?
    C. Call the hotel to see if they take pets?

 Check out 1 Corinthians 4:2 to see what Jasmine should do. Have you ever been in a situation like Jasmine where something kept you from doing what you promised? Were you faithful in that situation? How?

Doubting Thomas

As Cameron is checking out his books at the library, he turns around and almost runs over his friend Thomas. "Hey, Thomas, where have you been? I haven't seen you around much lately," Cameron says. "I've missed you at Sunday school the past couple weeks."

Thomas seems a bit uncomfortable. "Well, my mom and dad have been so busy fixing up the house and everything, we haven't had much time for church," Thomas explains. "I guess I'll come back again when we're not so busy." Cameron feels hurt as his friend runs off. He always has a good time with Thomas at Sunday school, and he thought Thomas did too. Cameron wishes his friend would be more faithful. What do you think Cameron should do?

Should Cameron . . .

- A. Report Thomas to the Sunday school police and have him picked up?
- B. Invite Thomas to come to Sunday school with him sometime so he'll get back in the habit of coming?
- C. Ignore Thomas the next time he sees him, because Cameron doesn't want to be friends with someone like him?

 For help in knowing what Cameron should do, look up Jude 1:22.
Do you know someone who needs to be encouraged to be more faithful? What could you do to encourage them?

The correct answer is B.

Delivery Time

Jordan's church is sponsoring a big spring festival in a couple of weeks. There's going to be some entertainment and food for the adults, games and crafts for the kids, and even some special events like a moon walk and pony rides. The church is hoping the entire community will come and is trying hard to get the word out. As their contribution to the festival, the children in Jordan's Sunday school class have each been given a stack of about three dozen flyers to hand out to neighbors and friends. It's been a busy week for Jordan, and it's not until Saturday after-noon that he notices that the stack of flyers are still sitting on his bedroom floor. Jordan doesn't really feel like walking around the neighborhood now. What do you think Jordan should do?

Should he . . .

    A. Throw the flyers out the window and deliver them by "air mail"?

    B. Not worry about it—his neighbors probably got a flyer from someone else in his Sunday school class who lives in the neighborhood?

    C. Take the flyers around now?

 Read Luke 16:10 for help in knowing what Jordan should do. If you are learning to say this verse from memory, practice saying it now to someone in your family.

Talk with your mom or dad about why it is important for each person to do his or her part in a project, no matter how small. What does the Bible say happens when you are faithful in the small things? What happens when you are not?

The correct answer is C.

The Final Exam

Today is the big science test. Tori has studied very hard for it over the past several days. She needs to get a good grade on this test to bring her grade in science from a C to a B. Her dad has promised her that he will take her to the opening day of the *Great Adventure* amusement park if she gets all A's and B's. Tori quickly goes through the first ten test questions. This is going to be easier than she had thought. Then she gets to question fifteen. She looks at the four choices. Tori knows this question. She can remember reading about it. She just can't remember the answer! Then the girl in front of her gets up to sharpen her pencil. Tori has a clear view of the girl's paper— and, if she wants, the answer to fifteen. What do you think Tori should do?

Should Tori . . .

    A. Do her best by choosing the answer that sounds right to her?
    B. Glance at the other girl's paper to help her memory?
    C. Ask the teacher if she can have a tiny hint on question 15?

 Look at Proverbs 21:3 for help in knowing what Tori should do.
Talk about times when it might be easy to be tempted to cheat a little. Do you think God wants us to be faithful in doing the right thing, even if the outcome is less than perfect?

The correct answer is A.

Review Time!

Think of three ways that God has been faithful to you this month.

1.

2.

3.

Bonus

List three ways you have been faithful to God or a person you know.

1.

2.

3.

Repeat your memory verse to a relative or friend who doesn't live in your house. (The verse is printed on the page just before March 1.)

Controlling the Tongue

What do you think is the most powerful part of your body? If you're a soccer player, you might say your legs. If you swim, it might be your arms. But do you know that the most powerful part of anyone's body is the tongue? With our tongue, we can say words that will help others, or we can say words that will hurt. What we say affects others even more than what we do.

Think of how you use your tongue throughout the day. Do you use it to say untrue words about people? Are your words angry or kind? Do you say words to comfort a friend or to make a friend feel bad?

How we use our tongue to speak is very important to God. The Bible is filled with directions on how to be wise and careful about what we say. James, the writer of the book of James, says that no one can control the tongue. But with the help of God the Holy Spirit, we can learn to think before we speak.

As you work through this month's *Sticky Situations,* think about the way you speak. If you tend to say the first thing that comes to mind, ask the Holy Spirit to help you wait before speaking. If you tend to say unkind words, the Holy Spirit can help to soften your spirit and your words.

Memory Verse: The tongue is a small thing, but what enormous damage it can do. A tiny spark can set a great forest on fire. And the tongue is a flame of fire. James 3:5-6

Picture Day

Callie gives her best smile when the photographer says, "Okay, say cheese!" This is going to be the best school picture yet. The ice-blue sweater she has "borrowed" from her older sister's closet is the perfect touch to her outfit. All Callie has to do is get home before her sister comes home from volleyball practice and hang the sweater back in her closet. Her older sister will never know—until the pictures come back. By then, Callie figures, it will be too late for her sister to do anything to her. Callie's plan works except for one tiny detail—lunch! Callie's best friend accidentally spills her fruit drink all over Callie. A large pink stain now covers her sister's once-blue sweater. Callie tries clean up the stain, but it won't go away. What do you think Callie should do?

Should Callie . . .

    A. Run home, hang up the sweater in her sister's closet, and pretend she doesn't know a thing about it?

    B. Give the sweater to her sister and say, "April Fools! Your blue sweater is really pink"?

    C. Admit what happened to the sweater and offer to do her sister's chores for a month as payback?

 Read Mark 4:22-23 to find out what Callie should do. What are some things that can happen if you try to cover up something you do wrong?

The Missing Umbrella

Michael is working on his spelling when he catches a flash of yellow out of the corner of his eye. A boy across the room is slipping something yellow into his backpack. Michael quickly looks away. It's not just any boy. It's Rob, the biggest and meanest boy in the school. It is an unwritten rule that you don't mess with Rob, and Michael makes a point of following that rule. Michael goes back to work. At the end of the day, however, one of the girls in his class says she has lost her new yellow umbrella. Michael looks to see if anyone else saw what Rob did. No one seems to have a clue. But if he tells on Rob, he is sure to pay for it on the playground after school. What do you think Michael should do?

Should Michael . . .

    A. Offer to buy the girl another umbrella in order to keep the peace?
    B. Talk to the teacher after class and tell her what he saw?
    C. Forget about it because he wasn't sure it was the umbrella—it might have been a banana?

 Read Zechariah 8:16 for help in knowing what Michael should do.
Talk with your mom or dad about a time when telling the truth would be hard.

Surf's Up!

Trevor and Grant are goofing around at Trevor's house on a rainy Saturday. Grant suggests that they surf the Internet for a while. He knows some cool sites that have some great games to play. Trevor's dad, though, has told him never to be on the Internet unless he is there. Trevor tells Grant about his dad's rule. "C'mon, Trevor," Grant says. "We'll be on and off before you know it."

Trevor wavers, "I'm not sure, Grant. My dad told me no, and besides, you know what we just learned in Sunday school about obeying our parents."

Grant says, "Oh, Trevor. You obey your parents most of the time, don't you? Your dad will never know about this. It's no big deal."

What do you think Trevor should do?

Should Trevor . . .

    A. Tell Grant he really wants to wait until his dad gets home; then they can surf the Net?
    B. Put a picture of his dad by the computer so he can go surfing and say to himself that he is obeying because his dad's picture is there?
    C. Suggest they go over to Grant's house and surf the Net?

 Check out 3 John 1:3-4 to know what Trevor should do. Talk over with your family the rules you have about using the computer (or TV) at your house. Name reasons why you should tell the truth about whether or not you obey the rules.

The correct answer is A.

Stick to the Truth

As Sumiko approaches the playground, she wonders what's going on. All her friends are in a big circle, talking. "Hey, what's going on?" she asks.

"Haven't you heard the news? Mrs. McAfee got really sick, and now we have a substitute for the rest of the school year," one friend informs her.

Another chimes in, "Yeah, and we heard it's Mrs. Holt! She's really old, and she hates boys."

Another girl contributes this piece of news: "My older brother had her for a sub once, and he said she is totally mean. You have to sit in your desk the whole day."

Sumiko knows exactly who Mrs. Holt is. She is Sumiko's neighbor, and although a bit gruff, she is really nice. What do you think Sumiko should do?

Should Sumiko . . .

- A. Keep quiet and let her friends find out for themselves about Mrs. Holt?
- B. Tell her friends that once Mrs. Holt chased her and her brother down the block for walking across her grass?
- C. Tell her friends that Mrs. Holt is really nice once you get to know her?

 Look up Numbers 13:30-32 to find out what Sumiko should do. Talk with your mom or dad about what you could say if someone said unkind things about one of your neighbors.

The correct answer is C.

Close Cousins?

Kelly's cousin is spending the weekend with Kelly and her family. It's been a long time since Kelly has seen Tiffany— probably when they were four years old. But Kelly remembers they had a lot of fun together. Even though it's been a couple of years, Kelly is sure they will get along just fine. But as soon as Tiffany walks in her room, Kelly can tell she is in for a long weekend. Tiffany doesn't like anything. She doesn't like the same music. She doesn't like to play the same games. She doesn't even like to watch the same TV shows as Kelly. By the end of the first evening together, Kelly is about ready to blow a major fuse. As she helps her mom with the dishes after dinner, her mom asks her how things are going with Tiffany. What do you think Kelly should say?

Should Kelly . . .

A. Really unload and tell her mom all the things that are wrong with Tiffany?
B. Tell her mom that this is absolutely the last time she wants Tiffany to visit?
C. Ask her mom for help in knowing what to do with Tiffany?

 For help in knowing what Kelly should do, read James 5:9. Is there someone you tend to grumble about? Think of some things you can do to keep yourself from being that type of grumbler.

The correct answer is C.

Bonus Time

Tony carefully counts out the dollar bills and the big pile of change. After weeks of doing chores and keeping up with his reading, Tony has earned enough money to buy one of the latest Monster Maniacs comic books. Word is out around school that the comic-book store has the newest Monster Maniacs. Tony sees at least three at the store that he wants. Tony finally takes two up to the register to make a last-minute decision. He has enough money for just one, so Tony ends up picking the latest one. When he gets home, he pulls out the Monster Maniac. Imagine his surprise when he discovers the store clerk made a mistake and slipped both comics into his bag! What do you think Tony should do?

Should Tony . . .

A. Yell, "Bonus!" and keep both magazines?
B. Read both comic books before deciding which one he wants to keep?
C. Return one of the comic books right away and tell the clerk what happened?

Take a look at Psalm 15:1-2 for help in knowing what Tony should do.
If you received a "bonus" like Tony's, what would you do? Would you keep your tongue still and not say anything? Or would you use your tongue to tell the truth?

The correct answer is C.

Complaints, Complaints

Since the weather has been getting better, Sean and his friends have been planning their first campout of the season. Of course they only "camp out" in Sean's backyard, but it's still sleeping outside in a tent. They have been busy getting things ready—that is, until Sean's parents hear the weather report for the weekend. The forecast calls for a big drop in the temperature and a late spring snowstorm! Sean's parents and the other parents all agree that the boys must change their plans. Now Sean and his friends are left with a bag of marshmallows and no place to roast them. Craig officially begins the complaint session: "It's all your parents' fault, Sean. They're the ones who said no first. It probably won't snow at all." The others quickly join in. Sean secretly agrees with his parents' decision. What do you think Sean should do?

Should Sean . . .

    A. Suggest that the boys have an indoor campout?
    B. Agree that his parents sure spoiled the weekend for everyone?
    C. Tell the boys that his parents never let him have fun—they wouldn't even let him go fishing once because it might rain?

 Check out Acts 23:5 to know what Sean should do.
Talk with your parents about a time when you were upset with a decision they made or a teacher made. How did you handle it? Were you tempted to say bad things about that person?

The correct answer is A.

You've Got Mail!

Todd finishes his homework and has some time before baseball practice. He wanders into the family room and is happy to find that the computer is free. Todd logs on and discovers that one of his friends from school has sent him an e-mail message. *Cool*, thinks Todd as he opens it up. He never gets any e-mail. His friend has sent him a chain e-mail. Todd is supposed to forward the message to five more friends. If he doesn't, it promises that an awful virus is going to hit his computer. Todd quickly reads through the e-mail he is supposed to send. It's a joke about one of the girls in his class at school. It is supposed to be funny, but Todd thinks it's mostly gross. Todd knows his friend will ask him the next day about the e-mail. What do you think Todd should do?

Should Todd . . .

A. Send the message on to five other friends to protect his computer from getting a virus?
B. Delete the message and tell his friend that his computer crashed last night and won't be fixed for at least a year?
C. Delete the message and tell his friend he didn't think the joke was funny?

 Read Ephesians 5:4 to know what Todd should do.
With your mom or dad, role-play a situation where a friend wants you to share a dirty joke. Come up with several ways to respond in that situation. Whether you speak by e-mail or in person, you can please God by controlling the words you share.

The correct answer is C.

The Last-Minute Loss

Becky races up the court, yelling to her teammate Mandy to pass her the ball. It is the final minute in the basketball game. Becky's team is only a point behind. A last-minute basket will make them the winners! Becky can feel the excitement in the gym. If only she could get Mandy's attention! She shouts again and then watches in horror as Mandy stops and shoots. Nooooooo! Mandy is the worst shooter on the team and the very last person you want to take the final shot. Becky wants to cry as she hears the ball clank off the rim. The buzzer signals the end of the game, and the *other* team begins to cheer. As Becky leaves the floor, she runs into Mandy. What do you think Becky should say?

Should Becky say . . .

   A. "Nice try. Next time maybe you'll make that shot"?
   B. "I can't believe you took that shot. Didn't you hear me
      screaming for the ball? I could have won the game"?
   C. Nothing—just glare at her?

 Look up Ephesians 4:29 to know what Becky should say. Think of a time when you messed up. What words made you feel better? What words made you feel worse?

The correct answer is A.

Who Says?

Cassandra catches up to her friends walking home after school. They are arguing about which second grade teacher is better—Mrs. Stewart or Mrs. Burton. "Well, Mrs. Burton lets us have *two* recesses every day. And we never have homework on the weekend," Sara declares.

"Big deal," Megan angrily answers back. "Mrs. Stewart gives out candy almost every day—and we learn more because we *do* have homework to do."

The girls glare at each other. Then Sara turns to Cassandra, "Tell Miss Smarty-Pants which teacher is better. You have Mrs. Burton too." Cassandra thinks Mrs. Burton is a wonderful teacher. What do you think Cassandra should do?

Should Cassandra . . .

A. Tell Megan she doesn't know what she's talking about—Mrs. Burton is the best second-grade teacher?
B. Refuse to be part of the argument and say both teachers are great?
C. Tell both friends they are being dumb to waste their time on such a silly argument?

 For help in knowing what Cassandra should do, read 2 Timothy 2:14.
How do you respond when someone wants you to be part of a silly argument? Think of three ways to avoid arguments.

The correct answer is B.

The Last Word

Devon's little brother runs in the back door, tears running down his face. "Mom, Mom, Devon hit me," he cries. Devon is right behind his brother when his mom gives him that "you have some explaining to do" look.

"I didn't hit him, Mom," Devon begins. "I might have given him a little push. But he was bugging Patrick and me. We wanted to play race cars alone!"

His mom gives him another look. "Devon, I told you before you went out that you would have to watch your brother while your dad and I finish cleaning in here. Now either you all play together or Patrick will have to go home."

Devon's younger brother smiles at him and says, "I told you so." Devon is about to explode. What do you think Devon should do?

Should he . . .

    A. Say nothing and walk outside to play?
    B. Tell his brother this is absolutely the last time he will play with him?
    C. Start calling his brother a "tattletale baby" and see what his mom does then?

 Read James 3:2 to see what Devon should do.
Talk about times when it is difficult for you to control your tongue.
Reminder: Don't forget to work on your memory verse for April. (You'll find it on the page just before April 1.)

The correct answer is A.

Trash Talk

Corey rushes through his chores. It isn't every day that the older boys down the street invite him to play basketball with them. Corey races over on his bike. "Hey everyone, this is Corey. Corey, you can be on my team," his neighbor Jason says. Jason is a really good basketball player. Everyone says he is going to be a star when he gets to high school.

As the boys run up and down the playground court, they begin talking trash, using bad language. When Corey misses a basket, he yells loudly, "Nuts!" The other boys fall down laughing. "Is that the best you can do?" one boy hoots. "If you want to play with us, you better learn to talk trash and do a lot better than 'nuts'!" Corey feels his face get red and hot. What do you think Corey should do?

Should Corey . . .

    A. Ask Jason to teach him some trash talk?
    B. Tell the boys he only talks trash when he takes out the garbage?
    C. Find another group of kids playing a game where trash talk isn't going on?

 Take a look at Matthew 12:36-37 for help in knowing how Corey should handle this situation.
If you had to give an account of your words for today, how would you describe your words? Talk with your mom or dad about words that are okay and words that aren't.

What a Mess!

Hannah knows the moment her dad walks in the door that she is in trouble. Her dad had left Hannah, her older sister, and her younger brother home and had gone out on some errands. Dad had given each one of them a list of chores to do before he got home. Somehow the time slipped by and Hannah did not pick up the family room as she was supposed to do. In fact, the room is even messier now because Hannah has gotten out some old magazines to flip through. Part of her snack is still on the coffee table, and her backpack from school still sits in the middle of the floor. "What happened here? Didn't you do anything I told you to do?" her father asks her. What do you think Hannah should do?

Should Hannah . . .

- A. Apologize and tell her dad she forgot all about doing her chores?
- B. Tell her dad that she had the room all cleaned and then her younger brother came in and made a mess again?
- C. Tell her dad that she was doing her homework and was going to do her chores after she had finished?

 Check out Psalm 34:12-13 to know what Hannah should do. Talk with your family about some things that can happen if you make excuses rather than tell the truth. What does God want us to do?

The correct answer is A.

Just a Joke

Lainey is at a friend's sleepover when the conversation gets around to the boys in class. Her friend giggles, "I bet I know who you like. You like Luke, don't you?"

Lainey's face turns beet red. She thinks Luke is cool, but she doesn't want that to get all over school! Quickly, Lainey decides what to do. "I do not like him. But you want to know who does? Jessica does," Lainey says, naming her best friend. "But don't tell anyone because Jessica will get mad."

Later that week Jessica comes storming up to Lainey. "How could you tell that big-mouth Stacy that I like Luke? Now everyone is teasing me about it! I thought you were my best friend!" Lainey feels bad. She didn't mean for it to get back to Jessica. What do you think Lainey should do?

Should Lainey . . .

A. Say, "Hey, I was only joking! Can't you take a joke?"
B. Tell Jessica that Stacy misunderstood her; she said Alexa, not Jessica?
C. Tell Jessica she's sorry and that she'll clear it up with Stacy?

 Look up Proverbs 26:18-19 to know what Lainey should do. Talk with your family about the difference between being funny and hurting someone by your words.

The correct answer is C.

15

The Uncontrolled Tongue

April

In the book of James, James writes about the uncontrolled tongue. He says the tongue is a small thing, yet it can do great damage. To review what James says the tongue is like, use a red or orange crayon to color in all the spaces with a dot. (You could use both colors to make your picture look very "hot.")

Unscramble the words below to find out what else James says about the tongue.

D A N E T H N O G E T U   SI   A

___ ___ _____ __ _

A L E M F   FO   I R F E.

_____ __ _____.   James 3:6

Answer: And the tongue is a flame of fire. James 3:6

Cleanup Time!

Max always wants to be first, to be the best, or to win. Today each team at the Boy Scout weekend camp has to clean up the area around their tent, get their tent in order, and collect some firewood before breakfast. The team that finishes first gets extra swim time in the afternoon. As team leader, Max is sure he and the other boys on his team could get the job done . . . if only Andrew wasn't on their team. Andrew is the slowest-moving person Max has ever met. And he isn't very neat either. Already the other boys are up, dressed, and ready to go. But Andrew is still in his sleeping bag! What do you think Max should do?

Should Max . . .

    A. Pour some cold water on Andrew's face and yell at him to get him moving?

    B. Order Andrew to get out of his sleeping bag immediately or he'll be kicked off the team?

    C. Help Andrew get going and assign him small tasks to get done?

 Take a look at Proverbs 10:32 to see what Max should do. Together with your mom or dad, think of a chore that needs to be done in your house. Think of three ways to ask someone in the house to do that task. How do you like to be asked to get something done?

The correct answer is C.

Have You Heard . . .?

Lakisha can't help but overhear the two girls talking in front of her on the bus. Lakisha leans forward so she can hear better. "So what happened after the teacher caught Whitney cheating?" one of the girls asks.

Lakisha takes in a sharp breath. Whitney is one of the smartest girls in the class. Why would she cheat? Lakisha listens for the answer. "Well, she started to cry and told her teacher . . ." Lakisha can't hear the rest because one of the boys behind her begins talking loudly.

When she gets to school, one of Lakisha's friends greets her, "Hey, did you hear that Whitney got the highest grade on the math test?" This is Lakisha's chance to tell what she heard. What do you think Lakisha should do?

Should Lakisha . . .

A. Tell her friend what she heard on the bus about Whitney's true secret to good grades?
B. Say nothing since she doesn't know the full story?
C. Just say, "Well, we'd all get good grades if we got a little help," and let her friend figure out the rest?

 For help in knowing what Lakisha should do, read Exodus 23:1.
With your mom or dad, role-play the situation above using the three different options. What happens with each one?

I'm Better than You!

Will and Ethan are good friends who always try to see who can get the best grades. The boys are two of the smartest kids in the class, but Ethan always seems to beat Will in math. That's one subject that just seems to come easier for Ethan. The class has a big review test on everything they have covered since the beginning of the quarter. Will spends hours studying for the test. He really wants to do well—and he really wants to beat out Ethan and get the highest grade. When the tests are handed back, Will gets 100%. He glances over at Ethan and sees he only got a 98% on his paper. Wow! He has done it. He finally got a better grade in math than his friend. What do you think Will should do?

Should Will . . .

A. Not say anything but pump his fist in the air?
B. Drop his paper on the ground so everyone can see it?
C. Put his test paper away and congratulate Ethan on doing so well?

 Read 2 Corinthians 10:18 to know what Will should do. Think of something you do very well. Do you brag about what you can do? What *should* you do?

The correct answer is C.

The Right Words

When school gets out, Danielle looks for Stacy. The two usually walk home together. But Danielle doesn't see Stacy anywhere this afternoon. She feels bad because she has some big news for Stacy—Danielle just found out that she and her family are going to Hawaii for vacation! Danielle just has to tell Stacy all about it. When she gets home, she calls Stacy right after finishing her snack. "Stacy, hi, it's Danielle. Guess what? I've got the greatest news!" Danielle begins. As she pauses for Stacy to respond, Danielle can tell that something is wrong by the tone of Stacy's voice. Stacy sounds like she has been crying and doesn't seem very interested in what Danielle has to say. What do you think Danielle should do?

Should Danielle . . .

    A. Ask Stacy what's wrong and save her news for another time?
    B. Tell Stacy her news first—that should cheer Stacy up?
    C. Tell Stacy she'll call her back when she's in a better mood?

 Check out Proverbs 25:20 to see what Danielle should do. Think of at least three things to say to someone who is going through a hard time. What do you think is the best way to cheer that person up?
Reminder: Don't forget to work on your memory verse for April. (You'll find it on the page just before April 1.)

Too Much Talk

Ashley loves to talk! She and her friends spend hours in her room talking about their favorite TV shows, teachers, foods, school subjects, and vacations. Whatever the topic is, Ashley has something to say about it. Sometimes her parents have to limit her talk at the dinner table so her brother can get a word in!

Today Ashley is going to help one of her mom's friends. Her mom's friend has two little girls—one who still is a baby and a three-year-old named Leah. Ashley's job is to play with Leah while the mom takes care of the baby. The mom tells Ashley that Leah is a bit shy. Ashley has never met anyone who is shy. For once she doesn't know what to say. How is she going to handle someone who doesn't like to talk very much? What do you think Ashley should do?

Should Ashley . . .

A. Carry on a conversation for the two of them?
B. Try to find out what kinds of things Leah likes to talk about and give her a chance to talk?
C. Complain to the mom that she can't get Leah to talk?

 Read Proverbs 10:19 to see how Ashley should handle the situation.
Think of three reasons why talking too much can lead to problems. Have your mom or dad tell what they do when they find themselves talking too much.

The correct answer is B.

Miss Rag Bag

One girl in Jennifer's class stands out from all the rest of the students. This girl grew up in another country. Her English is hard to understand, and she wears clothes that are very different. Often her sweater doesn't match her pants, or her skirt might be two sizes too big. None of the stuff she wears is ever in style, and a lot of it certainly isn't new. Jennifer thinks that this girl's family gets their clothes from the local Salvation Army store. A couple of Jennifer's friends nickname the girl "Miss Rag Bag." Today, as Jennifer and her friends are waiting for the bus, the new girl walks by. One of Jennifer's friends calls out, "Hey, Miss Rag Bag. Where did you get that orange sweater?" Another friend joins in. What do you think Jennifer should do?

Should Jennifer . . .

    A. Quietly tell her friends to stop making fun of the girl?
    B. Give the girl some fashion tips, like, "Lose the orange sweater"?
    C. Laugh with her friends without saying anything?

 Check out Proverbs 17:5 to know what Jennifer should do. Discuss with your mom or dad reasons why some people make fun of those who don't have much money or who are different. Role-play what you would say to Jennifer's friends in this situation.

The Lunch Lady

"So what did she say to you today?" Jeremy's friends ask him when he sits down at the lunch table. Jeremy knows exactly who his friends are talking about—Mrs. Morris, the mean lunch lady. Every day she stands behind the lunch counter and almost growls at the students. When she hands out the lunches, she never smiles. She says things like "Don't spill the soup" or "Your hands are dirty—go wash your hands." She never says anything pleasant. No one can figure out why she works in a school because it doesn't look like Mrs. Morris enjoys being around kids. Jeremy's friends always try to get a rise out of Mrs. Morris. When Jeremy sees that he forgot his milk and has to get back in line, his friends dare him to say something terrible to Mrs. Morris. What do you think Jeremy should do?

Should Jeremy . . .

    A. Grab his milk and shout, "Hey, lady, why are you so crabby?"
    B. Smile and say "thank you" no matter what Mrs. Morris says to him?
    C. Try to get her to smile by making silly faces?

 For help in knowing what Jeremy should do, read Proverbs 16:24.
With your mom or dad, think of someone you know who could use some kind words. Send a card or say something kind to that person today!

The correct answer is B.

The House of Cards

It's rained all day. Adam has played all his video games at least twice, has gone through his comic books, and still is bored. He gets out a card game and spends the rest of the afternoon building a house of cards. By the time he finishes, it is nearly as tall as him. Adam is pleased with his work. He runs off to find his dad. "Hey, Dad, you've got to come and see what I made," he says as he drags his father from in the front of the TV set. When they enter Adam's room, Adam finds his cards all over the room. "What happened!?" he shouts.

Just then his little brother comes in. "Adam, let me tell you what happened," his brother begins. Adam is in no mood to listen to his little brother. What do you think Adam should do?

Should Adam . . .

A. Tell his brother he's not interested in hearing what he has to say because it's obvious what happened?
B. Shout and scream at his brother for what he did?
C. Give his brother a chance to explain what happened?

 Take a look at James 1:19 for help in knowing what Adam should do.
With your mom or dad, come up with a plan for listening first, then speaking, especially when you are angry. Your plan may include counting or going to another room and coming back.

What Happened?

As soon as Nicole's teacher walks back in the room, Nicole knows her class is in big-time trouble. Mr. Stone just left the room for a few minutes to talk with another teacher. But a few minutes is enough time for a lot of students to make trouble, and that's all Nicole's class needed! It started with two boys throwing paper balls at each other. When one missed, the paper ball hit a girl sitting in the front of the class. She threw it back, and then the whole class joined in, including Nicole! When Mr. Stone walks back into the classroom, the floor is covered with paper balls. "What on earth happened here?" he wants to know. "I expect someone to tell me." As the silence grows, Nicole begins to wiggle in her seat. What do you think Nicole should do?

Should Nicole . . .

- A. Tell Mr. Stone that the boys in the back of the class started a paper-ball war?
- B. Wait for someone else to say something?
- C. Tell Mr. Stone that the whole class was throwing paper balls?

 Look up Ecclesiastes 3:1, 7 for help in knowing what Nicole should do.
Together with your mom or dad think of a time when it is good to say nothing. Then name a time when it is good to speak up.

The correct answer is C.

A Little Respect

Juan and his friends are hanging around his house after school. The conversation turns to one of the kids in Juan's class who is leaving school and being taught at home. Juan knows the boy and his family from church, and he knows that there are many reasons why the boy is going to be homeschooled. Jordan jumps right in, saying what he thinks: "Well, you know they go to that church on the corner. The people at that church teach that no one can go to public school, and the people there can only be friends with other church members."

Another of his friends says, "Yeah, that church is really weird. My mom said they don't like people who go to other churches."

Juan's friends don't have a clue what they are talking about. Someone needs to let them know what's true. What do you think Juan should do?

Should Juan . . .

A. Start laughing and say, "I can't believe how dumb you guys are"?
B. Quietly explain the truth about what his church teaches?
C. Decide there's no point in talking to these guys?

 Check out Colossians 4:5-6 to know how Juan should answer his friends.
What would you say if someone said something about your church that you knew was incorrect? What would be a wise way to use your tongue in that situation?

The correct answer is B.

Making Plans

April

Eric is looking forward to the weekend. He has been asked to go with Nathan's family to the lake. They are going fishing, sailing, and swimming. As Eric thinks about what he should bring, his mom calls for him. His best friend, Michael, is at the door. "Hey, Eric, want to go to the ball game with me and my family this Saturday? We've got great seats!" Michael tells his friend. Eric doesn't want to hurt Michael's feelings. Should he tell him what he has going on this weekend? What do you think Eric should do?

Should Eric . . .

    A. Tell Michael that he doesn't really like baseball anymore?
    B. Explain that he already has plans for the weekend with Nathan?
    C. Say he'll go but plan to come down with a mysterious illness the day of the game?

 Take a look at Proverbs 24:26 to know what Eric should do. Think of a time when you kept back information from a friend about something. What happened?

Do You Want to Know a Secret?

Giselle's friend Samantha has been acting strange. She stays away from the other girls during recess and doesn't seem to laugh as much as she used to. Giselle wants to find out why! She spots Samantha by the swings and goes over to talk with her. "Samantha, you haven't been acting like yourself lately. Is something wrong?" Giselle asks.

Samantha looks around and says, "My parents have been fighting a lot. I'm afraid Dad may leave. Promise me you won't say anything?"

Giselle spends the rest of recess with Samantha talking about her problem. When she gets back in the classroom, one of her other friends says, "So what's up with you and Samantha? What's the big secret?" What do you think Giselle should do?

Should Giselle . . .

- A. Tell her other friend it's none of her business?
- B. Tell her friend about Samantha but make sure she promises not to tell anyone else?
- C. Say that Samantha is going through a hard time and needs a little time by herself?

Read Proverbs 20:19 to know how Giselle should handle this situation.
Talk with your mom or dad about what kinds of secrets should be kept and what kinds of secrets may need to be shared with an adult who can be trusted. If someone is in danger, for example, a teacher or parent should know about it.

The correct answer is C.

Flattery Will Get You . . .

Shannon gives Crystal a long look when she sits down for lunch. "I thought you didn't like to hang around with Erin because she brags too much. Now you're always with her," Shannon says.

Crystal explains, "Well, Erin's family just got a built-in pool. I figure if I'm nice to her now, I'll get asked to go swimming a lot this summer. You should do the same!"

Just then Erin comes up with her lunch. "Have you guys seen my new backpack?" she asks, showing off a shiny neon green bag with bright orange and pink blobs all over it. Crystal says, "Oh, Erin. You always have the coolest stuff. Don't you like it, Shannon?"

Shannon thinks the backpack is ugly. What do you think Shannon should say?

Should Shannon . . .

    A. Agree with Crystal that it is the coolest backpack she has ever seen—and get her bathing suit ready?
    B. Tell Erin she never would buy anything in such an awful color?
    C. Say, "It's certainly the style," and then talk about something else?

 Check out Psalm 12:2-3 for help in knowing what Shannon should say.
Role-play a situation in which you give someone a real compliment and one in which you are just flattering the person. What do you think is the difference?

The correct answer is C.

Want to Fight?

Chris and his brother are in the middle of a heated game of Monopoly. Chris is really getting upset because his brother, who is younger, is winning the game. One more stop on Broadway, and Chris is finished. Not only is his brother winning the game, but he also is rubbing it in a lot. He keeps saying, "I can't believe I'm beating you! I've never beat you before. Just wait until I tell my friends." Chris's brother keeps this up while Chris is trying to take his turn. He warns his brother to be quiet. But that doesn't stop his brother. Chris is upset and knows how to get his brother upset too—just tell him, "I'm letting you win." That should get a real fight going. What do you think Chris should do?

Should Chris . . .

    A. Use his secret weapon and tell his brother, "You're so lame. You can't even tell when I'm letting you win"?

    B. Patiently explain to his brother that the game has nothing to do with skill, but with luck?

    C. Congratulate his brother and say he wants a rematch someday?

 Read Matthew 5:9 to know what Chris should do.
Think of a time when you and a brother, sister, or friend were trying to start a fight. What words start a fight? What words stop a fight?

The correct answer is C.

Review Time!

Think of three ways you can use your tongue for good purposes.

1.

2.

3.

Bonus

What are three ways the tongue can be used to hurt others?

1.

2.

3.

Say your memory verse to someone who is the same age as you. (The verse is printed on the page just before April 1.)

Obedience

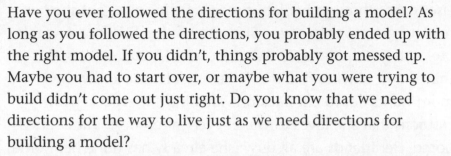

Have you ever followed the directions for building a model? As long as you followed the directions, you probably ended up with the right model. If you didn't, things probably got messed up. Maybe you had to start over, or maybe what you were trying to build didn't come out just right. Do you know that we need directions for the way to live just as we need directions for building a model?

In his Word, God gives us all the directions we need on how to live. Many times he tells his people that if they follow his directions, all will go well for them. But if they don't, things will not go well at all. The Old Testament is filled with stories of what happened to people when they didn't obey God. We probably could add a few examples ourselves!

Obedience is doing what we are told to do immediately, willingly, and completely. God wants us to obey him because he knows what is best for us. Obedience is not always easy. It may mean giving up something—even some of our friends.

We should obey what God says not only because it is for our best, but also because we love Jesus. John says that the mark of a follower of Christ is obedience. As you work through this month's *Sticky Situations,* think about your own obedience to God, to your parents, and to others in authority over you.

Memory Verse: Those who obey God's word really do love him. . . . [They] should live their lives as Christ did. 1 John 2:5-6

Is It Okay?

Lisette flips through her latest magazine for girls, but she has read it from cover to cover. She stares at her fish for a few minutes and watches it lazily swim in circles. *Enough of this,* she thinks, and turns to find the TV remote. Lisette knows her mom wants her to cut back on watching TV, especially the cartoons that she loves to watch every afternoon. But Lisette is bored. Her friends are all busy; she already has done her homework; and there is nothing else to do. She looks down at the TV listing in the newspaper. There are plenty of TV shows to fill her afternoon. What do you think Lisette should do?

Should Lisette . . .

    A. Put the remote back and look for something else to do?
    B. Go back to watching the fish?
    C. Watch only the educational channel—that should make her mom happy?

 Look up 1 Corinthians 6:12 for help in knowing what Lisette should do.
Together with your mom or dad, make a "Do" list and a "Don't" list: things your parents would like you to do and things they don't want you to do. How can you keep from doing the things on the "Don't" list?

Try Again

Nick throws his bat to the ground. He tries not to look at his other teammates as he walks back to the dugout, but he can feel their eyes on him. The bases were loaded, there were two outs, and Nick went down swinging! Not only did he strike out, but he also popped out and grounded out earlier in the game. He hasn't done one thing right the entire game. Later, as Nick is picking up his stuff to go home, his coach stops him. *Uh-oh,* Nick thinks, *here it comes.* His coach says, "Nick, I was watching you bat, and I think I know what you're doing wrong. How about coming to practice a bit early tomorrow, and we'll see if we can't work a few things out?" After the way he played today, Nick isn't so sure there is *any* hope for him to play better. What do you think he should do?

Should Nick . . .

- A. Take his coach up on his offer and keep trying?
- B. Tell his coach to save his time and offer to become the bat boy?
- C. Tell his coach thanks, but he's already decided to quit baseball for good?

 For help in knowing what Nick should do, read 1 Corinthians 9:25-27 for some good advice from Paul.
Ask your mom or dad to tell about a time when they faced a difficult challenge and felt like quitting.

The correct answer is A.

Help Wanted

Tyler tosses his mitt on the floor. "What's for dinner?" he shouts as he comes into the house. He and his friends have been playing baseball in the park for the past two hours. It was a great game, but Tyler is tired and hungry. He finds his mom on the phone.

"Yes, Mrs. Murphy. He's right here. I'm sure he'll be glad to come right over," Tyler hears his mom say to his elderly next-door neighbor. *Not Mrs. Murphy,* Tyler thinks. His next-door neighbor is forever asking him to do things for her. She must have seen him coming home from the park. Sure enough, when his mom hangs up she says, "Tyler, could you please go over and help Mrs. Murphy take in her groceries? I told her you would come over before dinner." That's the last thing Tyler wants to do. What do you think he should do?

Should Tyler . . .

    A. Tell his mom he hurt his shoulder throwing the baseball and shouldn't be lifting heavy objects like grocery bags?

    B. Ask his mom if he can help Mrs. Murphy later—like next week?

    C. Go over and help Mrs. Murphy?

 Read Romans 6:13 for help in knowing what Tyler should do. Together with your mom or dad, make a list of all the ways you can use your body to do God's work.

The Best Choice

Rhonda's parents want her to read thirty minutes every day. Every time she completes a book she receives ten points. For every fifty points she can go to the toy store and pick out a stuffed animal. The first book Rhonda selects is a mystery. The second book is about Abe Lincoln as a boy. But it's taking too long to get through these books. Rhonda will never read enough to get her fifty points. She goes up to her room, looking for a new book to read. There's a mystery that she hasn't read yet, but it has 256 pages. Then she finds a pile of comic books from a friend. Her mom said she could read *anything,* although her mom *also* said Rhonda would get the most out of books that challenge her. What do you think Rhonda should do?

Should Rhonda . . .

- A. Choose the mystery book next?
- B. Read ten comic books in thirty minutes to make up for one regular book—that would be a challenge?
- C. Just skim through the rest of the books she has to read?

 Look up Proverbs 13:1 for help in knowing what choice Rhonda should make.
Think of a time when you had a choice about how to obey a parent or teacher. Did you take the easy way out or accept a challenge? Which do you think would please God most?

The correct answer is A.

Pick up Your Stuff

Friday is David's grandpa's seventy-fifth birthday. His parents are planning a big party. All of David's aunts, uncles, and cousins are coming over. His parents have spent the morning cleaning, baking, and getting the house ready. David's mom comes to the family room, where David and his brother had been playing. His brother has left for a trumpet lesson, so David's mom looks straight at him. "Young man, I want you to pick up all your stuff and straighten up this room," she tells him. As David goes around the room looking for his things, he sees that a good deal of the mess really belongs to his brother. He knows his brother doesn't want him to touch anything of his. What do you think he should do?

Should David . . .

    A. Pick up *all* the stuff in the room and deal with his brother later?
    B. Pick up only his stuff and let his mother deal with his brother?
    C. Rake his brother's stuff into one big pile and tell him he didn't touch any of it?

 Read Jeremiah 7:23-24 to find out how God wants us to obey him and others.
Talk about the situation with your mom or dad. Why isn't it good enough for David to pick up only his stuff? Remember that God gives us families to help us learn to obey instead of just doing whatever we want. Obeying at home is one way to obey God.

The correct answer is A.

The Best Thing

Keenan begins grumbling before his family even leaves the church parking lot. "Can you believe this?" he asks his mom and dad. "Our Sunday school teacher gave us homework to do over the week. And she says she is going to call us during the week to see how we're doing on it! What does she think this is, school or something?" All week Keenan avoids his Sunday school homework—and the telephone. He learns that his teacher left a message reminding him to do the homework. Keenan has made it all the way until Saturday night without opening his Bible. He is about to settle in with a big bowl of popcorn and one of his favorite videos when his mom asks if he has anything he needs to do for Sunday. What do you think Keenan should do?

Should Keenan . . .

- A. Say yes and do his work before watching the video?
- B. Promise that he'll bring in double the amount of offering for the next two weeks instead of doing the homework?
- C. Jot down a few notes on the ride between home and church tomorrow morning?

 Take a look at 1 Samuel 15:22 for some help in knowing what Keenan should do.
What are three ways you can obey your Sunday school teacher? Together with your mom or dad, thank God for your Sunday school teacher and all the things you are learning.

The correct answer is A.

No Skateboarding Allowed

The town has fixed up the small park in Arun's neighborhood. There are new swings, a teeter-totter, and cool climbing equipment—monkey bars, slides, and a swinging bridge. Arun and his friends like to hang out there and play tag on the equipment. Today Arun and a friend are practicing some skateboarding tricks in Arun's driveway when some older boys from the neighborhood skateboard by. "Hey, we're going over to the park to try out the new playground. Want to come?" they ask Arun and his friend. The playground would make for great skateboarding—there are all sorts of stairs and levels to do neat tricks. But there also are signs that clearly say no skateboarding is allowed.

Arun's friend jumps up and grabs his skateboard. "Come on, Arun, get your skateboard. Let's go," says his friend. What do you think Arun should do?

Should Arun . . .
    A. Call the police department and alert them?
    B. Tell his friend he'll take a pass?
    C. Go and watch to see if anyone gets hurt?

 Check out Romans 12:2 for help in knowing what Arun should do.
Think of some other ways Christians sometimes copy the behaviors of this world. What are some activities you may need help in avoiding?

The correct answer is B.

Spring Cleaning

Every spring Kelly's parents choose one Saturday when the entire family will clean up the yard and the garage. Everyone gets something to do, even Kelly's little brother. This year Kelly's job is to clean out the big box in the garage. It's the box where she and her brothers and sister usually toss their Rollerblades and whatever else they happen to have in their hands at the time. Kelly spends Friday night at a friend's home. When she returns, her family is already busy working. Kelly's dad says, "Put your things away. We need you to come help us out here." Kelly stayed up late the night before and really wants to take a nap before doing her cleaning. What do you think she should do?

Should Kelly . . .

A. Tell her dad she'll get to her job sometime before the next big spring cleaning?
B. Take a nap first and then go do her work?
C. Do her work first and then take a nap?

 Read 2 Chronicles 24:5 for an example of how the Israelites responded to the call to obey God.
Discuss with your mom or dad the difference between being slow to obey and obeying right away. How quickly do you obey—are you an eager beaver or a slow tortoise?

The Baby-Sitter

Austin is right in the middle of his video game when he hears his dad calling, "Austin, I need you upstairs."

"Just a minute, Dad," Austin replies. He has never gotten this far in this game. A few more rounds and he will beat his older brother's score!

When he goes upstairs his dad says, "Please watch your little brother while I finish getting supper ready."

Austin complains, "Why can't Zach watch him?"

His dad answers, "Zach needs to get his homework done. I'm asking *you* to watch your little brother." Austin looks at his one-year-old brother, who at the moment is stuffing his hand in his mouth. Austin grumbles, "I can't do anything if I have to watch you." What do you think Austin should do?

Should Austin . . .

A. Play with his little brother?
B. Put his brother in the playpen, throw a few stuffed animals in there, and go finish his game?
C. Do exactly as his father said but keep complaining loudly so his father is sure to hear him?

 For help in knowing what Austin should *not* do, read 2 Chronicles 25:2.
Discuss with your mom or dad why C is not the best answer even if Austin *is* doing what his dad wants him to do. Talk about how we obey God when we don't act upset about having to obey the people he has given us to care for us.

The correct answer is A.

Miss Popularity

Nikki is the most popular girl in her class, so Bethany is very happy when she is asked to come to Nikki's birthday party. Bethany spends a lot of time picking out just the right gift and choosing just the right outfit to wear to the party. At the party Nikki tells everyone, "Let's do makeovers." The girls all run up to Nikki's room, where she pulls out a drawer of makeup— lipstick, blush, mascara, and eye makeup. "Do me first," one girl says.

"No, me. You went first last time," says another.

It's obvious to Bethany that these girls do this a lot. Bethany's parents don't let her wear makeup yet, but Bethany wants to fit in with her new friends. What do you think she should do?

Should Bethany . . .

A. Let the girls give her a makeover and wash it off before going home?
B. Tell the girls she'd rather just watch?
C. Say that she ate too much cake and doesn't feel well, so she needs to go home?

 Read Matthew 1:18-24 to see how Joseph obeyed God even when others might have thought his actions were strange. Talk with your family about some of the rules you have in your family that may be different from those of your friends. Talk about why these are good rules and how you can help one another remember to obey them.

The correct answer is B.

No Signs Here!

Wendy and her friend Brooke have spent several hours with Brooke's parents walking around the zoo on a hot spring day. While Brooke's parents are getting some drinks, the girls are told to wait on the bench. Across from the bench is a cool fountain and pool. Just sitting near the fountain makes the girls feel cooler. "Hey, I've got an idea. Why don't we stick our dusty feet in the fountain?" Brooke suggests. "It will feel great!" Wendy looks around and points out that no one else is doing this. But Brooke asks, "Do you see a sign saying you can't? Well, do you?" Wendy has to admit there is not a sign anywhere saying to keep your feet out of the fountain. But she knows that the water would get very dirty if everyone did this. What do you think Wendy should do?

Should Wendy . . .

    A. Stick a big toe in the water so she won't really be putting her feet in the water?

    B. Follow Brooke's lead—after all, there is no sign?

    C. Tell Brooke she thinks the girls should stay on the bench and cool off their feet later?

 Read Acts 5:29 for some help in knowing what Wendy should do.
Talk with your mom or dad about the reasons why you should obey God. Do you need a sign to tell you how to act?
Reminder: Don't forget to work on your memory verse for May. (You'll find it on the page just before May 1.)

May Baskets

Dante's art class at school is making May baskets for the people at a local retirement home. The teacher has asked students to bring in silk flowers and other materials to decorate the baskets. First, though, the students have to weave the baskets from strips of construction paper. In order for them to have enough baskets, each student has to make five. Art is not one of Dante's best subjects. He's all thumbs! It takes Dante twice as long as the other students to make one basket. The teacher gives Dante some tips on how to make the baskets and says Dante can finish the baskets at home. With a bit of practice, she says, Dante's baskets will look just as nice as the others. Dante is not so sure. What do you think Dante should do?

Should Dante . . .

    A. Throw the rest of the baskets together and get it over with?
    B. Spend as much time as necessary with his teacher to do the baskets right?
    C. Take the stuff home and get his mom to make the rest of the baskets for him?

 Check out 2 Timothy 1:7 for help in knowing what Dante should do.
Name some activities you are involved with that require discipline and practice. What are some benefits of that discipline? What is difficult about it?

Give It Up!

Alexis and her friends have been asked to help get ready for the church's spring dinner. They are to stuff plastic bags, which someone else will take to neighborhood homes. Each bag has a flyer about the dinner, a refrigerator magnet, and some other stuff about the church. When Alexis and her friends arrive, there are five hundred bags to be filled. Halfway through the morning, Alexis and her friends have stuffed only about 150 bags. One of her friends says, "This is too hard. We'll never get all of these done."

Some of the boys who are helping with a project down the hall stop by and start laughing. "When do you think you'll have those done—in time for next year's dinner?" Alexis is ready to quit. What do you think she should do?

Should Alexis . . .

A. Keep doing what she was asked to do, working on stuffing those bags until the job is done?
B. Tell the adult in charge she has a blister on her finger and has to go home?
C. Shove the empty bags in a closet and say to everyone, "We're done"?

 Take a look at Nehemiah 4:10-14 to see what Nehemiah did when the job God wanted him to do was hard to finish. Talk with your family about jobs that are hard to finish. What can you do to help one another obey God by finishing the jobs he wants you to do?

The correct answer is A.

Follow the Rules

Bart has been working on going up to the next level in his church's Wednesday night club. He has finished all the homework and has learned all the Bible verses. He has missed only one night. Now the only thing left to do is a three-hour community service project that the club has lined up. But Bart and his family are visiting his grandparents that weekend. Bart works it out with the club leader to come up with his own service project. He will spend three hours at a local nursing home. It's down to the last week before everything has to be finished, and Bart still needs to do his community service. The only problem is that this week is already packed. Bart doesn't know how he is going to fit in a trip to the nursing home. What do you think Bart should do?

Should Bart . . .

A. Count three hours of the visit to his grandparents as his community service?
B. Ask his club leader if he could do it over the summer when things are less busy?
C. Drop one of his other activities to get the community service project done in time?

 Read 2 Timothy 2:5 for help in knowing what Bart should do. Talk with your mom or dad about the types of jobs that you often try to get away from having to do. Think about what it means to be like an athlete who trains to play a sport. Does a good athlete try to get out of getting ready for a game?

The correct answer is C.

Follow Directions

God gave his people the Ten Commandments, which were rules to help the people live good and holy lives. Jesus, in his teachings, gave us the same rules, but he said them a little differently. Draw a line between each commandment on the left and how Jesus says it in the New Testament. You'll find six of the Ten Commandments. Can you find the other four in Exodus 20?

A. Do not worship any other gods besides me.

B. Do not misuse the name of the Lord your God.

C. Remember to observe the Sabbath day by keeping it holy.

D. Honor your father and mother.

E. Do not testify falsely against your neighbor.

F. Do not covet.

1. Don't be greedy for what you don't have (Luke 12:15).

2. Children, obey your parents because you belong to the Lord, for this is the right thing to do (Ephesians 6:1).

3. I tell you this, that you must give an account on judgment day of every idle word you speak (Matthew 12:36).

4. The Sabbath was made to benefit people, and not people to benefit the Sabbath. And I, the Son of Man, am master even of the Sabbath (Mark 2:27-28).

5. You must worship the Lord your God; serve only him (Matthew 4:10).

6. But I say, don't make any vows! If you say, "By heaven!" it is a sacred vow because heaven is God's thrown (Matthew 5:34).

Channel Surfing

Alan's older brother is supposed to be watching him while his parents are out. But his brother is upstairs finishing his homework. "Is it okay if I watch TV before bed?" Alan calls upstairs. His brother grunts, so Alan takes that as a yes. He sits down with the remote, but he can't find anything he is interested in. There are a few sitcoms, some baseball games, and a program about birds in the Amazon. Alan flicks through a few more channels and stops. He watches the TV for a minute and can tell that the show he's watching is the one he hears his friends talk about in school. It is the hottest TV show this year, partly because it shows a lot of fighting and killing. While his parents haven't said he can't watch the show, Alan knows he probably shouldn't watch it. Still, it looks interesting. What do you think Alan should do?

Should Alan . . .

    A. Watch the birds of the Amazon or a ball game?
    B. Watch the TV show his friends like so he can see for himself how much fighting there is?
    C. Keep channel surfing, but spend a few more minutes on that program when it comes around again?

 Look up Colossians 3:2 for some good advice for Alan. Make a list with your mom or dad about items to think about that are heavenly rather than earthly. List some ways you can focus on those things.

The correct answer is A.

Going to the Races

Saturday is the day of the huge sailboat race for all the area scout troops. Peter and his dad have spent nearly a month getting his entry ready. Last night Peter finished his boat. It's a beauty, and Peter is sure that it will do well. The winner will receive a gift certificate at the local sporting goods store. Peter already has picked out the canteen he wants for summer camp. When Peter gets up on Saturday, rain is coming down in buckets. About an hour later his scoutmaster calls and says the race will be held the following morning. After hanging up, Peter realizes that means the race will be held during church. There isn't anything special going on that day at church, but Peter and his family always go. Peter really wants to race his boat. What do you think he should do?

Should Peter . . .

- A. Skip the race this year?
- B. Go to the race and promise to "make up" the missed day at church?
- C. Go to the race and come late to church?

 For help in knowing what Peter should do, read Deuteronomy 30:19-20.
Discuss with your mom or dad what it means to obey God and commit your life to him on a daily basis.

Do Over!

Jenna's parents are having a big dinner party for her dad's office workers this weekend. All week they have been busy getting everything ready. On the morning of the party, Jenna's mom asks her to set the table. She shows Jenna how to fold the napkins just right; where to put the knives, forks, and spoons; and where to place the fine water glasses. When Jenna has finished the table, she thinks everything looks beautiful. "Come see, Mom," she calls.

Her mom takes one look at the table and says, "Honey, you did it wrong. You'll have to do it over again." Jenna is terribly disappointed. She thought she had done it right the first time. What do you think Jenna should do?

Should Jenna . . .

A. Leave the room, saying, "I quit; do it yourself"?
B. Argue with her mom that her way to set the table is better?
C. Listen carefully to her mom's directions and do it again?

 Read Deuteronomy 32:3-4 to see how one Bible character reacted to the Lord's discipline.
From the Bible verses you just read, describe how Moses reacted when God told him he couldn't go into the Promised Land. Talk with your mom or dad about a typical reaction to being disciplined. What can you learn from Moses?

Teacher Appreciation?

Gil's arms still hurt as he walks to school on Monday. He spent all of Saturday morning scrubbing the chalkboards in every classroom at school. *It isn't fair,* he thinks as he rubs his arms. He was caught drawing some rather unkind pictures of other classmates on the chalkboard while his teacher was talking with another teacher in the hall. But it had been his friend's idea. Gil thinks his teacher was too hard on him, but she didn't think so. (His parents didn't either.) As he gets to school, one of his classmates asks if Gil would mind drawing a picture on the card for teacher appreciation week. At the moment, Gil doesn't feel much like appreciating his teacher. What do you think Gil should do?

Should Gil . . .

    A. Tell his classmate to check back later; maybe he'll feel like doing it then?

    B. Draw a picture for his teacher and include a note of apology?

    C. Draw one of his now famous unkind pictures (like the ones on the chalkboard)?

 Take a look at Job 5:17 to see how Gil should react to being disciplined.

Have your mom or dad tell about a time when they learned something from being disciplined.

Reminder: Don't forget to work on your memory verse for May. (You'll find it on the page just before May 1.)

Honor and Obey

Christina and her friends are talking at lunch about their plans for the weekend. Emily sits down and suggests, "Hey, why don't you come with me and my older sister this weekend? We're going over to the mall to hang out for a while." The other girls respond excitedly. "Great idea!" "I want to go and check out that new store with all the hair clips and stuff." The girls begin making plans about what time to meet, where, and what time they should plan on coming home. Christina, though, has remained quiet. Her parents don't like her to go to the mall just to hang out, even if there is someone going with them. As they leave for recess, Emily asks her, "What about you, Christina? Can you come?" What do you think Christina should do?

Should Christina . . .

A. Tell her friends that her parents don't want her hanging out at the mall and suggest another activity?
B. Say, "My parents are so mean. They won't let me go, I know it"?
C. Tell her friends she has to cut her dog's toenails on Saturday?

 Check out Ephesians 6:1-3 for help in knowing what Christina should do.
Discuss with your mom or dad what it means to obey and what it means to honor someone. Can you obey someone without honoring them? Brainstorm ways in which you can do both.

The correct answer is A.

Benched!

Cody's soccer team is having an excellent season, and he is one of the major reasons for the team's success. Cody plays goalie and during the season he has played in ten shutout games. Today, if he can prevent the other team from scoring a goal, he will have eleven shutouts—the most ever in park district play. Cody is all set for the game. He wants to make the record book. At halftime, Cody's team is ahead three to zero. As he gets ready to run back on the field, Cody's coach tells him to take a seat on the bench so a teammate can have a chance to play goalie. This is going to ruin Cody's chances for the shutout record. The other kid isn't as good a goalie as Cody and probably will blow the shutout. What do you think Cody should do?

Should Cody . . .

- A. Take a seat on the bench and cheer for the new goalie?
- B. Refuse to come out of the game and suggest that the boy play another position?
- C. Explain to the coach why he doesn't want to sit on the bench, and beg to stay in the game?

 Read Acts 15:36-38 to see how John Mark had to give up something—traveling with Paul.
Talk with your mom or dad about a time when obeying meant someone in your family had to give up something. How did this become a learning and growing experience?

It's Too Hard!

Kendra had no idea how successful her recycling efforts would be. She saw the idea on a TV show and asked her teacher if the class could have a recycling bin just for scrap paper. Soon more classes had recycling bins, and from there it spread through the whole school. Kendra and her friends even made some posters to help kids learn about the importance of recycling. Now her principal wants to know if Kendra will attend the next school board meeting and propose that *all* the schools in the whole district take part in the recycling program. Kendra has trouble speaking in front of her class, let alone a group of adults! Besides, who would really listen to a kid? Certainly not the school board! What do you think Kendra should do?

Should Kendra . . .

- A. Tell her principal to forget it; she's just a kid?
- B. Dress up in her mom's clothes and put on lots of makeup so she'll look older when she appears before the school board?
- C. Work with her teacher and principal to come up with a good plan for the school board?

 For help in knowing what Kendra should do, read Exodus 6:10-12; 7:1-2, 6.
Look at the example from the Scripture passage. Discuss with your mom or dad what might have happened if Moses had given up and hadn't obeyed God. What *did* happen because he was obedient?

The correct answer is C.

I Won't Be Your Friend!

Craig and his best friend, Loren, have spent the afternoon building a go-cart in Craig's basement. They have put away their supplies and have some time before Loren's mom comes to pick him up. They go outside and Loren sees that Craig's neighbor has a trampoline. "Way cool," Loren says.

"Yeah, we get to go on it when my neighbor is home," Craig tells him.

Loren says, "Let's go on it now!"

Craig shakes his head. "No one is home now."

Loren begs even harder, "Puh-leassse! We're only going to bounce on it." Craig still shakes his head no.

"Craig, c'mon. I'm not going to be your friend unless you let me!" What do you think Craig should do?

Should Craig . . .

    A. Let Loren jump on the trampoline once or twice and hope no one sees him?

    B. Tell Loren he has other friends to play with and doesn't want to be his friend anyway?

    C. Tell Loren he'll call him when his neighbor is home and they can go on the trampoline then?

 Read 2 Chronicles 18:5-7 to see how a king reacts to the only prophet who tells him the truth.
Sometimes doing the right thing—or saying the right thing—will bring opposition. Role-play with your mom or dad what you would say to Loren.

The correct answer is C.

Step by Step

Everyone knows that Elly's teacher gives her classes big projects. But since the school year is almost over, Elly didn't expect to have such a huge project to do. Guess again! Each student has to do a book report *and* make either a mobile or diorama of a scene from the book. There is only a week to get it all done! Elly sits at her desk in her room and stares at the calendar on the wall. Elly is a good worker, but she works slowly. No matter how many ways she looks at it, she can't think of a way to get the project and a book report done on time. Her tears start to fall on her computer keyboard. What do you think Elly should do?

Should Elly . . .

A. Keep crying and then tell her teacher she lost the assignment?
B. Plan the steps needed to get the assignments done and work on the assignments one step at a time?
C. Worry about it until the night before and then tell the teacher she didn't have enough time to do the project?

 Check out Joshua 3:9-17 to see the difficult job that faced the Israelites and how they were able to do it.
Does God want you to obey a teacher or parent by doing a difficult job? With your mom or dad, make a list of the steps you need to take to get the job done. Now take that first step!

The correct answer is B.

Listen Up!

Seth can't wait to enter the scouts' model airplane competition for parents and sons. His dad isn't around much anymore, but his grandpa says he will help. He promises they will begin building the model over the weekend. Saturday comes, and Seth is up early, ready to get started. But Grandpa calls and says, "I'm sorry, Seth, but we're going to have to wait until later to begin the plane. I've got to run in to work this morning. You can take out all the pieces to make sure we have everything, but don't do anything until I get back. If you don't do it in the right order, you could mess the whole thing up." Seth is upset. He dumps out all the pieces on the table and looks at the directions. *This looks simple,* Seth thinks. He doesn't need to wait for Grandpa. What do you think Seth should do?

Should Seth . . .

- A. Wait until his grandpa comes to help?
- B. Surprise his grandpa by coming up with his own way to put the plane together?
- C. Fold the directions into a paper airplane and enter that in the competition?

 Look up 1 Chronicles 15:13-15 to see what happened when the Levites didn't follow God's directions exactly!
List three reasons why it is important to follow all directions. Think of three reasons why it's especially important to follow God's directions.

The correct answer is A.

No One Is Looking

Nolan and his classmates are getting ready for the school principal to visit the classroom. Nolan's teacher, Mrs. Todd, wants to make everything perfect. All morning the class has cleaned up the room, put up some of their artwork, and straightened up their desks. Now Mrs. Todd is making them write a letter to the principal, telling her about everything the class has studied. As the class works, Mrs. Todd walks around the room, checking on neatness and spelling, and reminding the students to use their best handwriting. Nolan is busy working on his letter when he sees some kids over in the corner tossing papers and giggling. Mrs. Todd has stepped outside the door and is talking with the principal. No one is looking! What do you think Nolan should do?

Should Nolan . . .

A. Make a bigger wad of paper and throw it across the room?
B. Continue working on his letter?
C. Fold up his letter as if it's done and watch the other kids?

 For help in knowing what Nolan should do, read Philippians 2:12.
Think of the people who help guide you to do the right things. Why should you do what they say when they are not with you?

It's the Rule

Today Roberto plans to meet his pal Blake at the corner and ride to school together. Blake is already there when Roberto pulls up. "Hey, I'll race you to school!" Blake yells, pedaling off as fast as he can go. Roberto speeds along behind him. As they near the school, Roberto gets off his bike. Blake keeps going. Then, seeing that Roberto is no longer behind him, he stops and calls back to his friend. "Hey, what are you doing? We haven't reached the playground yet!"

Roberto calls back, "Don't you remember? The principal says we have to walk down this block because there are too many cars and kids."

Blake makes a face. "That's a stupid rule. I'm not going to follow it. Let's go! Last one to school is a rotten egg!" Roberto watches as Blake pedals away. What do you think Roberto should do?

Should Roberto . . .

 A. Get everyone to disobey the principal's stupid rule?
 B. Finish the race—he doesn't want anyone to think he actually is a rotten egg?
 C. Let Blake win, and walk the rest of the way to school?

 Look up Romans 13:1-2 for help in knowing what Roberto should do.
Read the Bible passage aloud. What is the reason the Bible gives for obeying those in authority? Make a list of people in authority over you. Why should you obey them?

The correct answer is C.

But I Don't Want To!

Kirsten puts the last stuffed animal on her bed. It has taken her nearly the whole morning, but Kirsten finally has cleaned up her room as her mom asked her to do. She has picked up all the dirty clothes on the floor, put the books back in her bookcase, and put away all the games. She calls her mom to come look at her room. If her mom gives the okay, she still will have time to play with her friends before her grandparents come. Her mom looks at her room and says, "Kirsten, you have done a great job. Now I have one more thing for you to do. Would you please help your little sister clean up her room?"

Help her little sister—the one who threw her stuff all over the room and then blamed Kirsten? Kirsten wants to scream, "No fair!" What do you think she should do?

Should Kirsten . . .

A. Give her mom the number of a good cleaning service?
B. Tell her mom she has other plans and run out the door to meet her friends?
C. Help her sister and then go play with her friends?

 Look up Jonah 1:1-10 to see what happened to one Bible character who said "no way" to God.
Role-play the situation above to see what might happen next if Kirsten will not help her sister. What might happen next if Kirsten agrees to stay and help? What lesson can you learn from Jonah (and Kirsten)?

The correct answer is C.

Mind over Matter

The weekend finally arrives, but not soon enough for Amy. All week Amy has waited for Friday night when she is going to spend the night with her new friend, Meg. She has packed everything she needs, including her toothbrush and her special nighttime friend, Mr. Bunny. She doesn't care if Meg sees it because she knows that Meg has a special "blankie." The only thing she wonders about is what video they will watch. Amy has heard Meg talk about the types of movies her family rents, and sometimes these movies aren't the ones her mom and dad let her see. Several times Amy has asked her what videos they're going to watch, but Meg just shrugs her shoulders and says, "I'm not sure—whatever my mom and dad pick up on their way home." Amy has some movies she could take over just in case. What do you think Amy should do?

Should Amy . . .

    A. Watch whatever Meg and her family show to be polite?
    B. Bring some of her own videos and suggest she and Meg watch them?
    C. Put on a blindfold and hide in a closet if the movies are not the kind her parents let her see?

 Check out Daniel 1:8 to see how one Bible character handled a similar situation.
Think of a time when you faced a situation like Amy's. What steps could you take ahead of time that would help you handle that situation better? What did Daniel do?

Do What You Want?

Renée spent the weekend at Laura's house, and she was surprised. Laura can do whatever she wants to do! Her parents are divorced, and her mom works a lot of nights. So Laura's older sister is in charge. But her sister just says yes to whatever Laura asks. If Laura wants to eat two bowls of chocolate ice cream right before bedtime, it's okay. If Laura wants to stay up late to watch a scary movie, it's fine with her sister. When Renée thinks about her own home with all the rules they have, she begins to think that Laura is lucky. At Laura's house, she stayed up as late as she wanted. She ate lots of ice cream. And she watched tons of movies. Now Renée is back at her house, and her mom is telling her it's time to go to bed. What do you think Renée should do?

Should Renée . . .

A. Politely tell her mom that she is going to stay up later now?
B. Get herself ready for bed on the double?
C. Tell her mom she's going to have a big bowl of ice cream first?

 Read Judges 21:25 to find out about a sad time when God's people did whatever they wanted instead of obeying him. What do you think would happen today if all people did whatever seemed right in their own eyes?

The correct answer is B.

Review Time!

List three things you learned this month about being obedient.

1.

2.

3.

Bonus

List three ways you can obey your parents, your teacher, or another adult.

1.

2.

3.

Say your memory verse to one of the people whom you have obeyed. (The verse is printed on the page just before May 1.) Does this verse name someone you want to be like?

May

Serving & Stewardship

Serving or helping others is not just a nice activity that we do when we have nothing better to do or when we feel like it. For true followers of Jesus, service is a way of life. We are to serve others because we want to, and we're to do it to the best of our ability. Jesus is our model. He said, "For even I, the Son of Man, came here not to be served but to serve others, and to give my life as a ransom for many" (Matthew 20:28).

Serving others has nothing to do with how many things we do well, how old we are, or how much we have to give—whether it's time, money, or other gifts. It has everything to do with the way we feel about others' needs. If we want to be a servant, we must look for ways to help others and do whatever is necessary to help someone in need.

Learning to serve by using our time, money, and abilities wisely is called stewardship. God has given each person special abilities, talents, and gifts. We are to use everything we have to help God's kingdom grow.

As you work through this month's *Sticky Situations*, think about the way you feel about helping people. Do you see helping others as a way to serve God? Or is it a duty, something that you have to do or else?

Memory Verse: But among you it should be quite different. Whoever wants to be a leader among you must be your servant, and whoever wants to be first must become your slave.
Matthew 20:26-27

What about Me?

It is Shauna's ninth birthday, and everyone in her family is coming over for a party. In her family the birthday girl always gets to choose her own cake. No one else knows what kind of cake is chosen, so everyone looks forward to seeing the surprise cake. This year Shauna has chosen an angel food cake with lots of whipped cream and big, yummy strawberries. When Shauna's mom brings out the cake with nine birthday candles, everyone claps! After blowing out the candles, Shauna waits for the first piece. Her mom cuts the first slice, hands it to Shauna and says, "Here, Shauna, help me serve the cake. Give this one to your grandpa." What about her piece? What do you think Shauna should do?

Should Shauna . . .

A. Hide the first piece under her chair and serve her grandpa the next piece?
B. Serve everyone else first and then take her own piece of cake?
C. Wait until she sees which is the biggest piece and take that one?

 Read Numbers 15:39 to see what Shauna should do.
God told the Israelites to hang tassels at the bottom of their clothes. This would help them remember to serve others (especially God) ahead of themselves. Think of something you can make or do that will help you remember to serve others.

The correct answer is B.

Excuses, Excuses

José is late getting to Sunday school, but now he's glad he's sitting in the back of the room. His teacher is looking for volunteers to help set tables for the church dinner that evening. José's family is planning to go, but he really doesn't want to come early to set tables. As Mr. Nelson goes around the room, José hears excuse after excuse. "Sorry, we're not going to the dinner." "I can't because I have to take care of my little sister." "I have to practice for my piano lesson this afternoon." "We're going to visit my grandparents in the city."

Finally, after only one girl has agreed to come, Mr. Nelson comes to José. "What about you, José? Can you come?" he asks. There really is no reason why José can't come. What do you think he should do?

Should José . . .

- A. Tell Mr. Nelson that he is really bad at setting tables; his parents won't even let him do it at home?
- B. Say he has to practice for the upcoming computer-game contest; he wants to take first place this year?
- C. Tell Mr. Nelson he can come and he will even ask his older brother if he'll come too?

 Check out Judges 6:14-16 to see what excuse one Bible character gave God when asked to do something.
What are some times when you are likely to make excuses rather than do what you can to help? Make a promise card to give your mom or dad for an excuse-free service.

The correct answer is C.

The Greeter

Heather wants to cry. Her class is planning the end-of-the-year program for parents. The teacher wants her students to give a short review of everything the class has studied. As Mrs. Templeton goes over the parts, Heather's classmates all agree to do something. But Heather can't draw, and she is not very good at speaking in front of people. It doesn't seem as if there is *anything* for Heather to do. Mrs. Templeton asks, "Now, does everyone have something to do?"

Heather raises her hand timidly. "I can't do any of that stuff." Mrs. Templeton looks at her kindly. "Why, Heather, with that great big smile of yours, you will be the perfect greeter when the parents arrive." Heather hasn't thought of that! What do you think she should do?

Should Heather . . .

A. Give a great big smile and say yes?
B. Tell Mrs. Templeton she'll just plan on not coming to school that day?
C. Refuse because being a greeter isn't important enough?

 For help in knowing what Heather should do, read 1 Corinthians 12:27.
With your mom or dad, make a list of all the different "jobs" that go on in your house. Is one job more important than another? Are all the jobs necessary to making the house run smoothly? Talk about how this is also true in other places, like school and church.

The correct answer is A.

The Greatest

It is the last day of school, and all of the kids are talking about what they will do this summer. Josh is going to help with the vacation Bible school at his church. He will paint decorations, cut out some pieces for the crafts, and run errands with his mom. Soon some friends come up to Josh, and they begin telling what they're going to do. "I'm going to be on the swim team and I'm going to win some first-place ribbons," says one friend.

"That's nothing. I'm going to a basketball camp 150 miles from here for two whole weeks!"

"Well, my family and I are going to Europe," shares another. "What will you do, Josh?"

Wow, Josh thinks. *Everyone is doing such great things.* What do you think Josh should say?

Should Josh . . .

A. Tell his friends that he will be the director for his church's vacation Bible school?
B. Make up something really great—like the town mayor has picked him to lead the Fourth of July parade—and hope no one goes?
C. Tell his friends he is going to help out at his church's vacation Bible school?

 Take a look at Matthew 23:5-6, 12 to see how Jesus feels about bragging.
Listen to the news and find out if some people are saying great things about themselves. Do some people wait for others to say good things about them? What does Jesus say about those who exalt themselves?

The correct answer is C.

Not My Job

Rashid's job at Sunday school this month is to make sure the classroom is neat and clean before the end of class. Today the class has worked on a project involving a lot of cutting. They got a late start on the project, so the teacher lets them work a bit longer. It is almost time for church when they finish. After putting away his own things, Rashid looks around the room. Paper scraps are everywhere! Rashid quickly gets everyone's attention and says that *everyone* needs to help clean up the room. As the class begins picking up paper, Rashid sits back in his chair. "Hey, Rashid! Aren't you going to help out?" one student calls. What do you think Rashid should do?

Should Rashid . . .

    A. Tell the student that picking up paper scraps is not part of his job?
    B. Tell the student that his job is to tell everyone else what to do?
    C. Get down and start picking up scraps?

 Read Luke 22:26 for help in knowing what Rashid should do. Jesus said that leaders should be servants. Discuss with your mom or dad what you think Jesus means. Can you think of any examples from Jesus' life or from other Bible stories that show how to be a servant-leader?

The correct answer is C.

Summertime Blues

Dale flips through the book he just got from the library. He really doesn't feel like reading. Trouble is, there isn't anything that Dale feels like doing. Most of his friends are on vacation. He already has been to the pool a zillion times. He has read all the books in the Z-*men* series. He has even gotten tired of playing his new video game that he got for his birthday. That night he says to his dad, "I'm bored. There's nothing to do."

"Well," his dad says, "Mrs. Henry at church is looking for some help stuffing envelopes for a big mailing coming up. You could ride your bike over there and see if you can help." Stuffing envelopes? That sounds even more boring than sitting around at home. What do you think Dale should do?

Should Dale . . .

    A. Tell his dad he'd rather go to a good movie?
    B. Agree to ride over to church the next day and help Mrs. Henry stuff envelopes?
    C. Ask how much Mrs. Henry is willing to pay for someone to stuff the envelopes; if the price is right, he'll go?

 Look up Philippians 2:5-7 for help in knowing what Dale should do.
As you read the Bible passage, discuss with your mom or dad how Jesus felt about the work God had given him to do. How does the way you feel about serving and helping others need to change?

Show a Little Kindness

Nobody wants to be Maureen's partner in Sunday school. It isn't because she is stupid or anything. Maureen is, well, just different. Sometimes she smells funny. Her hair always looks like she combed it with an eggbeater. She often wears the same outfit three days in a row. Her shoes are all scuffed and beat-up. Theresa knows that Maureen lives in a small house at the edge of town. The yard always has rusty cars and at least a dozen kids running around. And Theresa has heard there is never enough food at home for Maureen to get a good breakfast. Theresa feels sorry for Maureen but doesn't really know what to do about it. Today Theresa sees that once again Maureen is sitting by herself. What do you think Theresa should do?

Should Theresa . . .

A. Try to ignore Maureen and just talk to the other kids?
B. Make a promise to herself that she'll ask her mom if someone can do something for Maureen's family?
C. Sit with Maureen, be her friend, and give her a breakfast bar?

 Read Psalm 41:1-2 to see what Theresa should do. With your mom or dad, make a list of blessings God has given you and your family. Think of ways you can share those blessings with others who have less than you.

Allowance Time

Beginning this summer, Ian is getting an allowance. After much talking with his parents, they finally have agreed that an allowance will help Ian learn how to save and spend money. His mom and dad have helped Ian set up a savings account at the local bank. They have even bought him a book where he can write down what he spends his money on each month. Ian's parents agree to buy his food, clothes, shoes, and school supplies, but Ian will have to buy any extras. Today is Ian's first allowance day. As his mom gives Ian his allowance, she asks him, "Now that you have an allowance, what do you plan to do about your church offering?" Wow! Ian has not thought about that. What do you think Ian should do?

Should Ian . . .

    A. Set aside the same amount each week to give as an offering to God?

    B. Give whatever he has left over as an offering?

    C. Figure God owns everything in the world and doesn't need any more from him?

 Read Deuteronomy 14:22-23 to see what Ian should do. Read the Bible passage aloud. Why is giving God a tithe, or ten percent of your money, so important? What do you do for an offering? What changes might you make?
Reminder: Don't forget to work on your memory verse for June. (You'll find it on the page just before June 1.)

The correct answer is A.

The Best Gift

For Gemma's "golden birthday"—she's turning nine on the ninth—she and her mom are planning a "girls' day out." The two of them are going to spend the day downtown. Gemma's mom plans to get tickets to see the ice-skating show. After the show they will eat at one of Gemma's favorite restaurants. A few days before their day out, her mom has some bad news. "Gemma, I'm sorry, but this Saturday I am going to have to work at the nursing home. My sub just called and said she has a family problem. If you want, you can come with me and help with the folks there. Then we'll grab something to eat later, and next week we'll go downtown." Gemma feels like crying. The plans for a day with her mom are dead. What do you think Gemma should do?

Should Gemma . . .

A. Tell her mom she'll stay home to have a "pity party" instead of a birthday party?
B. Ask her favorite aunt to "sub" for her mom and take her to the show?
C. Go with her mom and help the people at the nursing home have a good afternoon?

 Check out Acts 20:35 for help in knowing what Gemma should do.
Everyone enjoys getting presents. But what do you think Jesus means when he says that it is better or "more blessed" to give? Can you think of a time when you felt like that?

The correct answer is C.

Don't Look the Other Way

Every Wednesday afternoon Darrin and his mom take the bus and go downtown for Darrin's piano lesson. His piano teacher gives lessons from a studio he has leased in an office building near the center of town. Darrin loves going into town and seeing all the buildings and the people. There is only one thing Darrin does not enjoy. Every afternoon when they get off the bus, Darrin and his mom see a man dressed in raggedy clothes asking people for money so he can eat. His mom always hurries Darrin past the man and tells him not to look at him. Darrin, however, can't get the man's eyes out of his mind. It bothers Darrin, but he doesn't know what he can do about it. He's only one kid! What do you think he should do?

Should Darrin . . .

    A. Walk by, looking the other way?
    B. Ask his mom if they could pack a brown-bag lunch for the man?
    C. Ask his mom if they could change bus routes so they won't have to walk by the man anymore?

 Read Proverbs 28:27 for some help in knowing what Darrin should do.
It may not be possible to help all the people you see on the street. But what are some other ways you can help needy people? Name at least three things you may be able to do as a family to help those who are poor.

The correct answer is B.

What a Disaster!

Lindsay watches with disbelief as the pictures on TV show a city in another state that has been hit by a bad flood. She never would have believed that water could cause that much damage. There are pictures of families sitting by wet furniture, and there are stories of people who had to be rescued from their rooftops. At the end of the news story, people are asked to send money to help the flood victims. Lindsay really doesn't understand why she and her family should do that. After all, these people live in another state, in a place she has never heard of before. They don't know her, and she certainly doesn't know anyone from there. What do you think Lindsay should do?

Should Lindsay . . .

A. Ask her dad to flip the channel because the story about the flood is ruining her appetite?
B. Ask her family if they could send some money to help the flood victims?
C. Hope that the people in that town have friends and family members with lots of money?

 Check out Matthew 25:31-40 for help in knowing what Lindsay should do.
Sometimes when there's a report about something terrible that has happened in a faraway place, it's easy to think someone else will take care of it. Why does Jesus say you should help?

Share and Share Alike?

Kayla and her parents have been redoing her bedroom. It took weeks of shopping to find the right bedspread and matching curtains. Her dad and mom painted the room, and she picked out a cool wallpaper border as the finishing touch. Kayla is so happy. She thinks her room looks great! Which is why she is upset about having to share her room—especially with Darlene! Darlene is the daughter of her mom's college roommate. The last time Darlene came to visit, she spilled nail polish on Kayla's bedspread, threw dirty clothes all over the room, and left dirty dishes and glasses on the dresser. If Kayla shares her room with Darlene, it will never, ever be the same. What are her parents thinking? What do you think Kayla should do?

Should Kayla . . .

A. Rope off a small corner of the room where Darlene can stay and mark everything with "Don't Touch—This Means You" signs?
B. Send Darlene to a local hotel?
C. Tell her parents what she is worried about and come up with a plan on how to handle Darlene?

 Check out Luke 6:38 to see what Kayla should do. With your mom or dad, talk about what you think the Bible verse is teaching. What does the Bible verse have to say about the way you treat others? What can you expect in return?

The correct answer is C.

The Birthday Check

Ellis will soon be eight years old. Every year Ellis receives a birthday card with a check from his Uncle Rick. Last year Uncle Rick sent him thirty dollars. This year Ellis can't believe his eyes when a check for fifty dollars comes floating out of the card. Wow! He can buy a lot of good stuff with that! Ellis's dad promises to let him look at the newest video games. While sitting in church Ellis hears the minister talk about a nearby homeless shelter. The shelter helps homeless women and children. They need money for new toys for the children. Ellis starts to feel guilty about his fifty-dollar check. Maybe he ought to give some money to the shelter. What do you think Ellis should do?

Should Ellis . . .

A. Talk with his parents about giving part of his money to the shelter and using the rest to save up for a video game later?
B. Drag some of his old, broken toys out of the back of the closet and give those to the shelter?
C. Forget about the shelter and buy his video game, because after all, the money is his gift?

 For help in knowing what Ellis should do, look up 2 Corinthians 9:7.
After reading the Bible verse, come up with at least three ways that God wants us to give when it comes to our money. How are you doing in the giving department?

Do a Little Dance

If there's one thing that everyone knows about Cammie, it's that she is a dancer. She has just found out that she can go to an advanced dance class in the fall—one that will prepare her for toe shoes! When her Sunday school teacher says that they are going to hold a talent show to help raise money for the homeless, everyone turns to Cammie. "Cammie, why don't you dance for the talent show?" her teacher suggests. "We would love to see you, and it would help a lot of people." Cammie loves to perform, but she is afraid that she might hurt herself. She doesn't want *anything* to keep her from going to that class in the fall. What do you think Cammie should do?

Should Cammie . . .

- A. Agree to dance for the talent show?
- B. Tell her teacher she needs to stay off her feet until the fall?
- C. Offer to show a videotape from her last dance program instead?

 Look up 1 Peter 4:10-11 for help in knowing what Cammie should do.
Make a list of talents and abilities you have. Plan some ways you can use them to help others.

A Call to Action

If we say we love God and love others, it will show in what we do. Using the symbol bank below, decode the following message about how our actions help others know who we are.

SYMBOL BANK

A B C D E F G H I J K L M N O P Q R S T U V W X Y Z

__ __
☆ ◆ ☆ ☆ ✹ ★ ☆ ✧ ★ ☆ ✡ ◤ ✧ ☆ ★ ✹ ✧ ★ ✾ ☆ ★ ✧ ✹

__ __ __ __ __ __ __ __ __ __ __ __ __ __ __ __ __ __ __
✹ ★ ★ ☆ ★ ✧ ◭ ✧ ★ ★ ☆ ★ ♣ ◤ ✧ ✧ ◤ ☆

__ __
✧ ✹ ★ ★ ★ ✧ ✧ ★ ★ ◤ ☆ ◤ ✹ ✧ ☆ ☆ ★ ✧ ✧ ♣

__ __ __ __ __ __ __ __ __ __ __ ____ ____
☆ ☆ ♣ ✹ ✧ ◆ ✹ ◤ ✧ ◤ ✹ ★ ★ ✧ ★ ☆ ★ ★ ◭

__ __ __ __ __ __ __ __ __ __ __ , __ __ __ __ __ __ __
✾ ☆ ★ ✧ ★ ♣ ◤ ★ ★ ★ ✧ ✧ ✧ ☆ ☆ ✹ ★ ☆ ✹

__ __ __ __ __ __ __ ? 1 John 3:17
☆ ✧ ✹ ◤ ★ ★ ☆

The Accident

César drinks his milk in one gulp and stuffs a couple of cookies in his mouth. If he hurries he can get over to his friend's house just in time to catch the first games of the summer Olympics. César and his friend have agreed never to miss a basketball game if they can help it! This morning César had to attend his sister's softball game, so he is running late. As he pedals his bike over to his friend's house, he sees a little boy lying on the ground, crying. As César turns to get a better look, he can tell that the boy has fallen off his bike and has badly skinned his knee. César looks around—no one sees the boy but him. If he stops to help the boy, however, he'll miss the first part of the Olympics! What do you think César should do?

Should César . . .

- A. Say a quick prayer for the boy's knee to heal, then keep going?
- B. Call out, "Are you okay? I'll call 911 when I get to my friend's house"?
- C. Stop and help the boy?

 Read James 2:15-16 for some help in knowing what César should do.
People with needs are all around you. Think of two or three that you know and brainstorm ways you can serve them today.

The Food Drive

Vanessa's church is having a food drive for a family that has had a lot of medical bills and now doesn't have much money for food. Vanessa and her family have worked hard during the week, collecting food from their block. On Sunday she and her family bring in ten bags of groceries. When Vanessa walks into Sunday school, one of her friends tells her, "Hey, did you hear? Kim's family brought in ten bags of groceries." There is Kim in the center of a group, bragging about how hard *she* worked. What do you think Vanessa should do?

Should Vanessa . . .

   A. Say, "With all the food we've collected, the family should have lots to eat for a long time"?
   B. Tell Kim's family you want to have a food-drive playoff to see who can collect the most food?
   C. Say, "Well, we collected ten bags too, and I know for a fact that I worked harder than anyone."

 Check out what Jesus has to say in Matthew 6:2-4 about doing good deeds.
Discuss with your mom or dad different reasons people help someone else. What does the Bible verse say should be your reward for helping others?

Is That Your Best?

Sydney is very busy. On Mondays she has piano lessons, on Tuesdays she has gymnastics, and on Wednesdays and Saturdays she usually can be found on the softball field. Her mom just signed her up for an art class on Thursdays, so if you want to catch up with Sydney, it had better be after church on Sunday. Her Sunday school teacher wants the class to help out with monthly service projects she has scheduled. The teacher is asking who can help pull weeds at the church on Saturday morning. That's the same time as Sydney's ball game. Sydney can't be two places at once. What do you think Sydney should do?

Should Sydney . . .

    A. Pull weeds for five minutes before the game?
    B. Ask if some of the service projects can be done on Saturday afternoons so she can take part in them?
    C. Ask the group to leave some weeds for her to pull on Sunday?

Read Malachi 1:6-8 to see how God wants his children to "sacrifice," or give up things for him.
What things have you given up or sacrificed by giving them back to God? Are you giving your best to God or not?

Give a Little Bit

Barrett has counted the money in his Mars bank and learns
that he has thirty dollars. His mom tells him he can use the
money to buy whatever he wants. After buying some stuff, all
Barrett has left is a dollar and some change, which he plans to
use to buy candy. At Bible club on Wednesday night a visiting
missionary tells stories about living in a small village in Africa.
Then the leader passes around an offering basket. The money
from the offering will help the missionary with his work. Barrett
wants to give something, but all he has in his pocket is the
dollar and some change. He doesn't think a dollar will do
much good. What do you think Barrett should do?

Should Barrett . . .

   A. Wait until he can give more money to the missionary and pray
      every day?
   B. Give what he has?
   C. Forget about it, knowing there are plenty of people with more
      money who can help out?

 For help in knowing what Barrett should do, read
John 6:8-13.
This probably is a familiar story to you, but consider what
might have happened if the young boy had thought like
Barrett. What does this Bible story teach you about what God
can do with even your "little" gifts?

Keeping Back

Each week Anton receives ten dollars in allowance money. From that amount four dollars goes into savings, four dollars is his own spending money, and two dollars is for his weekly offering at church. For the past several months Anton has been saving his money for a new computer game. With all his savings, Anton has thirty dollars. In the newspaper ads Anton notices that he can get the computer game he wants for forty dollars. If he uses all of his allowance this week he can buy the computer game. It would mean that he won't be able to bring in his church offering for this Sunday. But he could pretend he didn't get his allowance money. What do you think Anton should do?

Should Anton . . .

A. Wait to buy the game until he has saved up enough money without using his offering money?
B. Use all his allowance to buy the computer game and take in an empty offering envelope to make it look good?
C. Stick an IOU in the offering basket—God will understand that he had to have the computer game now?

 Look up Acts 5:1-4 for help in knowing what Anton should do.
In the Bible passage, what was Ananias's biggest mistake? What do you think God cares more about—the amount of money you give, or your telling the truth about what you can give?

Attitude Adjustment

Tanya is helping her parents plan a birthday party for her younger sister. A dozen four-year-olds will be at the party, and Tanya has agreed to help with some games and do some face painting. The day before the party, Tanya's best friend, Rachel, calls and wants to know if she can go to the movies tomorrow. Tanya can't go because of the party, but she asks Rachel if she would like to come and help her with the birthday party instead. "It's going to be a lot of fun," Tanya tells her friend. "You can help me with the face-painting."

There is silence on the other end of the phone line. "Sounds pretty boring to me, but I don't have anything else going on. I suppose I could come by and help," Rachel finally says. Tanya isn't sure she really needs *that* kind of help. What do you think Tanya should do?

Should Tanya . . .

    A. Tell her friend to get real and change the way she feels about little kids if she wants to stay friends?

    B. Tell Rachel that's okay, but she won't help *her* the next time she asks either?

    C. Ask her friend if she'd like to come and help with the food?

 Check out what 1 Corinthians 13:3 says about our attitude in serving others.
Can you think of a time when someone refused to help you? What was *your* attitude? Think of ways you can show love when it comes time to help that person.

The correct answer is C.

Keep the Change?

The kids from Jamie's day camp are going to the city zoo. The night before the field trip Jamie begs her dad for some money to buy something at the zoo's gift shop. Her dad pulls out a $20 bill and says she can buy something for $5, but she must bring back the change. Jamie and her friends have a great time at the zoo. Before they leave for home, her group stops at the zoo gift shop. Jamie soon sees that there isn't much to buy for $5. She could get a small change purse or an orange plastic molded animal. But what she really wants is the cute stuffed monkey for $17.99. Jamie's dad always tells her not to buy junk. Dad wouldn't want her to buy one of those cheap gifts when she could buy the monkey. Besides, she still will bring back change! What do you think Jamie should do?

Should she . . .

A. Buy the monkey and tell her dad she lost the rest of the change?
B. Buy the orange molded animal and toss it in the back of her closet when she gets home?
C. Save the money and not buy anything this time?

 Read Luke 16:12 for help in knowing what Jamie should do. Why shouldn't Jamie buy the orange molded animal? Talk with your family about the kinds of things you can and can't afford to buy right now. Pray that God will help you all agree on these things and stick to your family budget.

The correct answer is C.

The Money Trap

Wade can't help but stare as he walks into his friend Alan's home. It is huge! The front hall alone is bigger than Wade's bedroom, which he shares with his younger brother. Not only does Alan have his own room, but he also has his own computer! And telephone! And TV! Wade's family doesn't even own a computer, and his family of eight shares one phone and one small TV set. "Wow, you have a really cool house. What do your parents do?" Wade asks.

"Oh, they work in big offices downtown," Alan says.

Later that night Wade is quiet, thinking of Alan's huge home and all the things his friend has. His dad asks, "What's up, Wade? Something wrong?" What do you think he should say?

Should Wade . . .

    A. Ask his dad if they can move to Alan's neighborhood?
    B. Ask his dad why he doesn't get a better job, like Alan's parents, so they can have more things?
    C. Share his feelings with his dad about what he saw at Alan's house?

 Read Matthew 6:24 to see what may help Alan think about how important money is or is not.
What do you think Jesus wants us to learn about money?
Talk about ways money can become a "master," with us as slaves.
Reminder: Don't forget to keep working on your memory verse for June. (See the page just before June 1.)

The correct answer is C.

Never Too Young

The church's annual missions conference is coming up in a few weeks. This is a huge undertaking that attracts more than four hundred people each year. It takes an army of volunteers to make it work. Mason's dad is helping prepare the food for the big dinner. His mom is helping arrange transportation and housing for the speakers. Even his older sister is involved—she plans to help out in the nursery. Everyone, it seems, has a job to do except Mason. On Sunday in church the pastor asks for more people to help in a few key areas, like cleanup and decorations. Mason would love to help out, but he doesn't think anyone would take him seriously because he is only seven. What do you think Mason should do?

Should he . . .

    A. Keep quiet because no one will listen to a seven-year-old?
    B. Come to the program and offer to help out with something he can do—like pick up the trash?
    C. Wait a few more years until he can run the whole thing?

 Read Jeremiah 1:4-9 to see how one Bible character felt about being too young to serve God—and what God said to him.
Do you think anyone is too young to serve or help others? Name ways everyone at your house can serve at home, at church, and among your friends.

The correct answer is B.

The Dirty Job

Latrelle's scout troop is having its first campout of the season. It is time for the troop to get dinner ready, and the scout leader has posted the job each one is to do. Latrelle is happy to see that he has cleanup for tonight. After a long day of canoeing, Latrelle has nearly fallen asleep when the dinner bell rings. He joins the line of hungry boys, following the smell of a bubbling stew. After two big helpings, Latrelle finally feels full. He is getting ready to go bug hunting with some friends when the call for cleanup sounds. Latrelle almost forgot that he is on cleanup. He joins the boys in the kitchen and looks with horror at the number of dirty, sticky pots waiting to be scrubbed. "Okay, boys, who wants to be chief washer?" the scoutmaster asks. No one says a word. What do you think Latrelle should do?

Should Latrelle . . .

    A. Leave for a minute and hope by the time he returns someone has taken the job?

    B. Offer to be the chief washer tonight?

    C. Say that he will pick up all the trash around the camp with a toothpick as his cleanup duty?

 Take a look at John 13:3-5 for how Jesus modeled serving others.

Think of all the dirty jobs that have to be done in your home, in your church, and in your community. What would happen if nobody did those jobs? What dirty job can you take on to help your family?

The correct answer is B.

The Answer Is Yes

When Jessica walks in the door, she sees a long white envelope addressed to her on the kitchen table. It is from Mrs. Thompson, her fourth-grade Sunday school teacher. Jessica loves Mrs. Thompson's class. One of her latest projects is putting together a group of kids and teens to do programs for inner-city kids. Jessica opens the letter and sees that Mrs. Thompson wants her to be a part of this group. Jessica needs to talk about this with her mom and dad. It is going to take a lot of time, and Jessica already is very busy. She really would like to have a carefree summer and not have to think about helping others. What do you think Jessica should do?

Should Jessica . . .

    A. Throw away the letter and forget about it?
    B. Let the group get started without her and then see how much time is really needed to be part of the group?
    C. Talk over with her parents the summer plans that would please them—and Jesus—most?

 Look up Matthew 9:9 to see how one man responded to Jesus' invitation.
When it comes to serving, do you offer to help right away, or do you wait and see if it's something you want to do? Based on what you read in Matthew 9:9, what do you think Jesus wants us to do about obeying him and helping others?

Let's Work Together

Liliana and her friends have spent the entire afternoon down in her basement playing. They have played games, worked on some craft projects, and started to try on some old costumes Liliana's mother just found in the attic. When Liliana's mom comes down to tell the girls it is time to leave, she is not happy about the mess in the basement. It looks as if it has been hit by a huge storm! Pieces of games are in different places. Scraps of material and glitter are on the floor. And clothes are thrown everywhere. Her mom looks at Liliana. "This basement needs to be cleaned up right now! I don't care how you do it, just get it done!" What do you think the girls should do?

Should they . . .

- A. Each take a part of the basement and start cleaning?
- B. Run out the door and leave the mess for Liliana to clean up—after all, it's her basement?
- C. Draw straws; the shortest one has to clean the basement by herself?

 Find out how the Israelites handled a huge task they were facing by reading Nehemiah 3:1-2, 28-32.
Talk about times when the people in your family have cooperated to get a job done. What happened when everyone did his or her job? What happened when someone didn't do his or her job?

The correct answer is A.

For You!

Grant struggled in math and reading throughout the year. Three weeks ago his mother hired Mrs. Anderson to be his tutor for the summer. She is one of the toughest tutors in town. Grant feels as if he has spent the whole month of June with Mrs. Anderson. He doesn't really like her either. She doesn't smile much and always makes him do his work over when it's wrong. But she is fair, and he has to admit she has been helping him. Today as he leaves for his time with Mrs. Anderson, his mom hands him a brightly wrapped package. "Here. This is a present to thank Mrs. Anderson for the way she is helping you," she says. A present for Mrs. Anderson? Grant feels as if he should be the one to get a present for giving up so much of his summer! What do you think Grant should do?

Should Grant . . .

A. Give the gift to his Sunday school teacher instead—Grant really likes her better?
B. Give Mrs. Anderson the gift and tell her thank you?
C. Open the gift for himself and hope it's something good to eat?

 Look up Proverbs 18:16 to see what Grant should do. Think of three reasons why you like to receive gifts. Now think of three reasons why you like to *give* gifts. Why do you think it's important to give others gifts?

The correct answer is B.

Shop till You Drop

Everyone at day camp looks forward to the last Friday in the month. During the month Mrs. Smith hands out "Smith Dollars" to students who take part in sports, crafts, and other activities. At the end of the month students can spend their money at the Smith Shop and buy books, cool erasers, stickers, and other stuff. Stacy has been saving up her Smith Dollars to buy a book that has been in the store the past couple of months. She has enough money now for the book *and* a couple of other smaller items. As her table is called to shop, Stacy sees that one of the kids from her table has stayed behind. "Aren't you going to shop, Kirk?" she asks.

"Nah, I don't have enough money to even buy an eraser," he says. Stacy looks at her neat stack of Smith Dollars. What do you think Stacy should do?

Should Stacy . . .

    A. Offer Kirk some of her money so he can buy something too?
    B. Hurry and buy her book before someone else does?
    C. Let Kirk look at one of the erasers she bought?

 Check out Psalm 112:5 for help in knowing what Stacy should do.
The Bible verse talks about being happy to share what you have. Think of times when you can happily share your time, your abilities, or the things you own.

Review Time!

List three things you learned this month about serving others the way Jesus served.

1.

2.

3.

Bonus

Come up with three new ways you can serve others at home or at school.

1.

2.

3.

Say your memory verse to someone you have served recently. (The verse is printed on the page just before June 1.)

Friends & Family

Two of the greatest gifts that God gives us are family and friends. How would you describe yourself as a friend? Are you loyal, kind, and caring? How do you act around your family? Do you look for ways to live peacefully with your brothers or sisters and to please your parents? Or is your main concern how many times you can "win" at home?

One of the best examples of friendship in the Bible is the close relationship between David and Jonathan. Their friendship was based on their commitment to God and to one another— nothing, not even a jealous father and king, was going to get in the way of their friendship. Do you have a friend like Jonathan or David, one on whom you can count no matter what? Are you that kind of friend?

Families, too, are one of God's greatest gifts. God planned for families to love, respect, encourage, help, and understand one another.

As you work through this month's *Sticky Situations,* see how you measure up as a friend. And what changes, if any, do you need to make in your relationships at home?

Memory Verse: Follow God's example in everything you do, because you are his dear children. Live a life filled with love for others, following the example of Christ, who loved you and gave himself as a sacrifice to take away your sins. Ephesians 5:1-2

It's in the Cards

Janelle and her friend Denise are hanging out, like they often do on a summer afternoon. Both girls are hit hard by that "there's-nothing-to-do" bug. "Wanna go Rollerblading?" Janelle suggests.

"Nah, my blades are broken. How about going to the park and playing tag?" Denise counters.

"Nah, there's only two of us, so that won't be too much fun," Janelle says.

"I know!" Denise brightens up. "My older sister just got some tarot cards. Let's tell each other's fortune."

Janelle remembers she has heard in Sunday school that the Bible says to stay away from fortune-telling. But she doesn't want to hurt her friend's feelings. What do you think Janelle should do?

Should Janelle . . .

    A. Go along with her friend—after all, it's only a game and they aren't real fortune-tellers?

    B. Suggest the girls set up a fortune-telling booth to make a little money on the side?

    C. Tell Denise she doesn't want to do that, and then come up with something else to do?

 Take a look at Deuteronomy 13:6-8 to see how serious it is to God when someone tries to steer you away from him. Sometimes even your good friends can suggest things to do that may steer you away from God. Role-play with your mom or dad what you might say to a friend in a similar situation.

The correct answer is C.

Get the Facts

Joy's park-district art class has a thief. Someone has lost a new box of crayons. Another friend had a plastic snake that some-one took from his backpack. Even Joy has lost a set of neon-colored markers. She had just been ready to use them, and the next thing she knew they were gone! Everyone was talking at lunch that day about the things that were missing. "Well, I think I know who it is," says one of Joy's friends. "I think it's that new boy, Dylan. He's always so quiet. He never talks to anyone." Dylan and his family just moved in next door to Joy. He *is* quiet, but Joy thinks that's mostly because he is new. She doesn't think he would steal anything. As she is walking home with Dylan that afternoon, however, Joy sees what looks like a brand-new pack of crayons in Dylan's backpack. What do you think Joy should do?

Should Joy . . .

    A. Not say anything until she has more proof?
    B. Shout, "Stop, thief"?
    C. Ask Dylan, "Hey, where'd you get those crayons? They look like Maria's missing box of crayons"?

 Read Job 6:14 for some help in knowing what Joy should do. Talk with your mom or dad about how you would feel if you were falsely accused of something. Can you think of a time when you have been?

You Should Know Better

When Dave first hears the news about his good friend, Spencer, he doesn't believe it. Spencer got into trouble with his day camp director when, on a dare, he pulled the fire alarm and ran through the camp yelling "Fire!" When firefighters came on two big fire trucks, they learned it was a false alarm. Now Spencer has to stay right with the director for a whole week. He can't even play with the other kids. When Dave gets home from piano lessons, he sees Spencer's dad bringing him home from day camp. Spencer looks like he has been crying. Spencer sees Dave and comes over but doesn't say anything. Dave hasn't talked to Spencer since the day his friend yelled "Fire!" What do you think Dave should do?

Should Dave . . .

    A. Say, "How could you do something like that? Did you leave your brains home that day, or what?"
    B. Start laughing at Spencer and pretend to put out a fire with a big hose?
    C. Say, "Hey, Spence. I'm sorry about what happened. Looks like you feel pretty bad about it."

 Check out Job 16:2-3 for some good advice for Dave. When you have done something wrong or are going through a bad time, how do you want your friends to help you? What would you say to Spencer?

Stand by Me

The baseball game is really close. In the ninth inning, Shiv's team is ahead by only one run. The other team has last bats, though, and now Shiv's team is in trouble. The bases are loaded, but there are two outs. All they have to do is get this last batter out, and the team can celebrate. Shiv looks over at his friend in right field. "Two outs," he calls. "We've got this guy!" Ravi nods and gets ready. The pitcher goes into his windup, releases the ball, and *thwack!* The ball goes sailing into right field. Ravi follows it all the way, adjusts his glove, and then—drops the ball! Two runs score, and the game is over.

As the other team celebrates, Shiv and his teammates walk off the field, heads down. One of the boys says to Ravi, "Does your mitt have a hole in it or what?" Shiv knows his friend feels just awful. What do you think Shiv should do?

Should Shiv . . .

   A. Ignore Ravi—he dropped the ball, so let him handle it?
   B. Tell Ravi, "You'll catch the next one; don't worry about it"?
   C. Suggest Ravi put something sticky on his mitt to keep the ball from dropping?

 Read Psalm 55:12-14 to see how David felt when a friend turned his back on him.
Think of a friend you know who is going through a difficult time. Think of two things you can do for that friend.

Fight Fair

Natalie's best friend is mad at her. Natalie was supposed to go over to Julie's house one evening to help her make some no-bake cookies. But Natalie had to help her mom with some errands instead. Natalie left a message with Julie's sister, but Julie must never have received it. Now Julie isn't talking to her. Natalie sees Julie swinging in her yard with two other girls. As she walks toward Julie, she can hear her saying in a loud voice, "Here comes Miss Nose-in-the-Air. She thinks she's too good to spend any time with me." *This is so unfair,* Natalie thinks. Julie is being stubborn and not letting her have a chance to explain. And on top of that, Julie also is making fun of Natalie in front of the other girls. What do you think Natalie should do?

Should Natalie . . .

A. Walk away and cool off before talking to Julie again?
B. Tell Julie, "Well at least I'm not Miss Stubborn-as-a-Mule"?
C. Remind Julie of the time she forgot to wait for her after school, leaving her to walk home by herself in the rain?

 Look up Proverbs 17:9 for help in knowing what Natalie should do.
When you are talking with a friend who is upset with you, sometimes it's hard not to bring up past wrongs. It's easy to bring up more personal things you know about the person. Talk with your family about some things you can do in the future if someone is upset with you.

The correct answer is A.

The Odd Couple

Down the block from Clay's house is a run-down old house that once was a mansion. It has four stories, a huge front yard, a long tree-lined driveway, and big pillars in the front. But the shutters are falling off, the trim needs paint, and the lawn is full of weeds. The two people living in the home are as run-down and odd as the house. They hardly ever go outside. For fun, some of Clay's friends ride by and shout at them. Then the boys take off on their bikes laughing. Today, as they ride their bikes to the park, Clay's friends suggest they throw some rocks at the house. "Maybe we can get both of them to chase us! That would be really funny!" his friends say. What do you think Clay should do?

Should Clay . . .

- A. Suggest the boys toss marshmallows instead?
- B. Tell the boys they should leave the people alone; after all, they are neighbors?
- C. Offer to be the lookout so if the two people do come out to chase the boys, the boys will get a head start?

 Read Proverbs 11:12 for help in knowing what Clay should do.
Do you have a neighbor or friend or family member who is "different"? How do others treat this person? Think of two ways you can be a good neighbor to the person who is different.

A True-Blue Friend

As Olivia joins some friends she hears one say, "I just can't stand her. She is so bossy."

"Yeah, she never listens to anyone else, and she says things that aren't kind," another girl adds. "Did you hear what she said to me yesterday? She told me I should never wear anything red because it makes me look like a tomato!"

Who are they talking about? Olivia wonders.

"Yeah, that April sure can be a jerk," the first girl says. April! Olivia and April have been good friends for years. April can be bossy, but there are a lot of things Olivia likes about April. She can be funny, she is always willing to help with math, and although she has a lot of stuff, she always shares. What do you think Olivia should do?

Should Olivia . . .

A. Keep quiet and not admit to being friends with April?
B. Tell her friends that April once told her not to wear yellow because it made her look like a banana?
C. Share some of April's good qualities with the girls?

 Read Ruth 1:14-18 for an example of how true friends stick together no matter what.
Ask your mom or dad to talk about her or his loyal friends. Discuss what it means to be a loyal friend.

Friends Forever?

Monica reads the note again. It is from her friend (or onetime friend) Vanessa. For the first couple of weeks of the summer, she and Vanessa were together almost every minute. But Vanessa is a grade ahead of Monica, and now Vanessa only wants to hang out with her older friends. It is pretty much the same thing all week long and on the weekends, too. She never calls Monica to do anything anymore, and the times Monica has asked her to play, Vanessa always is "busy." Now Vanessa has just sent Monica a note asking if she wants to go to the amusement park with her and her family on Saturday. In the note Vanessa said that she misses Monica and still wants to be friends. What do you think Monica should do?

Should she . . .

    A. Tell Vanessa she would love to go to the amusement park with her and her family?
    B. Suggest they "do lunch" when she is less busy?
    C. Ask Vanessa what happened to her other friends?

 Check out Proverbs 17:17 for help in knowing what Monica should do.
Role-play with your mom or dad how you would answer Vanessa's note. If you and a friend drifted apart, how might you handle it?

July

Good Neighbors

Zach promises his mom that he will finish mowing the backyard this afternoon. His dad has been teaching him how to cut the grass, and Zach has been given the job of doing the backyard. It is flat and wide open, so there aren't any tricky turns. Before Zach goes out to cut the grass, his friend Drew calls wanting Zach to come over and play ball that afternoon. Drew has to go to the dentist now, but he will be home later. That's perfect for Zach. He can cut the grass and still go to Drew's house. As Zach is getting the mower out of the garage, his mom calls to him, "Remember the Wilsons' baby. She's napping now, and the lawn mower will wake her. Maybe you ought to mow later." If Zach does that, he will miss Drew and a chance to play ball. What do you think Zach should do?

Should Zach . . .

> A. Tell the Wilsons to close all their windows because he's going to mow now?
> B. Mow later and promise Drew he'll play ball another day?
> C. Cut the grass with a big pair of scissors so he won't make any noise?

 Read Proverbs 27:14 for some advice on being a good neighbor.
Have your mom or dad help you make a list of ways that you are a good neighbor. Come up with at least one thing you can do today to be a good friend and neighbor.

Plan B

Leo and his friend Jamal are helping plan the Sunday school picnic. Every year the third and fourth graders are in charge of the games. "I know, let's play Red Rover, Capture the Flag, and Spud," says one girl. Those are the same games they play every year.

Leo sees his friend waving his hand. Jamal begins, "I think we should dress up like clowns and do tricks and hand out balloons."

The other kids say things like: "I don't have a clown costume." "I don't know how to do any magic tricks." "Does that mean I have to wear a red nose?"

Jamal turns to Leo, "What do you think?" Leo's friend always has different ideas. What do you think Leo should do?

Should Leo . . .

A. Ignore Jamal and stick to what has worked before?
B. Have everyone sign up for clown classes and try it next year?
C. Suggest the group discuss Jamal's idea and think about what might work?

 Read Proverbs 27:17 for some help in knowing what Leo should do.
Read the Bible verse aloud. Discuss with your mom and dad what it means for a friend to "sharpen" a friend. How can you help your friends think through new ideas they may have? Reminder: Don't forget to work on your memory verse for July. (You'll find it on the page just before July 1.)

The correct answer is C.

Let's Get Together

Naomi's swimming teacher tells the summer class at the "Y" that there is going to be a race next week. The swimmers can swim alone or with a partner. Naomi really loves to swim and knows she has a good chance to win by herself. She isn't interested in a partner because no one would be as fast as she is. Naomi has all but decided to swim solo when her good friend Elantra calls her that night. Elantra asks Naomi to swim with her in the race. Elantra is good at swimming. But she isn't as fast as Naomi. What do you think Naomi should do?

Should Naomi . . .

A. Tell her friend that she wants to swim alone?
B. Agree to work with Elantra because two are better than one?
C. Make Elantra pass a test first to see if she is good enough to swim with her?

 Check out the principle the Bible gives us in Ecclesiastes 4:9-12 about working with others.
Think of a time when you worked by yourself and of another time when you were with a partner. Which did you like better? What are some good things that happen when you work with others?

The Last Word

Yikes, thinks Emmett. Here comes Last-Word Luke, heading straight toward him! Last-Word Luke is one of those kids who always has to have, well, you guessed it, the last word. Emmett is just about to warn his friends, but Luke reaches the group before he can. "What's happening?" he asks. The boys have been discussing who will be the best basketball player on the local high school team this fall. Emmett and most of his friends agree it will be Too-Tall Thaddeus Strong.

Luke, of course, disagrees. "Are you kidding? The best player will be Swish Stevenson. He's my man!" Emmett has read about Swish. Because of poor grades he may not even be playing next year. What do you think Emmett should do?

Should Emmett . . .

    A. Keep quiet and agree to disagree with Luke?
    B. Present a five-page "fact sheet" to Luke on why Swish will be the loser and Too-Tall will be the best player?
    C. Suggest the group take a vote and vote out Luke's choice?

 Look up Proverbs 17:27 for some help in knowing what Emmett should do.
Do you know someone like Luke? What do you think it means to agree to disagree? Talk with your mom or dad about ways you can do that with any person like Luke who may come into your life.

It's Lunchtime

Alec whistles as he leaves the house for the last day of vacation Bible school. It is going to be a good day. No, make that a great day! Today, in honor of his ninth birthday, his dad has made him his absolute favorite cookies (chocolate chip) to share with his class. *And* he made him two of his absolute favorite kind of sandwich—peanut butter and honey with a touch of banana! Yep, it is going to be a great day. All morning, Alec waits for lunch. Finally, Alec and his classmates file into the church fellowship hall. Alec takes out his first sandwich and is about to take a big bite when his friend Ted screams, "Oh, no!" Someone at the table has spilled milk—all over Ted's lunch. Ted tosses his soggy sandwich into the wastebasket. Lunch is over for him. What do you think Alec should do?

Should Alec . . .

A. Tell Ted, "I always dip my sandwich in my milk. It tastes really good"?
B. Stuff both sandwiches in his mouth and say, "*Thorry,* Ted. I ate my lunch"?
C. Offer Ted one of his sandwiches?

 For help in knowing what Alec should do, read Philippians 4:14.
Talk with your mom or dad about a time when a friend helped you when you were in trouble. Think of a time when you helped a friend.

The correct answer is C.

I've Got Dibs!

Grace and her sister Kaitlyn are going to visit their grandparents at their beach house for two weeks. As the older sister, Grace is in charge of making sure Kaitlyn doesn't run through the house with sandy feet or swim right after lunch. Grace is looking forward to staying in that special room at Grandma and Grandpa's house on the third floor. She has to climb a little ladder to get up there, and it's a small room. But it has a wonderful octagonal window from which you can hear the ocean waves and get a great breeze. This is Grace's favorite place in the house. When they arrive, she and her sister run into their grandparents' arms. As they bring their suitcases inside, Grace hears Kaitlyn ask, "May I please stay in the little room this time, Grandma?" What do you think Grace should do?

Should Grace . . .

A. Drop the suitcase and run as fast as she can to claim the room?
B. Let Kaitlyn choose where she wants to sleep and take whatever room is left?
C. Declare that the little room is off-limits to anyone under the age of five?

 Read Genesis 13:5-9 to see how one Bible character handled sharing space.

When you and a brother, sister, or friend want the same thing, how do you decide who gets it? Talk with your family about three ways to handle those types of decisions in the future.

The correct answer is B.

Best Friends

One of the best examples of friendship in the Bible is the close relationship between Jonathan and David. Jonathan was King Saul's son, and David was to replace Saul someday as the king of Israel. There could have been hard feelings between the two of them, but David and Jonathan agreed to be friends and to care for each other throughout their lives. Connect the dots to find out what Jonathan gave to David as a sign of their friendship. (You can read about it in 1 Samuel 18:1-4.)

David . . . met Jonathan, the king's son. . . .
They became the best of friends.

1 Samuel 18:1

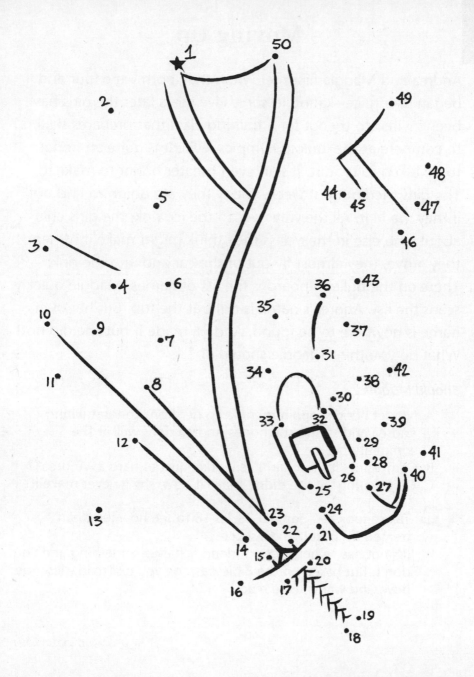

Moving Up

Andrea and Maggie first met when they both were four and began taking ice-skating lessons. Five years later the girls have been invited to try out for a training class that prepares skaters to compete at the Junior Olympics level. It is quite an honor to be asked to try out. It's an even greater honor to make it! The girls tried out last week. Today they are going to find out if they made it. All the way over to the ice rink, the girls chat about who else in their class they think might make it. When they arrive, they almost fly out of the car and into the rink. There on the bulletin board is the list of names. Maggie quickly scans the list. Andrea's name is right at the top. But her own name is nowhere to be found. Andrea made it but she did not! What do you think Maggie should do?

Should Maggie . . .

A. Not let her disappointment keep her from congratulating Andrea and saying she hopes Andrea does well at the competitions?
B. Complain, "It's not fair! I've worked just as hard as Andrea"?
C. Quit skating—if she didn't make it now, she'll never make it?

 Take a look at 1 Samuel 23:16-18 to see how Jonathan treated his best friend's success.

It's not easy when a good friend achieves something and you don't. But based on the Bible passage you just read, describe how God wants us to react.

A Friend in Need

Simone doesn't want to admit it, but she is scared. Tomorrow her mom is going into the hospital for surgery. The doctors think she may have cancer, and the surgery will provide answers. Simone is scared for her mom. She is scared to find out if it really is cancer, and she is scared for her brothers and sisters. What will happen to them if her mom has cancer? Since Simone is the oldest, she is trying to be brave. She let her little sister sleep with her last night; and she tried to keep a brave smile on her face at breakfast. But at Sunday school Simone finally loses it and bursts into tears. Her friends gather around her. "What's wrong, Simone?" they ask. Simone really doesn't want to bother her friends with her troubles. What do you think she should do?

Should Simone . . .

A. Tell her friends she has something stuck in her eye?
B. Tell them about her mom and ask her friends to pray for her and her family?
C. Shrug it off and say she was thinking about a sad TV show she saw last night?

 Read Daniel 2:17-18 to see the first thing Daniel did when he was facing a difficult situation.
Is it easy or hard for you to share your problems with friends? Is there a problem you should share right now? Do it!

The correct answer is B.

Join the Crowd

Brendan doesn't have a lot of friends. He is quiet and on the shy side. He likes to play computer games and build stuff with his connector kits. So at the beginning of summer, when the boy across the street started to pal around with him, Brendan was very happy. Logan is a friendly, outgoing boy who likes anything athletic. He has been teaching Brendan how to play hoops. And Brendan has taught Logan how to beat the newest computer game. The only problem with Logan is that he also is part of a larger group of boys that were known last year as the bullies of the school. They pick on younger kids and are known as troublemakers. Logan only acts that way when he is with them, but Brendan doesn't know what will happen once school begins again this fall. What do you think he should do?

Should Brendan . . .

    A. Begin to lift weights so he can be a good bully?
    B. Practice picking on his younger brother so he can fit in with Logan's crowd?
    C. Be Logan's friend but stay clear of his other friends?

 Check out Proverbs 13:20 for help in knowing what Brendan should do.
Work with your mom or dad to define "the wrong crowd."
Describe the kind of friends you would like to be around.

The correct answer is C.

One girl in Clarissa's Sunday school class is different from the other kids. Cheyenne suffered a crippling illness as a baby, and now she walks with a limp. She also slurs her words so that she is hard to understand. Cheyenne is not as quick to get stuff as the others. She often makes funny noises in the middle of class, which gets all the other kids laughing. Cheyenne doesn't play like the other kids, so Clarissa doesn't like to play with her. At a Sunday-evening family time at church Clarissa's dad says quietly, "Why don't you invite the girl over there to play some games with you?" Clarissa looks over to see who her dad is talking about. It's Cheyenne! Just because Clarissa is in Sunday school with Cheyenne doesn't mean that she has to be her friend, too, does it? What do you think Clarissa should do?

Should Clarissa . . .

A. Say, "Maybe later," and then run off to play with her other friends?
B. Invite Cheyenne to play the games with her and make sure she is included?
C. Get one of her other friends to play with Cheyenne?

 Check out Philemon 1:16 to see how God views all his children, no matter what their differences.
Think of someone you know who may be different from your other friends. According to this Bible passage, how are we to treat other Christians? Think of two things you can do to make that person feel loved.

The correct answer is B.

Keeping the Peace

Lucas bangs open the door, throws down his backpack, and breathes a sigh of relief. Home at last! It has been one of those horrible days at the baby-sitter's house. Lucas dropped his box of sixty-four crayons all over the floor in her family room. She yelled at him because he wouldn't share his newest race car. He forgot to bring his supplies for an art project, so he couldn't get started on it with the other kids. Lucas is so glad to be home. All he wants to do is watch TV. Lucas grabs some cookies and heads for the TV set. His little sister is watching her favorite TV show starring Fa-Fa and Tinky-Bink. That's the last thing Lucas wants to watch! But if he changes the channel, the wailing will begin! What do you think Lucas should do?

Should Lucas . . .

A. Do something else until his sister is done watching the program?
B. Use the remote and tell his sister that he doesn't know how the channel got changed?
C. Make a deal with his sister that she can watch her TV show on all the days that have a *J* in them?

 Read Psalm 133:1 for some help in knowing what Lucas should do.
Think of three things that can lead to unhappy moments in your house. Now think with your mom or dad about three ways you can keep the peace in your family.

The correct answer is A.

Report-Card Day

It seems to Takashi that nothing comes easily for him the way it does for his older brother, Izumi. It seems as if Izumi doesn't have to work at all, and he still gets good grades. Takashi, however, has to work hard just to get a B. So when his mom started the two boys on piano lessons earlier this summer, Takashi was not happy. Something else for Izumi to beat him at, he thought. Surprisingly, though, Takashi has been enjoying his piano lessons. The boys take lessons at different times, so Takashi really doesn't know how Izumi is doing. But one afternoon he hears Izumi practicing. It's a lesson that Takashi worked on a week ago—and he can play the piece much better! He can't believe it! He can do something better than Izumi! What do you think Takashi should say?

Should Takashi . . .

A. Run around the room shouting, "I can play better than you"?
B. Tell his brother to get up and let a real pro play the piece as it is supposed to be played?
C. Tell his brother to keep practicing—he can do it?

 Read Genesis 37:5-8 to find out what happened when one brother bragged about himself to his other brothers. Share a time when one of your brothers or sisters (or a friend) began bragging about himself or herself. How did it make you feel? What is another way to share with others the things you do well?

It's Your Turn

Carefully, Brianna gets out a big box from underneath her bed. She opens the box and takes out her photo album. She got a new one for her birthday, along with stencils, markers, and stickers to make some cool designs. She has been working on it since her birthday and is almost up to her kindergarten years. After working on it for almost an hour, she hears a knock on her bedroom door. It's her older sister, Danielle. "Hey, Brianna, can you do me a favor? It's my turn to set the table, but I really need to run next door before dinner. I promised to feed Mrs. Hazel's cat. Could you set the table for me, please?" Brianna is right in the middle of a new page. What do you think Brianna should do?

Should Brianna . . .

   A. Tell her sister no way; she's too busy right now?
   B. Tell her sister okay?
   C. Make a deal with her sister—she'll set the table for her tonight if Danielle will walk the dog the next three nights?

 To find out what Brianna should do, read Philippians 2:20 for an example to follow.
Think of a time when a brother, sister, or friend did a favor for you. Show your appreciation by making him or her a thank-you card.
Reminder: Don't forget to say your memory verse for July. (See the page just before July 1.)

The correct answer is B.

Brotherly Love

Byron's older brother, Jeff, seems to live to torment him. Byron can't walk by Jeff without getting a thump on the arm or a quick shove. The other day Jeff let Byron play baseball with him and his friends only because one friend got sick. Then Jeff yelled at Byron all the way home because he had dropped a fly ball and lost the game for them. Today Byron is working on his model airplane when Jeff comes knocking on his door. "Hey, little brother," Jeff said in his sweetest voice. Byron waits. "Do you think that I could borrow your bike? Mine has a flat tire. A couple of my friends and I were going to ride down to the park," Jeff says. "Please? I'll let you play ball with us again." Byron could ruin his brother's afternoon by saying no. What do you think Byron should do?

Should Byron . . .

   A. Let Jeff have the bike on the condition that he gets to play first base next time?

   B. Tell Jeff he suddenly has to use his bike to return his friend's flashlight that he left at the house two months ago?

   C. Let Jeff use his bike?

 Take a look at 1 Peter 3:8-9 for some help in knowing what Byron should do.

Think of a time when it's hard to be nice to your brother or sister. Think of two things you can do to show him or her kindness.

The correct answer is C.

The Birthday Gift

Lance knows exactly what he wants to get his dad for his birthday—a great big tin of chocolate chip cookies that he is going to bake himself. His mom agrees to let him have the kitchen one afternoon while his dad is out. As Lance is getting everything he needs, his mom comes in with Lance's little sister Emma. "Emma wants to help too," Mom says. Oh no! Not his little sister! "Emma will just mess things up," Lance is about to protest, but he catches his mom's "You better do what I say" look and stops just in time.

"Fine," Lance says instead. He hands his sister a measuring cup and the flour and turns to mix up the butter and sugar. When he checks on Emma, he discovers that most of the flour is either on the floor or on Emma. What a mess! What do you think Lance should do?

Should Lance . . .

    A. Start yelling at his sister, "Can't you do anything right—you've made a complete mess"?
    B. Show Emma how to measure out the flour correctly?
    C. Demand that his mother get Emma out of the kitchen before she makes a bigger mess?

 For help in knowing what Lance should do, read Galatians 5:14-15.
Read the Bible passage aloud. What do you think it means to "devour" someone? How can words do that?

The correct answer is B.

Kindness Counts

Evan runs from the playground, trying to keep the tears from falling. The mean words from his so-called friend are still ringing in his ears. Evan doesn't know why Rocky has begun calling him names, but he guesses that Rocky is trying to look cool in front of the older boys. Still, he can't believe that Rocky called him a four-eyed geek and all that other stuff. He and Rocky have been friends for a long time; now he isn't sure he wants to be Rocky's friend ever again. When he turns the corner to go home, Evan sees a black baseball cap in the middle of the sidewalk. It looks like Rocky's cap! When Evan picks it up, he sees it has Rocky's name neatly written on the inside seam. Evan picks it up and remembers all those nasty names Rocky called him earlier. What do you think he should do?

Should Evan . . .

 A. Take it over to Rocky's house and give it to Rocky's mom?
 B. Cross out Rocky's name and write in "Pinheaded Nerd"?
 C. Fill the hat with mud, sticks, and rocks, and leave it on Rocky's doorstep with a note: "To my good friend, Rocky"?

 Check out Ephesians 4:31-32 to know what Evan should do. Think of a time when a friend has made you feel bad. How did you handle the situation then? How might you handle the situation now?

The correct answer is A.

Playing Favorites

At least once every summer, Nancy's mom allows Nancy to invite a friend for a sleepover and then to spend the following day downtown. For the past two years Nancy has asked her best friend, Amanda, to come. This year Nancy's mom is going to take her to a tea at one of the nicest hotels in the city. Nancy doesn't know if she should invite Amanda, though. It's not that Amanda wouldn't enjoy it, but she doesn't really have the right kind of clothes for a fancy tea. Amanda rarely, if ever, wears anything new. Nancy has never seen her in nice clothes—the kind that you would need to wear to tea. She doesn't want to embarrass Amanda either. The more she thinks about it, the more Nancy thinks she ought to invite another friend—one who has better clothes to wear. What do you think Nancy should do?

Should Nancy . . .

A. Invite one of her better-dressed friends?
B. Offer to take Amanda and give her one of her old (but nice) dresses to wear?
C. Invite Amanda and go no matter what Amanda chooses to wear?

 Read James 2:1-4 to know what Nancy should do. Think of reasons you sometimes choose some friends over others. It might be because of what they have, their ability to play a sport, or something else. Ask your mom or dad to help you plan activities to do with all of your friends.

The correct answer is C.

Family Time

At Doug Potter's house Sunday afternoons are what his parents call "Potter Time." Every week one member of the family gets to pick what the family will do. Sometimes it's okay, but other times Doug ends up spending a perfectly fine afternoon wandering through a craft fair or seeing a stupid movie that his sister wants to see. (Nothing good like *Invasion of the Killer Grubs.*) Just once, Doug would like to do something else—like go over to his friend's house and play. Today is one of those days because it's his sister's turn to pick again. This time she picks taking a ride out to a petting farm and riding a pony. *Real excitement,* thinks Doug. He would rather go over to his friend's house. What do you think Doug should do?

Should Doug . . .

    A. Pretend he's come down with a sudden stomachache and hope his family will leave him home?

    B. Suggest that next weekend the family should take a break from each other?

    C. Go along with his family and enjoy the afternoon?

 Read Proverbs 11:29 for help in knowing what Doug should do.

Families are important to God, and getting along with your family is even more important. With your mom or dad, plan a family fun night for your whole family.

The Horse Show

Chantel's best friend, Preeti, loves horses! She has pictures of horses tacked on every space of wall in her room. She reads books about horses. She draws pictures of horses. She dreams about owning a whole stable of horses someday. Chantel, on the other hand, is afraid of horses! She shares her friend's interest as long as she doesn't have to get near a real horse. This Saturday Preeti is going to be in her first horse show. She has been taking jumping and riding lessons for a year and is ready to demonstrate her skills. She wants Chantel to come and see the show. Chantel would rather go to a craft show than watch horses running around a ring! What do you think Chantel should do?

Should Chantel . . .

    A. Go to the horse show and cheer Preeti on from the bleachers?
    B. Tell Preeti she is going to the craft show to get an idea for a gift for her?
    C. Ask Preeti to tape the horse show, and say she'll watch it in the safety of her own home?

 For help in knowing what Chantel should do, look up John 15:12-13.
You may never have to give up your life for a friend, but talk with your mom or dad about different ways you can show Jesus' kind of love to your friends.

The correct answer is A.

Play Ball!

Very upset, Raul throws down his mitt. The entire afternoon is ruined. Their last good baseball has just sailed over the fence and into the woods. The boys have spent nearly a half hour looking through the woods for the ball. They have come up empty-handed. That means the end of baseball until someone is able to buy a new ball. But no one has money. As the boys think about what to do next, one boy suggests, "Hey, I know. Payton has a ball! He's got a lot of them because his dad works for a sporting goods company. If we let him play, we'll never run out of baseballs." No one wants to say anything, but no one really likes Payton. He is always trying to pick a fight. But he does have baseballs! What do you think Raul and his friends should do?

Should they . . .

    A. Invite Payton to play as long as he'll supply the baseballs?
    B. Find another game to play until one of them can buy a new ball?
    C. Ask Payton to be the ball boy but don't talk to him?

 Read Psalm 28:3 for help in knowing what Raul and his friends should do.
Sometimes you might let someone think you want to be friends just because that person has something you want. Talk with your mom or dad about some other ways that Raul could handle this situation with Payton.

The correct answer is B.

Not Him!

When Weldon walks into Sunday school class, he does a double take. Sitting at the table, all by himself, is the meanest boy in the neighborhood. Mitchell is the only boy he knows who was kicked out of school for a month. On the playground everyone tries to stay away from Mitchell and his buddies. If you aren't paying attention, you could lose your lunch money. And now, here is Mitchell, sitting in Weldon's Sunday school class. Someone must have made him come as a punishment, Weldon decides. He is about to take his seat when his teacher calls him over. "Weldon, Mitchell is going to be joining our Sunday school class. Why don't you sit with him and help him learn the ropes?" Mr. Seeger suggests. What do you think Weldon should do?

Should Weldon . . .

- A. Pull Mr. Seeger aside and warn him that he had better watch the offering plate?
- B. Suggest that Mitchell might be better off at a different Sunday school?
- C. Sit with Mitchell and try to get to know him?

 Take a look at Acts 9:26-28 to see how one Bible character handled some pretty difficult introductions to a man a lot of people feared.

Think of someone in your neighborhood that you would vote "least likely to show up in Sunday school." Role-play with your mom or dad how you would react if that person were to walk into your class.

The correct answer is C.

Review Time!

List three things you learned about being a good friend this month:

1.

2.

3.

Bonus

List three things you plan to do to be kind to a brother, sister, or friend next month:

1.

2.

3.

Repeat your memory verse to a friend. (The verse is printed on the page just before July 1.)

Compassion & Forgiveness

Quick—what's your first response when someone does something to hurt you? Do you want to get back at that person? Or is your first response to forgive? Jesus gives us his law for forgiveness: "If you forgive those who sin against you, your heavenly Father will forgive you. But if you refuse to forgive others, your Father will not forgive your sins"(Matthew 6:14-15).

God forgives us, not because we are good and deserve it, but because he loves us. God has mercy on us—he forgives us because *he* is good. As we begin to understand God's mercy and his love for us, we will want to pass it on to others. When we realize that God doesn't treat us as we deserve, we will begin to treat others with mercy and love too!

When we understand that everyone needs God's forgiveness because everyone does things wrong, we begin to look at others differently. We can become more compassionate. That means we feel sorry for people. We want to share the hurts of others and to help them because we know we have similar problems and hurts. We show compassion for others when we treat them with kindness, when we offer comfort instead of judgment, and when we care for them the way that Jesus cares for us.

Look for opportunities to forgive others and to help them with compassion and love as you work through this month's *Sticky Situations*.

Memory Verse: Be kind to each other, tenderhearted, forgiving one another, just as God through Christ has forgiven you.
Ephesians 4:32

Man's Best Friend

After years of begging their parents for a dog, Angelo and his brothers finally get a golden retriever puppy. At first Angelo and his brothers can't leave the dog alone. But as the days go by, they are no longer as interested in the puppy. It not only is getting bigger (and less cute), but it also is becoming more interested in the boys' things. First it chewed up a cover on one of Angelo's books. Then it buried his brother's model car in the backyard. The boys are discovering that having a puppy is a lot more work than they thought. Before dinner Angelo's dad asks him to take the dog outside and play with it for a while. Angelo really wants to go over and see his friend's new bike. What do you think Angelo should do?

Should Angelo . . .

   A. Take the dog outside and let it run around while he reads a book?
   B. Tell his dad he'll play with the dog later, as in "when I get around to it"?
   C. Take the puppy outside and play ball?

 Read Proverbs 12:10 to know what Angelo should do. God wants us to be kind to everything he created—including animals! Make plans to do something kind for a pet today—yours or a friend's.

The correct answer is C.

The Class Thief

Last month at an Awana Club meeting, Erika stole a pencil case from Miguel. She returned the pencil case, and no one ever knew about it other than Miguel, Erika, and the club leader. This month the group is getting ready to do a short skit about Queen Esther, and Miguel has brought in some props for the group to use in the skit. As they are packing up their things to go home, one of the group members asks Erika to take care of the prop bag. Miguel glances at her. Erika sees Miguel looking at her and quickly looks away. Should Miguel tell the group about the girl's "past record"? What do you think Miguel should do?

Should Miguel . . .

- A. Say nothing and give Erika another chance?
- B. Make sure all his belongings are well marked so they won't get stolen again?
- C. Say in a loud voice, "Well, not to mention any names, but I sure wouldn't let anyone who steals things be in charge of the props"?

 For help in knowing what Miguel should do, read Luke 6:37. What is the danger of judging someone based on his or her past? Are there things you may have done wrong in the past but have changed since then? How do you want people to judge you?

The correct answer is A.

The Paper Trail

Darnel is glad summer school is almost over. Then his teacher hears him talking and makes him write one hundred "I will not talk in class" sentences. The worst part is that it wasn't even his fault. Someone else had asked him a question, and Darnel had just answered him! What else did Mrs. Stone expect him to do? Darnel stretches out his fingers one more time, packs up his stuff, and goes to find Mrs. Stone. He sees her hurrying down the hall. Just as she turns the corner, her shoe catches something on the floor and she goes flying! She goes one way and the huge stack of papers she was carrying goes another! Hundreds of papers float through the air and land throughout the hallway. It is an amazing sight. What should Darnel do?

Should he . . .

    A. Give Mrs. Stone his papers and ask if he can go outside now?
    B. Stand there laughing and shout, "I wish I had my camera"?
    C. Quickly move to help Mrs. Stone pick up her papers?

 Read the parable in Luke 10:30-37 for help in knowing what Darnel should do.
Jesus told this parable in answer to the question, "And who is my neighbor?" How would you answer that same question? To what people are you to show kindness?

The correct answer is C.

Comforting Thoughts

Carlos dribbles the basketball, waiting for his friends. Just as he is about to give up and go home, Riley and the others show up at the playground. "What took you so long?" Carlos asks.

"Aw, we were trying to convince Juan to come and join us. But he'd rather mope around," Riley answers.

After the game Carlos pulls Riley aside. "What's up with Juan?" he asks.

"Oh, I don't know. Something about his dad losing his job," Riley answers, and then takes off.

Carlos knows what Juan is going through. Carlos's dad lost his job last year. There were lots of tears and fears about having to move. Carlos feels sorry for Juan, but he also feels helpless. What should Carlos do to help his friend?

Should Carlos . . .

    A. Send Juan a good joke book to cheer him up?
    B. Write Juan a note about how he felt when going through the same experience and offer to talk with him about it?
    C. Forget about it—he got through it; so will Juan?

 Check out 2 Corinthians 1:3-4 for help in knowing what Carlos should do.
With your mom or dad, pretend that Juan wants to talk to Carlos about his situation. Role-play what you would say to Juan to help comfort him.

He Did It!

Over the weekend some kids used neon green paint to write nasty things about the park district sports director on the bathroom walls. So far no one knows who did it. But Rachel has an idea about one kid who might have done it. It's no secret that Jerome and the sports director do not get along. Jerome is one of those kids who gets to visit the director's office a lot. Rachel and her mom had been walking by the park over the weekend and had seen a group of boys near the place where the writing was discovered. She didn't get a real good look at the boys, but she did see a bike that is the same color as Jerome's bike. Today she sees a touch of green paint on the side of Jerome's shoe. What do you think Rachel should do?

Should Rachel . . .

    A. Let the sports director handle the investigation unless Rachel is absolutely certain of the facts?

    B. Tell the sports director she is sure it was Jerome?

    C. Dust the area for fingerprints and see if they match Jerome's fingerprints?

 For help in knowing what Rachel should do, read Exodus 23:7. It's easy to think something is true before having all the facts. With your mom or dad, talk about when it is best *not* to tell on someone and when it *is* important to express your concerns.

The correct answer is A.

The Missed Goal

Lucie does not like to play soccer. She isn't good at sports to begin with, and when it comes to soccer, she is horrible. She can't kick the ball very hard, and she hates running up and down the field. To make matters worse, she is on the same team as two of the best soccer players in the neighborhood. Most of the time they keep the ball away from Lucie, which is okay with her. But somehow in the game today, Lucie ends up with the ball and a chance to score on a wide-open net. She turns, kicks the ball as hard as she can . . . and misses by a mile. She can feel the glares of her two teammates as she runs back to her position. The next thing she knows, *WHACK!* She is hit in the head with the soccer ball. She turns around and sees the two girls giggling at her. What do you think Lucie should do?

Should Lucie . . .

- A. Trip the girls as they run by and say, "Oops! Did I do that?"
- B. Report the two girls to the National Association of Poor Sportsmanship?
- C. Not even look at the girls—just go back to playing the game?

 Look up Proverbs 19:11 for some help in knowing what Lucie should do.
Share a time with your mom or dad when you were really angry about something someone had done to you. How did you handle it? What would you do differently today?

Butterflies

Kristie's biggest rival on the swim team is her best friend, Robyn. She and Robyn met the first day of swim team when they were in first grade. Out of the water they are the greatest of friends. In the water it is a race to the finish! Most times they trade off who comes in first and second. But when it comes to the butterfly (the hardest stroke), Robyn is the best. Kristie can never beat her friend. And it doesn't help that Robyn rubs it in every time they get out of the water. Now Robyn is wearing butterflies on her T-shirts, shorts, hats—you name it, it has butterflies on it! Kristie tries not to let it bug her and keeps working on her stroke. Tonight they are both doing the butterfly. As Kristie finishes her race, she looks up and sees Robyn just touching the wall! Kristie finally beat out the Butterfly Queen. What do you think Kristie should do?

Should Kristie . . .

    A. Tell Robyn, "Good swim"?
    B. Pump her fist in the air and shout, "Yes!!! I beat Robyn"?
    C. Do a butterfly dance around the pool?

 Better look up Proverbs 24:17 to know what Kristie should do.
Think of a person who is good at something you do. How does it feel when they beat you out? How does it feel when you win? What is the best way to respond to winning and losing?

The Big Hurt

Ty has just finished practicing piano for the afternoon when he notices a boy skateboarding on the sidewalk in front of his apartment building. It's Damien, a neighborhood bully. *Why me?* thinks Ty. *Why, out of all the sidewalks in the city, did Damien choose to go skateboarding down my sidewalk?* That morning Damien was trying to bully the little kids on the playground, and Ty called him on it. Damien backed down, but his parting words were, "You just wait. You haven't heard the last from me!" Just as Ty is turning from the window, he sees Damien go down with a loud crash on the sidewalk. Damien is rolling around in pain. Blood is streaming from his knees and elbows. *Ugh,* Ty thinks. *That probably hurt a lot.* What do you think Ty should do?

Should Ty . . .

    A. Give Damien a mop and bucket of water and tell him to clean up the blood?

    B. Help Damien with some bandages and ointment for his wounds?

    C. Advise Damien that he should wear knee pads and elbow pads the next time he skateboards?

 Read 2 Kings 6:18-23 to see how one Bible character told the king to "take care" of Israel's enemies.
In the Bible passage Elisha was following the advice in Proverbs 25:21-22. Read those verses also. Then talk with your mom or dad about what it means to heap "burning coals" on an enemy's head.

The correct answer is B.

The Last Laugh

Heidi's best friend just did a very bad job of acting. The fourth-grade vacation Bible school class was putting on a skit for the second graders about the crossing of the Red Sea. Brianna hadn't learned her lines. When she did say something, she kept staring at a point on the back wall. It was so bad that everyone turned around to see what she was staring at! Even the second graders could tell that she was goofing up, and they began to giggle every time Brianna spoke. That had gotten the rest of Heidi's class laughing, and it had gone downhill from there. After the program Heidi and her friends are talking about the play. One girl begins acting like poor Brianna, and the girls laugh so hard they can't stop. Heidi has to admit the girl is funny, but she still feels sorry for Brianna. What do you think Heidi should do?

Should Heidi . . .

A. Tell her friends that Brianna probably feels bad enough without her friends laughing at her too?
B. Get everyone to start acting like Brianna?
C. Hide behind the slide and then laugh?

 Read Ecclesiastes 7:21-22 for help in knowing what Heidi should do.
Talk with your mom or dad about the difference between laughing *at* someone and laughing *with* someone.
Reminder: Don't forget to work on your memory verse for August. (You'll find it on the page just before August 1.)

The correct answer is A.

Sticks and Stones . . .

Today is the town library's summer spelling bee. Kelsey is sure that she has a good chance of winning. She and her dad spent last week reviewing all the words on the list. Kelsey is nervous at the beginning. But as the spelling bee goes on, she feels more sure of herself. Finally it comes down to Kelsey and Jacob, who moved into the neighborhood just a month ago. He is given a word to spell and tries hard to get it right, but he misses by a letter. Kelsey spells the word correctly and wins the contest! Later Jacob comes up to her and says, "Hey, it's the walking dictionary. So, Miss Smarty-Pants thinks she knows it all. Wait until next year—you're toast!" What do you think she should do?

Should Kelsey . . .

A. Give him the *L* sign and chant, "Loser, loser"?
B. Say, "Okay, buddy, spell rhinoceros," and leave?
C. Say, "Sorry you lost," and then walk away?

 Check out Lamentations 3:30-31 for some words that may help Kelsey know what to do.
Even though we may think that only sticks and stones can hurt us, words can and do hurt. Think of some of the things you have said to your friends and others recently. Do you need to ask for forgiveness? If so, don't waste a minute!

Bits and Pieces

Shelby knew even before her sister opened her mouth what she was going to say. The day before, Karina had begged Shelby for her shell collection. Karina wanted to take it to day camp because her group was studying the oceans. Shelby finally gave in and let her sister borrow her shell collection. Now Shelby looks at the bag of broken shells in her sister's hand. "I'm so sorry, Shelby. I was trying to be careful, but I saw a butterfly and went after it. I tripped and fell. Here's your shell collection," Karina says, a big tear trickling down her cheek. Every single shell is broken! Shelby is so mad! It took her nearly three summers to collect all those shells during family vacations at the beach. Shelby knew this was going to happen! What do you think she should do?

Should Shelby . . .

  A. Tell Karina she'll forgive her *after* she replaces the shells?
  B. Tell Karina she'll never let her borrow anything of hers ever again?
  C. Forgive her sister even though she's terribly disappointed and start collecting shells on the next family vacation?

 Take a look at Mark 11:25 for help in knowing what Shelby should do.
Think of a time when someone made a mess of something that was special to you. Was it easy for you to forgive the person? Why is it important to forgive even when it isn't easy? If you're not sure, read Mark 11:25 again.

The correct answer is C.

Not Again!

For about the tenth time Gordon looks out the window to see if his friend is coming. Gordon can't wait to show T.J. his latest experiment—complete with smoke. Finally T.J. calls to tell him he can't make it because he has to go to the dentist. Gordon hangs up the phone with a slam. This is the fourth time this week that T.J. called to say he couldn't come over. First it was chores he "forgot" to do. Then it was his mom who wanted him to go shopping. Then it was a make-up piano lesson. Now this. The next day T.J. walks up to him at the post office. "Hey, I'm sorry about yesterday. Can we get together this afternoon?" his friend asks. Gordon has forgiven his friend for standing him up three times. But four? That's asking too much! What do you think Gordon should do?

Should Gordon . . .

- A. Have T.J. sign a statement saying that he won't ditch Gordon again?
- B. Make plans to show T.J. the experiment that afternoon?
- C. Tell T.J. he's got other plans today?

 Read Luke 17:3-4 to see how Gordon should handle this situation.
Can you count the number of times God has forgiven you? Do you think there is a limit on how many times you need to forgive someone for the same wrong? What does the Bible say?

WWJD?

Savanna's Sunday school teacher gave her a WWJD bracelet for memorizing thirty Bible verses. Savanna is proud of her bracelet. She really worked hard at memorizing those Bible verses. No one else in the class has come close to memorizing as many verses as she has. Savanna wears her bracelet everywhere. Today an older neighbor girl takes a closer look at it. "Hey, where did you get that?" she asks. "What do the initials stand for?"

"The initials stand for 'What Would Jesus Do?' Savanna tells her.

"Only a real dork would wear something like that," says the older girl. Savanna's face is getting red. What should she say?

Should Savanna . . .

- A. Say that her Sunday school teacher gave her the bracelet for memorizing Bible verses?
- B. Tell the older girl that only dorks would say bad things about a bracelet like hers?
- C. Explain that the initials on the bracelet really stand for "Where Will Jackrabbits Dig?"

 Look up Romans 12:14 to know how Savanna should respond to her friend.
With your mom or dad, role-play the situation above. What else could you say to someone who makes fun of you because you are a Christian?

The correct answer is A.

Getting Even?

Allison doesn't know why, but Mary Kate, who lives down the street, will do everything she can to upset her. So Allison tries to stay away from Mary Kate whenever possible. Today, though, Allison is watching the clouds as she walks across the playground toward the swings. She is thinking about her family's plans for the weekend. All of a sudden Allison finds herself face first on the ground. Mary Kate tripped her and then ran away! Later Allison and her friends are talking about what to do about this girl. "I have a plan," one friend suggests. "Let's hide behind the bushes by the corner. When Mary Kate walks by, we let her have it with water guns. My brother has at least five Super Soakers we can use. Mean Mary Kate won't give you any trouble after that!" It sounds like a good idea. It sure would cool off Mary Kate. What should Allison do?

Should she . . .

   A. Let her friends hose down Mary Kate?
   B. Agree to the plan but only use little squirt guns?
   C. Tell her friends no thanks?

 Read Deuteronomy 32:35 for help in knowing what Allison should do. Note that God is the speaker.
Read the Bible verse aloud. Talk with your mom or dad about what it means for God to take care of justice rather than you taking care of justice.

Compassion Check

In the story of the Good Samaritan (Luke 10:25-37) we learn that our "neighbor" is anyone we meet who has a need. We also learn that compassion means acting to meet that person's needs. Take time to read the Bible story together with your mom or dad. Then look for fifteen words from the story in the Word Search.

WORD BANK

ATTACK	INN	JEWISH	MONEY	SAMARITAN
BANDIT	JERICHO	MEDICINE	NEIGHBOR	TEMPLE
DONKEY	JERUSALEM	MERCY	PRIEST	WOUNDS

Love your neighbor as yourself.
Luke 10:27

J	S	A	M	A	R	I	T	A	N
N	O	H	H	S	I	W	E	J	Y
E	T	E	M	P	L	E	E	S	E
I	Q	U	N	A	T	T	A	C	K
G	M	E	R	C	Y	B	F	L	N
H	M	P	R	W	T	A	L	E	O
B	K	E	A	S	L	N	O	E	D
O	E	N	L	O	R	D	N	N	I
R	Y	I	B	A	Y	I	T	I	K
F	R	G	A	E	S	T	X	C	P
P	L	T	N	J	E	U	H	I	I
A	W	O	U	N	D	S	R	D	C
V	M	T	S	E	I	R	P	E	E
O	H	C	I	R	E	J	X	M	J

The Big Mess-Up

Hunter hears his mom calling him to get up and get ready for church. But that's the last place Hunter wants to be. Boy, did he mess up! One of Hunter's friends dared him to take a comic book from the local newsstand. Just as Hunter thought he was getting away with it, a strong hand gripped his shoulder. "Where do ya think you're going with that comic book?" a deep voice growled. To make matters worse, Hunter lied to his parents about taking the comic book. He said his friend did it while he stood by. But then the newsstand owner called them. No, Hunter does not want to go to church. His parents may forgive him, but how can God ever forgive him? His mom still is calling. What do you think he should do?

Should Hunter . . .

   A. Dig deeper under the bedcovers and shout, "There's no one here by that name"?
   B. Ask God to forgive him because he's really sorry about stealing that comic book, then get ready for church?
   C. Go to church but keep his head down and stay away from the pastor?

 Take a look at Psalm 51:1-7, David's prayer for forgiveness after he messed up big-time!
Talk with your mom or dad about some of the things for which they—and God—have forgiven you. (Let your parent share something also!) Thank God that there is no sin too big for him to forgive.

Go Fish

Gwen's dad has promised to take Gwen and her brother fishing if they do well in their computer class. For Gwen this isn't too big a deal. She is very good with computers. But her brother, Gavin, has to work very hard. He likes computers, but he doesn't like to create letters or e-mail messages. It's not that he can't type—it's just that he is very slow. Gwen is pleased when she gets an A! Her dad is happy too. Then Gavin shows his grade to Dad and waits. It's a C. Gwen secretly smiles. Now only she and her dad will be going fishing! But wait. Dad is smiling gently at Gavin and saying, "You worked hard too, Gavin. You did your best. We'll all go fishing tomorrow." What could her father be thinking? Gavin didn't come close to doing as well as Gwen. What do you think Gwen should do?

Should Gwen . . .

    A. Tell her dad that a C doesn't qualify as "doing well"?
    B. Show how she feels about the fishing trip by dumping all the worms in Gavin's bed?
    C. Recognize that Gavin did work hard, and go fish!

 Read Jesus' story about two brothers—one who did very well and the other who messed up—in Luke 15:11-32.
Discuss with your mom or dad what this story teaches about God's forgiveness. How should you act toward those who mess up?

Forgive and Forget?

Last week, Blair and his friend Angelica got into a huge fight. Angelica said some things about Blair that really hurt him, including a comment that Blair was "as dumb as dirt." But the kids patched things up. Blair forgave Angelica for calling him dumb, and all went well until today. The kids are doing their homework for Awana Club. They work for a few minutes in silence until Angelica is so upset she throws her pencil across the room. "I just don't get it!" she says. Blair looks over at Angelica's book. Blair understands the puzzle. He's about to offer to help when Angelica's words from yesterday come back to him. If he's so dumb, maybe he shouldn't offer to help his friend. What do you think Blair should do?

Should Blair . . .

> A. Forget about Angelica's remarks and offer to help her?
> B. Ask Angelica, "Who's dumb as dirt now?"
> C. Keep quiet and let his friend figure it out on her own?

 Read Philemon 1:10 to see what advice Paul gave to a man whose slave had run away from him.
Think of a time when you said that you forgave someone but didn't really. Talk with your mom or dad about the actions that go along with the words "I forgive you."

The Fun Fair

Every summer Maria's church sponsors a fun fair, complete with prizes, games, cotton candy, and lots of other good things. Maria always goes to the fun fair with her best friend, Rosa. After she completes her chores, Maria gets on her bike and rides over to Rosa's house. She finds her friend on her knees in her mom's flower garden, pulling weeds. "I've got to weed these flowers for my mom before I can go anywhere," Rosa says, looking as if she is about to cry. Maria stares at the big garden. There is no way that Rosa will get those weeds pulled and still get to the fun fair. Maria knows how much Rosa enjoys going to the fair—about as much as she does! What do you think Maria should do?

Should Maria . . .

    A. Offer to bring some cotton candy back for Rosa?
    B. Shrug and say, "Oh well, there's always next year," and ride on?
    C. Offer to help Rosa pull weeds—working together they may both make it?

 Look up Mark 2:3-4 to see how four men saw the need of their friend and did something about it!
Make a list of friends or people you see every day. With your mom or dad's help, name a need that each one may have. Come up with one way you can help meet each need.

Watch Your Language

After dinner Chad hears his mom and dad talking about his friend Kent. Chad asks his dad what's going on. "Well, it appears that Kent said a few swear words to the playground supervisor at the park," his dad says. "He probably won't be playing there for a while." Sure enough, Kent doesn't show up at the park for the next couple of days.

Chad misses Kent. He is a great friend, always willing to help others, and a great ball player. But Chad also can't believe that Kent would be so stupid as to use swear words—especially with a playground supervisor! One afternoon the doorbell rings, and Chad is surprised to see Kent standing there. What do you think Chad should do?

Should Chad . . .

A. Ask Kent to come in—then check with his parents to be sure it's okay for him to get together with Kent?
B. Tell Kent that his house is a no-swearing zone, so stay out?
C. Ask Kent if he took "stupid pills" the day he used swear words?

 Take a look at 1 Timothy 1:15-16 to see how Paul describes God's forgiveness—no matter how badly we sin.
Ask your mom or dad to share a time when someone they knew got into big trouble. How did friends act around that person afterward? How did they act themselves?

Swing Time

Tucker and his best bud, Justin, are on their way to the neighborhood park. Tucker has been practicing a flip off the swings and wants to show Justin how to do it. As they come near the playground, they can see that the park is crowded. All the swings are taken up by younger kids. "Do you want to go home and come back later, or should we wait until one of those kids gets off the swings?" Tucker asks his friend.

Justin has another idea. "Look, we're bigger than those kids are. Why don't we just tell them to get off the swings or else?" he suggests.

Or else what? Tucker wonders. He doesn't want to get into a fight or anything. Maybe just a threat would do the trick. What do you think Tucker should do?

Should Tucker . . .

    A. Tell Justin he would like to wait?
    B. Tell the younger kids that he and Justin will pull them off if the kids don't let the two boys have the swings?
    C. Shout, "Ice cream truck!" and hope that some of the kids will leave the swings?

 Read Nehemiah 5:1-7 to see what happened when one group of Jews began picking on some helpless fellow Jews. Think of situations at home or in the neighborhood in which the younger kids get picked on. (If you're the youngest in your family, this may be easy!) What do you think God wants you to do when that happens?

The correct answer is A.

Pool Play

Drew and his buddies are enjoying a lazy summer day at the neighborhood pool. They find a nice grassy area to put down their towels. Then they race each other to the pool. Later they decide to take a break and go back to their towels. By this time many more people have come. A number of them, including a few parents with their babies, are sitting near the boys. After a while of sunning themselves, one of the boys suggests they toss their football around. The other boys eagerly jump up and spread out among the people. Drew doesn't know about his friends, but he knows *he* doesn't have the best arm in the world. He's afraid that he might nail one of the parents or kids near them with a bad toss. What do you think Drew should do?

Should Drew . . .

    A. Yell, "Heads up!" every time he tosses the ball?
    B. Suggest to his friends that they move their game to a less crowded part of the pool area?
    C. Let the ball fly—after all, the boys were there first?

 Check out Philippians 2:4 for a clue about how Drew should behave.
With your mom or dad, name three ways that you thought about the needs of others before your own today.
Reminder: Don't forget to say your memory verse for August. (See the page just before August 1.)

The Raffle

It's the end-of-summer reading party at the town library. Kids have helped to decorate the children's section with drawings of characters or scenes from their favorite books. It's one of Joanna's favorite times of the summer. The best thing about the reading party, however, is the raffle. Each year the children's librarian puts together a package of the newest books and other fun stuff. This year the package includes a book that Joanna really wants. The raffle is held right after lunch. When the winning number is given, Joanna's heart skips a beat. She misses winning the raffle by one number! As she walks home, Joanna's friend Megan joins her, carrying—you guessed it—the winning raffle package. "Look what I won! Isn't it great?" her friend gushes. What do you think Joanna should say?

Should Joanna . . .

- A. Shrug and say, "So what's the big deal?"
- B. Say she's got better books at home than the ones in the package?
- C. Congratulate her friend on winning the prize?

 Take a look at Romans 12:15 to see what Joanna should do. Think of the best news you possibly could get. How do you want your friends to act when you tell them? How do you feel when they aren't as excited as you?

Now Showing . . .

It's the first day that the newest *Space Zone* movie is showing at the local theater. Bryce and his friends are going to the very first showing. When school starts, they don't want to be the only ones who haven't seen it. To make sure they get good seats, they have their parents drop them off nearly an hour before show time. But other kids must have the same idea because there's already a long line. Bryce and his friends join the line. It's a nice evening, and they don't mind the wait. Finally the doors open, and the line slowly moves toward the ticket booth. As Bryce and his friends near the front of the line, Bryce sees a group of older kids who have just come. Rather than go to the end of the line, these kids have cut in front of three younger kids who are ahead of Bryce and his friends. The younger kids are upset, but the older kids just laugh. What should Bryce and his friends do?

Should they . . .

A. Report what happened to the theater manager?
B. Yell, "No cuts!" and hope the older kids hear them?
C. Say nothing and be thankful the older kids didn't pick on them?

 For a clue about what Bryce should do, read Hebrews 13:3. Read the Bible verse aloud. Talk with your mom or dad about what it means to "share the sorrow of those being mistreated." Think of one way you can do that.

The correct answer is A.

The Fallen Enemy

When Jasmine walks into the classroom on the first day of school, she can tell right away that something is wrong. Her teacher, Miss Wilson, is sitting at her desk with no smile on her face. As soon as everyone is sitting down, Miss Wilson explains that Jackson was hit by a car on his way to school. He has a broken leg and is in a lot of pain. Miss Wilson reminds everyone how important it is to be careful when walking back and forth to school. Then she suggests that each class member make a get-well card for Jackson. Jasmine gets out her colored markers. But she doesn't feel like making a card. Last year Jackson was mean to most of the kids in the class. Jasmine wouldn't be surprised if Jackson had run out in front of the car while chasing another kid. What do you think Jasmine should write in her card?

Should Jasmine . . .

    A. Write, "Sorry to hear about your accident—NOT"?
    B. Write, "Get well, but not too soon"?
    C. Write, "Hope you're back up and around real soon," and put a piece of candy in the card?

 Look up Psalm 35:11-14 to see how David responded when his enemies were ill.
Think of one or two things you might say to an enemy who is ill or experiencing a tough time.

My Brother's Keeper

Stephanie has to wait for her younger brother so they can walk home from school together. Today she is in a hurry to get home for a snack. Her brother is nowhere to be seen, so Stephanie leaves. When she gets home, she's surprised to see that her brother is already there. "How did you get home so quick?" she asks.

Her brother grins and says, "I took a shortcut with some other guys."

"What shortcut?" Stephanie asks.

It turns out that her brother tagged along with some older boys and went through several backyards. He says they're going to take another shortcut tomorrow. Mom and Dad have told Stephanie and her brother not to cut through the neighbors' yards. What do you think Stephanie should do?

Should Stephanie . . .

A. Let her brother go on his shortcuts, and wait for him to get in trouble?
B. Care enough about her brother to tell him that he shouldn't walk home with those older boys?
C. Tell her brother that it's not her problem if he gets hung up on a fence?

 Find out how Paul felt when others were led to do wrong things in 2 Corinthians 11:29.
Talk about how you feel when you see a friend or someone in your family going along with the crowd in doing something wrong. Role-play with your mom or dad what you could say to that person.

The correct answer is B.

Rules Are Rules

Haley and her friends have secret club meetings in her basement. At the last meeting the girls came up with a list of rules
for the club. The number-one rule is that if anyone misses a
meeting, that person is kicked out. Today at club Crystal tells
the group that she and her mom are going shopping downtown for school clothes next Saturday. Haley remembers that
next Saturday is a club meeting. She informs Crystal about
this, and Crystal says, "Yeah, I know. I'll have to miss that
one." If Haley lets Crystal miss a meeting, then the other girls
will probably do the same thing—and then there will be
nobody at club. What do you think Haley should do?

Should Haley . . .

A. Give Crystal a special job to do to make up for missing the
   meeting?
B. Tell Crystal she's out of the club if she misses next Saturday's
   meeting—no matter what?
C. Give Crystal a "pass" and forget about it—after all, club is
   supposed to be fun?

 Check out Hosea 12:6 for a clue as to what Haley should do.
Talk with your mom or dad about why rules are important.
Then talk about what makes a rule a good rule or a bad rule.
Share what you think it means to balance rules with love and
justice.

What's Mine Is Yours?

August

Caleb's older brother, Martin, is the star baseball player at the high school. Everyone admires him—including Caleb. But what no one knows about Martin is that he's absentminded. He loses track of his things, which is why he's asking Caleb if he can borrow his baseball glove for the next game. Caleb is honored. He has worked hard to get his glove into what Martin calls "playing shape." Martin tries out the mitt and says it is excellent. Caleb feels he's part of the team with his mitt out there. The team wins, but following the game Martin leaves Caleb's glove out in the field. It rains overnight, and Caleb's mitt is now a wet soggy mess thanks to his brother. Martin offers to buy Caleb a new mitt as soon as he gets some cash. What do you think Caleb should do?

Should Caleb . . .

    A. Tell Martin that he will wait and that he enjoyed seeing his brother use his glove in the game?

    B. Make Martin buy him the glove of his choice—one that is three times as expensive as his old glove?

    C. Accept the new glove but make Martin break it in for him?

 Read 1 Samuel 24:9-13 to see how David responded when he had a chance to get even with King Saul.
Talk with your mom or dad about "paying for the crime." In what ways do you make others pay for their mistakes, and when have you let someone off the hook?

The correct answer is A.

The Party List

Cassie's tenth birthday is coming up soon. Because she didn't have a party last year, her parents say she can have a big birthday party this year. She can have up to fifteen friends. Cassie sits down at the kitchen table with her parents to go over her class list. She comes up with fifteen names. Cassie puts a star by the name of each classmate she definitely wants to invite and a question mark next to those she is not sure about.

"What's with these question marks?" her mom asks.

"Well, these two are best friends, and neither one invited me to their party. This kid probably wouldn't invite me to his party. I'm not sure I want to invite those three," Cassie explains. Her mom gives her "the look." What do you think Cassie should do?

Should Cassie . . .

- A. Invite just the twelve friends who will probably invite her to their parties?
- B. Invite the fifteen kids to her party and forget about who will invite her back?
- C. Send out a survey to see who will invite her to their parties and then send out invitations?

For help in knowing what Cassie should do, read Luke 6:35-36.
Think of someone you know who does things in order to get something in return. How does that differ from what the Bible verse says to do?

The correct answer is B.

Just Say Hi

Lisa is helping her dad with the groceries. She looks for the brand of cereal her brothers like best and her father hates the most—chocolate marshmallow crunch. As she's looking at the boxes, Lisa sees another girl doing the same thing. It's Corinne, one of the meanest girls in the entire elementary school. Corinne never smiles, never says hi, and never, ever has anything nice to say. Lisa quickly looks back to the cereal boxes. Maybe she won't see her. Lisa pulls out any old cereal box and turns to leave. Just as she does, she sees Corinne coming toward her. There is no way she can pass by her without Corinne seeing her. What do you think Lisa should do?

Should Lisa . . .

   A. Look up, smile, and give Corinne a big hello?
   B. Pull down a bunch of cereal boxes and shout, "Earthquake"?
   C. Pretend she's really studying the cereal boxes very carefully?

 Take a look at Proverbs 11:17 for a clue as to what Lisa should do.
Talk with your mom or dad about what might happen if Lisa chooses to smile and say hello to Corinne. What kinds of good things happen to you when you show people some kindness?

Review Time!

Think of three things that you learned this month about forgiving others.

1.

2.

3.

Bonus

List three people you know who could use a little kindness in their lives. By each name, write down something kind you can do for that person.

1.

2.

3.

Say your memory verse to someone who has been kind to you.

Responsibility & Work

Responsibility is a big word that means taking care of the things that you are expected to do. What do your parents expect you to do at home? What responsibilities do you have at school? How about with your friends? A responsibility you have might be making your bed every morning. Or it might be making sure you bring your homework assignments home from school each day. Maybe it's taking the dog for a walk every afternoon.

Followers of Jesus also are given many responsibilities: to tell others about Jesus, to care for one another, to care for the animals and the world he has given us, and to use the gifts and abilities he has given us to help others. Whew! That may seem like a long list, but the good news is that God is with us and is able to help us take care of whatever responsibilities he gives us. In fact, the Bible is filled with many directions on how we are to take care of our work and responsibilities.

As you work through this month's *Sticky Situations* on responsibility and work, think of how you handle your responsibilities. Think about what you may need to change in how you do the work that is given to you.

Memory Verse: Work hard and cheerfully at whatever you do, as though you were working for the Lord rather than for people.
Colossians 3:23

The Picnic Problem

Sabina puts the last sandwich in the picnic basket. Finally, everything is ready. Now she just has to wait for her three friends. They have been planning this picnic for two weeks. Last week it rained and the week before that one of the girls got sick. Today the sky is blue. And, as far as she knows, everyone is healthy. Finally her friends arrive, and the girls walk down to the nearby park and pick a shady spot by a tree near the stream. They spend a wonderful Saturday afternoon eating, wading in the stream, and just gazing up at the clouds. When it's time to leave, the girls pack up their things. But there is no garbage can for their trash. They look at the pile of crumpled paper, banana peels, and other yucky-looking stuff. What do you think Sabina and her friends should do?

Should Sabina and her friends . . .

    A. Carry the stuff with them until they find a trash can?
    B. Throw the trash in the water and let the stream carry it away?
    C. Leave the stuff and let someone else come by and pick it up?

 Look at Genesis 1:28 to see God's instructions for taking care of his earth.
Talk with your mom or dad about several ways you and your family already take care of the world. Now come up with one or two more things you can do.

The correct answer is A.

Baby-Sitting Blues

Isaiah is saving money to buy a new CD player. To earn some money, he has agreed to take his baby brother to the park on Saturday mornings to play for an hour. It's a huge responsibility, but Isaiah actually enjoys playing with his brother. Isaiah is playing with his brother in the sandbox when he sees some of his friends coming down the sidewalk. He knows that if they see him he's going to be in for some major teasing. Isaiah tries to get his brother to go on the swings. (Swinging at least is still cool.) But his brother starts crying. His friends see him and start laughing. "Hey, Isaiah, what are you doing playing with a baby?" they call out. "Why don't you come play with the big boys?" What do you think Isaiah should do?

Should Isaiah . . .

A. Tell his friends that he's collecting sand for his seashell collection?
B. Tell his friends that his brother escaped from the house and he tracked him down at the playground?
C. Tell his friends that he takes care of his brother every Saturday—maybe they would like to join him sometime?

 Look at the example of Judah in Genesis 44:32-33 and see how to be brave as you accept responsibility.
Ask your mom or dad to share a time when they had to be brave in order to carry out a responsibility they had been given.

Training Camp

Camille is a good soccer player. In fact, she is one of the best goalies at her age level in the soccer league. Because she's done so well, her parents agree to send her to a soccer camp run by former professional players. Camille is so excited she can hardly wait. On the first day of camp the kids spend much of the morning running drills so the coaches can see what level they are—beginner, intermediate, or advanced. Camille feels that she has done well and hopes to move up to the advanced level. After lunch one of the coaches tells Camille that her skills are very good. "Would you mind helping some of the other kids who need more practice on their skills?" the coach asks her. It's not exactly what Camille has in mind. What do you think she should do?

Should Camille . . .

- A. Politely tell the coach she would rather move to a more challenging level?
- B. Thank the coach and say that she would be happy to help out the others?
- C. Agree to help but only if she can wear a whistle and make the kids run laps if they don't get it right?

 For help in knowing what Camille should do, read Luke 12:48.
Make a list of things that you do well. How can you use one of those skills to help others?

The correct answer is B.

The Visit

Diane's grandma and grandpa are coming for a visit, and that means one thing—cleaning! Every time her grandparents come, Diane's parents go into major-cleaning mode. The house is in a whirl until everything is in its place and everything is sparkling. But to get that done, Diane's parents need helpers. And those helpers are always Diane and her sister. The storm hasn't hit yet, but it's now just two days before her grandparents are to arrive. So Diane knows the cleaning storm is coming any minute. She and her sisters are watching TV when they hear their dad getting out the cleaning stuff. The girls exchange looks. They know it's about to begin. "Hey, girls, I need you to do a few things," they hear their dad call out. What should Diane and her sister do?

Should Diane and her sister . . .

    A. Run away and take cover?
    B. Look real busy when their dad comes downstairs and tell him they can help when they are finished?
    C. Ask their dad what they can do to get ready for the visit?

For a bad example, look at 1 Samuel 10:17-22 to see how the future king of Israel acted when it was his turn to step forward.
Describe how you often act when there is work to be done at home. How about at school? Do you run away, or are you ready to help?

You Have My Permission

Next Friday Tremaine's class is going on a field trip to the zoo as part of their study on the rain forest. They will be visiting the new Amazon exhibit, and each group has to study one animal of the rain forest while they are there. Tremaine's group is studying the scarlet macaw. When the students get to class, the teacher says that today is the last day to turn in permission slips for the zoo trip. Tremaine panics. He digs in his backpack and discovers the permission slip crumpled at the bottom. He forgot to give it to his mom! If he doesn't turn it in today, he won't be able to go. What do you think Tremaine should do?

Should Tremaine . . .

> A. Tell the teacher he forgot about the permission slip and ask if he can bring it in tomorrow?
> B. Fake his mom's signature and turn it in?
> C. Tell the teacher that a great big gust of wind swept the permission slip right out of his hands as he was walking to school and can he please have a new one to turn in tomorrow?

 Check out 1 Chronicles 21:1-8 to see how David acted when he made a big mistake.
Think of a time when you made a mistake and tried to cover up for it. What happened? How can you take responsibility for what you did when you do something wrong?

Pet Project

Tara begged her parents for months to get a pet, and finally they gave in. She now is the proud owner of a gerbil named Snickers. As part of the agreement, Tara has to feed the pet and give it fresh water each day, and she has to clean out its cage each week. So far Tara has followed through on her responsibilities, and Snickers is one happy gerbil. But now the fall session of dance classes is beginning. This fall Tara is taking more classes than ever. She has signed up for ballet, tap, and jazz. It's a busy schedule, with classes three times during the week and two classes on Saturday. Tara comes home very tired. She still manages to feed Snickers each day, but nearly three weeks have passed since she cleaned out the cage. Now a rather strong odor comes from her room. What do you think Tara should do?

Should Tara . . .

    A. Buy a can of air freshener for her room?
    B. Pay her best friend to come and clean out the gerbil's cage?
    C. Take the time to clean out Snickers' cage?

 Read 1 Kings 1:5-6 to see what happened when King David devoted all his time to being king and didn't take care of his responsibility to his family.
With your mom or dad, make a list of chores you do around the house. Think of how you spend your time. Do you have enough time to take care of all that you are expected to do? If not, what needs to change?

The correct answer is C.

Short Stop

Anthony and his pal Brandon are walking home from school and talking about how to beat the newest version of the Maggio Brothers video games. Anthony can't get past the drawbridge and the ugly monster. Brandon is trying to explain how he did it, but Anthony doesn't understand. "Look," says Brandon, "if you stop by my house, I'll show you."

Anthony knows that his mom told him to come home right after school. "Can't do it today," Anthony says.

"Aw, it will only take a minute. I've got everything set up," Brandon says. Soon Anthony finds himself being pulled into Brandon's house. When he walks in the door at home, he can tell that he is in big trouble. His mom begins, "So what happened?" What do you think Anthony should say?

Should Anthony . . .

- A. Explain that Brandon literally dragged him into his house to play a video game?
- B. Say that there was a huge backup of kids on the sidewalk and the walk home was very slow?
- C. Admit that he stopped at Brandon's house to check out his new video game?

 Read Matthew 27:15-24 to see how one Bible character tried to avoid responsibility by not making a decision.
Have your mom or dad share a time when they (or someone they know) gave excuses rather than taking responsibility for a decision they made. How do you suppose God feels about excuses?

The correct answer is C.

My Mission Field?

In Sunday school a missionary from Ecuador showed slides to Tanisha's class. The missionary spoke about living in the jungles of Ecuador. It sounded exciting but scary. Tanisha couldn't imagine herself living away from her CD player or video games. One of the last things the missionary told the class was that they didn't need to go to the jungles of South America to tell others about Jesus. (Tanisha gave a small sigh of relief to hear that!) Then the missionary said that *their* mission field was right in their own neighborhood. As Tanisha walks home from church with her family, she thinks about what the missionary said. She has never thought about her neighborhood as being a mission field. What do you think Tanisha should do with this new knowledge?

Should Tanisha . . .

A. Think of one or two friends with whom she can talk about Jesus?
B. Figure that the missionary really wasn't talking to her but to the boy sitting next to her?
C. Decide that she'll go right out there and tell her friends about Jesus—as soon as she has five more years of Sunday school?

 Check out Romans 1:5 to see your responsibility as a Christian.
Think of one or two of your friends who don't know Jesus as their Savior. Invite them to attend Sunday school or a church event with you.

The correct answer is A.

The Service Project

Once a month Amber's church sponsors a church-wide service project. Anyone can help, and Amber's family usually does. This month the project is making peanut butter and jelly sandwiches for homeless people. Everyone is placed on a team, and each team has to make two hundred sandwiches. Everyone has a different job to do. Amber has to put the finished sandwiches into plastic sandwich bags. As their team starts working, Amber sees that one of the girls is slow and spends a lot of time goofing around with her friends. At one point the girl leaves. She comes back ten minutes later, saying that she needed to rest her hand from spreading peanut butter. Amber sees that her team is really behind the others in getting the work done. What do you think Amber should do?

Should Amber . . .

    A. Kick the girl off her team and demand a new peanut-butter spreader?
    B. Do the best job she can and not worry about what the other girl does?
    C. Take over the girl's job and do both their jobs?

 Look up 1 Corinthians 3:8 for help in knowing what Amber should do.
What are some groups or teams to which you belong? How can you help the others work their hardest? Will you do your best even when some of the others don't?

The Star

Parker's older brother is a star. He's a star on the swim team. He's a star in the classroom. He's the best trumpet player in the band. There is nothing that Parker's brother can't do. Parker, on the other hand, hates the water. He does okay in school, but he really has to work hard. As for music, he tried to play the clarinet once but only made every dog in the neighborhood howl. Parker is good at just one thing, and that's building things with his connector blocks. Once he built a three-foot-high castle without using the directions. It was great to look at, but what good is that? The annual family reunion is coming up, and Parker dreads it. Everyone will talk to his brother, but no one will even look at him. What do you think Parker should do?

Should he . . .

   A. Put on a clown costume—that way no one will miss him?
   B. Be glad God gives each one of us special gifts, and not try to compare himself to his brother?
   C. Stay in his room unless someone needs something made with connector blocks?

 For a clue as to what Parker's thoughts should be, read Ephesians 4:7-8.
Make a list of everyone in your family. Now list a special gift each family member has. Think of ways to show you're glad for each one's special gift.

Bragging Rights

Bridget has been taking violin lessons since she was four years old. She loves playing and practices for at least a half hour each day. Bridget dreams of playing one day for a big crowd in a grand concert hall, and her teacher believes that she has the talent for it. Today is the music school's annual recital, and Bridget has worked hard getting her solo ready. Although she is nervous, she is sure that she will do a good job. When it's Bridget's turn, she takes the stage and makes no mistakes as she plays her violin. When she finishes, the people clap for a long time. Afterward, at the tea for those who played and for their parents, a woman comes up to Bridget and tells her how well she played. What do you think Bridget should say?

Should Bridget . . .

    A. Thank the woman, and then silently thank God for the gift he has given her?

    B. Thank the woman and tell her how hard she works to be able to play like that, what her practice schedule is like, and how much time she gives to it?

    C. Say, "Oh, it's nothing—anyone can do it"?

 Take a look at Romans 12:3 for a clue as to how Bridget should respond.
With your mom or dad's help, make an honest estimate of your abilities and talents. What do you do well? Why?

Extra Credit

Colin carefully colors in the last part of the map for his social studies project on the Iroquois. He leafs through his report. It looks great! Colin has spent nearly three days working on it. He and his mom spent an entire afternoon looking for facts about the Iroquois, and Colin spent another afternoon answering all the questions for the report. He proudly brings his report down to his mom. "This looks great, Colin," she says. "Did you answer the bonus question for extra credit? It's always a good idea to do a little bit more than what's expected." Colin goes back upstairs. What he really wants to do is go outside to play with his friends, not do *extra* stuff on his report. What do you think Colin should do?

Should Colin . . .

    A. Do the extra credit question?
    B. If he has time after playing ball, jot down a few sentences?
    C. Skip it because after all, extra means exactly that—it's extra, so you don't have to do it?

    Check out how Jacob went beyond what was expected of him in Genesis 31:38-42.
    Together with your mom or dad, talk about some good reasons for doing more than is expected of you. If you make that your habit, how will people come to think of you? Reminder: Don't forget to work on your memory verse for September. (You'll find it on the page just before September 1.)

The Big Job

Jennifer needs to do a service project for her scout troop. Her dad suggests that she offer to plant bulbs for the church. That sounds like a good idea to Jennifer—how hard can it be to put a few bulbs in the ground? *All you have to do is dig a hole, plunk the bulb in, and cover it up,* Jennifer thinks. *Piece of cake!* On Saturday Jennifer rides her bike to the church. Already a few adults and kids are working in different flower beds. The woman in charge directs Jennifer to where she will be working and hands her a bucket of bulbs. Jennifer can barely lift the bucket. There are over one hundred flower bulbs to be planted. Even if Jennifer starts now, it will take her all day to plant all these bulbs! What do you think Jennifer should do?

Should Jennifer . . .

A. Throw the bulbs into the air, step on them where they land, and squish them into the ground, calling them "planted"?
B. Ask a couple of her friends from the scout troop to come and help her?
C. Tell the woman in charge she can't possibly plant all those bulbs, and go home?

 Read Exodus 18:21-23 to see what Moses did to handle a big job.
Pretend you are Jennifer. How would you divide the work up to get the bulbs planted?

The correct answer is B.

Quitting Time

Dimitri and his younger brother are helping their dad rake the lawn. Each boy has one area of the yard that he is responsible for raking. Dimitri secretly considers himself lucky. His area of the yard has only two trees, but his brother's part has four trees. The boys start at the same time, but since Dimitri is older and has less leaves, he finishes quickly. *Good,* he thinks. *It's quitting time.* He still has time to catch up with his friends at the playground and shoot some hoops. He's about to put away his rake when he sees his brother sitting down for a rest. His brother has raked less than half of his part of the yard. He has a long way to go until he's done. What do you think Dimitri should do?

Should Dimitri . . .

    A. Slap his brother on the back and say, "Keep up the good work"?

    B. Show his brother how he rakes leaves so his brother can get done faster?

    C. Offer to help his brother finish up the yard?

Look up Numbers 32:16-19 to see how two tribes of Israel helped out the others even though their work was finished. Think of a time when you have been the last person to finish up a task or a chore. What would have helped you the most to get it done?

The correct answer is C.

More to Do

The more responsible we are—that is, the more we show we can take care of the chores and tasks given to us—the more responsibilities we will be given. Check out what Jesus has to say about this in the Bible verse on the right. Use the number code to help you.

THE MASTER WAS FULL OF

PRAISE. "WELL DONE, MY

GOOD AND FAITHFUL

SERVANT. YOU HAVE BEEN

FAITHFUL IN HANDLING

THIS SMALL AMOUNT, SO NOW

I WILL GIVE YOU MANY MORE

RESPONSIBILITIES. LET'S

CELEBRATE TOGETHER!" Matthew 25:21

Number Code

A = 1	B = 7	J = 13	Q = 19	X = 25
E = 2	C = 8	K = 14	R = 20	Z = 26
I = 3	D = 9	L = 15	S = 21	
O = 4	F = 10	M =16	T = 22	
U = 5	G = 11	N = 17	V = 23	
Y = 6	H = 12	P = 18	W = 24	

My Personal Best

Lance gets all his stuff together—a couple of pencils, plenty of paper, and the books he checked out on desert animals. His report is due Monday and needs to be done today since his family has church on Sunday morning and plans for Sunday afternoon. Lance doesn't mind spending time on the report. He wants to do a good job—and besides, it's raining! For about an hour Lance works hard. He's nearly finished when the phone rings. It's his friend Grant wondering if he wants to go to the movies. Grant's dad will pick him up in twenty minutes. Lance thinks that if he races upstairs and throws together a few sentences about scorpions, he probably can finish *and* still get to the movies. What do you think Lance should do?

Should Lance . . .

A. Tell Grant he can't go, then finish his report, giving it his best effort?
B. Scribble a few thoughts down on the last page and figure that his teacher probably won't read all of the report?
C. End the report where he stopped and write, "For more information, call Lance at 555-1256"?

 Check out Exodus 35:25-26 to see how the Israelite women devoted their skills to the building of the Tabernacle.
To what project or task do you need to give your best effort?

The Swing Set

Kirby's dad is building Kirby and his sister a new wooden swing set. It is going to be totally cool. It has a fort, three swings, monkey bars, and a twisting slide. Kirby can hardly wait to invite all his friends to come over and try it out. Today his dad is starting the project. He has all his tools laid out and is reading over the plans. Kirby is excited as he watches. He would love to hammer a few nails or drill a few holes. Kirby asks his dad, "Hey, Dad, can I help you with the swing set?"

Kirby's dad smiles. "Sure. Why don't you pick up all the scraps and throw them away. Then you can hand me the tools when I ask for them."

This is definitely not what Kirby had in mind. What do you think he should do?

Should Kirby . . .

A. Tell his dad, "Never mind. I just remembered I have to floss my teeth"?
B. Tell his dad that he really is more interested in using the tools than in holding them?
C. Ask his dad if he can also hammer a few nails or drill a few holes, then help out in whatever way his dad thinks is appropriate?

 To see how Ruth approached work that was tiring and not very exciting, look up Ruth 2:7.
Talk with your mom or dad about Kirby's situation. What might happen if Kirby does a good job helping out his dad with these small tasks?

The correct answer is C.

Get Going!

Paula has been asked to stand up in front of her class and tell about her family's trip to the Kennedy Space Center. Paula has lots of information and photos from their visit. As she looks over everything, however, she realizes that she doesn't know where to begin! Plus she wants to do a good job in front of the class. Paula spends one whole afternoon going through the material she picked up at the space center. She chooses several photos from their trip that might work on a poster. The more she looks over everything, though, the harder it is for her to know what to say. What does her teacher want to know about? What if she leaves out something important? Paula is ready to give up! What do you think she should do?

Should Paula . . .

A. Throw everything into a bag and use whatever she picks out for her talk?
B. Select the things that are most interesting to her and get started?
C. Go get a few cookies and let the project "sit" for a while?

 In Haggai 2:1-4, the Israelites faced the enormous task of rebuilding the temple in Jerusalem. Find out what message the Lord had for them.
Ask your mom or dad to tell about a time when they faced a big task. How does knowing that God is with you in whatever you do help you in facing the big jobs you may have?

The correct answer is B.

The List

The weekend is finally here, and Tashawna is looking forward to a lazy Saturday filled with nothing to do—especially no schoolwork! Her parents, however, have a different idea about how Tashawna will spend her time this weekend. When Tashawna comes down to the breakfast table, she discovers a list by her cereal bowl. Her parents have written down a list of chores that Tashawna has to do before she can play with her friends. Tashawna looks at the list: *Make your bed. Read for fifteen minutes. Put the dishes away. Clean up your room. Help Dad wash the car.* What are her parents thinking? This is the weekend. Tashawna is not supposed to have any work to do! What do you think she should do?

Should Tashawna . . .

    A. Accept her list of chores and get them done?
    B. Make a sign protesting unfair child-labor practices?
    C. Take the list and start calling herself Cinder-Tashawna?

 Read Colossians 3:23 for a clue about how Tashawna should respond.
What's your first response when your mom or dad asks you to do something around the house? Read the Bible verse aloud. How does hearing this change your attitude toward chores?
Reminder: Don't forget to say your memory verse for September. (You'll find it on the page just before September 1. Does it sound familiar? It's the same verse you just read for today!)

The Shortcut

This year, Ahmed has the same third grade teacher that his older brother, Sherif, did when he was in third grade. So far, it appears that Mrs. Wolfe is giving Ahmed's class the same kinds of assignments as she gave Sherif's class. For example, the big project now is to collect ten different rocks and identify them as part of the class's study of the earth. Sherif still has his rock collection sitting in his room. Ahmed is having a hard time finding different types of rocks. He has looked down at the park, in his backyard, and along the road. The best he can come up with is four kinds of rocks. The project is due on Monday, so Sherif offers to give him some of the rocks from his collection. What do you think Ahmed should do?

Should Ahmed . . .

   A. Take the rocks from his brother but scatter them throughout the yard so he can "find" them himself?
   B. Tell Mrs. Wolfe he could find only four different kinds of rocks?
   C. Continue searching for more rocks until he finds all ten?

 Read Proverbs 21:5 for help in knowing what Ahmed should do.
Think of a time when your family tried to take a shortcut in getting a project done. (Or ask your mom or dad to tell about a time when her or his family did.) What happened as a result of taking that shortcut?

The correct answer is C.

Great Opportunities

School has just started, and already Shari's mom is planning ahead. At the breakfast table this morning she is looking at all the programs being offered through the library during Thanksgiving break. "Take a look at this one," she says to Shari. "You could learn about ancient Egypt and build a model of a sphinx. Or you could take a story-writing class." To Shari everything sounds like school. And look at those starting times—8:30 A.M.! During Thanksgiving break? Shari's idea of a break leans a bit more toward the two R's—rest and relaxation—not the three R's of "reading, 'riting, and 'rithmetic." What do you think Shari should do?

September

Should Shari . . .

A. Tell her mom that she really is going to be too busy doing "other things" to sign up for a program?

B. Grunt, "I'll think about it," and hope her mother never brings it up again?

C. Tell her mom how she feels, but consider signing up for one of the programs her mom is suggesting—it may be fun, and she may even learn something?

 Take a look at Proverbs 24:30-34 for some advice on making the most of your opportunities.
Role-play the situation above. Pretend you are Shari's mom. What three good reasons can you give to Shari about why she should sign up for a class?

A Job Half Done

J.P. is not one of the smartest students in his class. In fact, he spends twice as long as anyone else in the class getting his homework done. And when it comes to remembering sight words, J.P. is behind everyone else. Today his teacher says that to encourage students to try harder to learn new words, she is starting a reward program. Each time a student learns a new sight word, that student will receive ten points. Each student who earns one hundred points by the end of the month will be able to come to a special breakfast with the teacher. J.P. hears a few students say that they will make the breakfast club by the end of the week. J.P. will be happy if he has learned one word by then! What do you think J.P. should do?

Should J.P. . . .

    A. Not even try—he'll never earn the one hundred points?
    B. Ask his teacher and parents for extra help, and work his hardest to make the goal?
    C. Keep on going as he is—if he makes it, fine; if not, he'll have a donut at home?

 Check out Proverbs 12:11 to see how J.P. should approach learning his facts.

Try It—You'll Like It!

Every school year Joy does the same things. She is in the church choir, she goes to Girl Scout meetings, and she plays soccer. Her mom usually signs her up for the activities, and Joy just goes. So she is a bit surprised when her mom asks her after dinner if she would like to join a new program in town that is teaching children acting skills. At the end of the session, the class will put on a short play for parents. Joy never really thought about acting before. The idea of acting on stage is a bit scary. And she's not sure if she can do it. She's never acted in anything, and what if she forgets her lines? Her mom tells her it will be a lot of fun. Joy is not so sure. What should she do?

Should Joy . . .

    A. Tell her mom maybe next year?
    B. Try it—maybe she'll like it?
    C. Tell her mom no way—she doesn't have "star quality"?

 Read Ecclesiastes 11:6 for help in knowing what Joy should do.
Think of a time when you tried out something new that you were unsure about. What did you learn from that experience?

The Art-Less Mural

Janae's art class is making murals for Parents' Night. Each group is given a different topic. When the groups are done, the murals will be put together to make one large mural that will hang in the front hall so all the parents can see it. Janae's group has to draw pictures about the special classes, like art, music, and physical education. The group is working hard on the mural. Each student has a specific part to draw. As they are working, Janae sees that the group next to hers is goofing off. They haven't done much work on their part of the mural, and what they have done looks awful. There are only a few splashes of paint and a drawing of something, but Janae has no idea what it is. If that's what that group's part of the class mural is going to look like, then the whole mural will look awful. What do you think Janae should do?

Should Janae . . .

- A. Keep busy helping her own group get its mural done and not worry about what the other group does?
- B. Offer some suggestions on what the other group could do with its mural?
- C. Inform the teacher that the other group is doing a terrible job and he had better do something about it?

 For help in knowing what Janae should do, read 1 Thessalonians 4:11.
Think of what may happen if Janae tries to tell the other group how to do its project. What may happen with that group? What may happen with Janae's group?

The correct answer is A.

The Chicken-Pox Kid

Elliott's little brother, Carter, just came down with the chicken pox. Carter is covered from head to toe with scratchy, itchy red spots. His mom is making him take oatmeal baths every two hours to keep him from scratching. If that's not bad enough, Elliott and Carter are supposed to go to their neighbor's birthday party today. Every year this kid has the coolest parties. Last year there was a magician. This year Elliott heard that they are going to have a clown who makes balloon animals. As Elliott leaves, he tells his brother that he'll bring him home a piece of cake. It's a great party. The clown is terrific. Elliott is about halfway home when he remembers the cake! He forgot to get a piece of cake for his brother. What do you think Elliott should do?

Should Elliott . . .

A. Call when he gets home and see if there is any cake left?
B. Go back and get a piece of cake for his brother?
C. Put on clown makeup and hope his brother forgets about the cake?

 Check out 1 Timothy 5:8 to see what Elliott should do. Read the Bible verse aloud. With your mom or dad, make a list of ways you can care for your relatives. Do something on your list today!

My Beauty Rest

Natalie is invited to be part of a small group of the children's choir which is going to sing with the adult choir for the missions festival. Only eight children have been invited to sing. The choir director told the children the importance of making each rehearsal. She gave them each a schedule that they need to go over with their parents. It has the practice dates and the dates when they are going to sing. Each member has to sign the slip along with a parent. Natalie and her parents are looking at the dates and putting each one on the calendar. A number of morning rehearsals fall on Saturday, which is the day when Natalie gets up late and spends most of the morning in her PJs watching 'toons. She's not sure if she wants to go to choir practice then! What do you think Natalie should do?

Should Natalie . . .

A. Ask the choir director if all of the Saturday practices can be changed to another day?
B. Tell her choir director thanks, but she really can't fit choir practice into her busy schedule?
C. Get up early on Saturday mornings, skip the 'toons, and go to practice?

 Take a look at Proverbs 31:15 for help in knowing what Natalie should do.
Have your mom or dad tell you if they are early risers or night owls. When do they get most of their work done? What are some things you might be able to get done on Saturday mornings?

The correct answer is C.

That's No Excuse

Darrell is on his first overnight camping trip. The troop arrived last night (in the rain) and spent about two hours setting up camp. The boys finally were able to fall into their sleeping bags after a soggy dinner of peanut butter and jelly sandwiches. This morning Darrell is last in line for breakfast and gets a plate of cold pancakes. At least it has stopped raining. Right after breakfast the boys pack up for a two-mile hike. When they finally get back to the campsite, Darrell's feet are killing him. His knee is hurt from tripping on the trail. He has at least a million bug bites, and he is tired! He has just flopped down on his sleeping bag when the scout leader pokes his head into the tent. "You guys have KP. Better get on it or we're not going to eat," he says. Darrell really doesn't feel like getting up. What do you think Darrell should do?

Should Darrell . . .

    A. Get up and get to work?
    B. Tell his scout leader he is sick and can't be around food right now?
    C. Say he's a terrible cook and he doesn't want to make the other scouts sick?

 For help in knowing what Darrell should do, look up Proverbs 22:13.
Have your mom or dad make a list of some of the excuses they hear throughout the day. Do you recognize any of them?

The correct answer is A.

A Polished Job

Every fall Fernando's mom gets out her silver, her crystal, and her fine china to clean. She usually asks Fernando and his older brother, Manny, to help with polishing the silver. Right after breakfast she puts the two boys to work. She shows the boys how to apply the polish and how to work hard to get off every dark spot. She lets the boys try a few of the pieces and looks over the finished product. When she can see that the boys know what they are doing, she goes off to tackle another chore, putting Manny in charge. The boys are busy working when Manny begins to check Fernando's work. "Hey, you missed a spot here," he says. "And you should do that one over again." Fernando is starting to get a bit upset. What do you think he should do?

Should Fernando . . .

A. Redo the ones that his brother pointed out?
B. Ask his brother who made him the Chief Silver Polish Inspector?
C. Start pointing out the flaws in his brother's work?

 Read Ephesians 6:7-8 to see what Fernando's attitude should be toward his work.
Think of a time when a friend or family member told you to do your work over again. How did you respond?

The Substitute

Faith's third grade teacher is wonderful. She's gentle and soft-spoken and always has a kind word to say to each student—no matter how badly you might mess up. Faith just loves her. So it comes as a huge shock when the principal greets Faith and her classmates one day with this news: "I'm sorry to tell you that Miss Anderson was in a car accident last night. She is going to be all right, but she will be out for at least two months recovering. Your new teacher is Mrs. Thatcher." From the very beginning the class can tell that Mrs. Thatcher is nothing like Miss Anderson. She rarely smiles. And if you mess up, watch out! Faith knows it's going to be a long, hard two months before Miss Anderson returns. What do you think she should do?

Should Faith . . .

    A. Organize a class strike and stop working until the principal gets them a nicer substitute?
    B. Pray that Miss Anderson will heal faster than expected and get back to class as soon as possible?
    C. Help Mrs. Thatcher get to know the class and do what she can to follow her directions?

 Look up Joshua 1:16 to see how the Israelites responded when Joshua became their new leader.
You probably have had a substitute in school once or twice. Imagine how that person feels walking into a strange classroom. Think of two things you could do to help that teacher.

The correct answers are B and C.

Review Time!

What are three things you learned about being responsible—doing the things expected of you—during this month? List them below.

1.

2.

3.

Bonus

Set three goals for taking on more responsibilities. Talk it over with your mom or dad to make sure your goals are reasonable.

1.

2.

3.

Repeat your Bible verse to one of your neighbors.

Wisdom & Humility

Who is the wisest person you know? The president? A famous scientist? Your mom or dad? King Solomon from the Bible? How about Jesus? There are a lot of people who know a lot of facts. We usually call them smart. But *wise* people have wisdom, and that is different. It is more than being able to add and subtract. It is more than being able to say a lot of memory verses. It is more than knowing all about God. Wisdom means using what we know to live in a way that pleases God.

The Bible tells us that God gives us wisdom (Proverbs 2:6) and that true wisdom begins with faith in God (Proverbs 1:7). The Bible calls wisdom "fear of the Lord." That doesn't mean to be afraid of God, but to give God the honor and respect he deserves, to live in awe of his mighty power, and to obey his Word. When the things we learn from God's Word change the way we act, think, and feel, then we are on the path to becoming wise young men and women.

Hand in hand with wisdom comes humility—being humble. That means we don't think we're better than we are. When we understand our weaknesses, we will turn to God and depend upon him for wisdom and strength. Having humility also keeps us from puffing up with pride. It helps us to think of other people as more important than ourselves.

As you work through this month's *Sticky Situations,* think about how you feel about yourself and others. Are there any changes you may need to make? Ask God to give you wisdom! He gives it freely to all who ask (James 1:5).

Memory Verse: Fear of the Lord is the beginning of knowledge. Only fools despise wisdom and discipline. Proverbs 1:7

1

Sunday School Blues

"It's not fair," grumbles Isabelle as she gets into the car after church. "What's not fair?" her dad gently asks. Well, it appears that Isabelle's Sunday school teacher is going to start giving the class homework assignments. If that's not bad enough, Mrs. Tucker is going to check their work every week. "Well, that doesn't sound so awful," her dad begins.

Isabelle doesn't let her dad finish before jumping in. "Dad! I've heard all those Bible stories a million, zillion times. I don't want to do the homework. It's going to be completely boring. Sunday school isn't supposed to be like school."

Isabelle's dad thinks she needs a major change in the way she thinks. What do you think Isabelle should do?

Should Isabelle . . .

A. Inform Mrs. Tucker that she has no intention of doing any homework—period?
B. See if she can learn something new from those familiar Bible stories?
C. Ask if she can go to another Sunday school class where they watch movies every week?

 Read Proverbs 1:7 for help in knowing what Isabelle should do. If you have been going to Sunday school for a long time, you may feel like Isabelle—you've heard all those stories at least a million times. Pray with your mom or dad, asking God to help you and your family keep learning new things from the Bible.

The correct answer is B.

Father Knows Best?

After dinner Colin hangs around the table as his mom and dad finish their coffee. He keeps drumming his fingers on the table until his mom finally asks, "Colin, what's up? Don't you have some homework to do?"

Colin takes a deep breath and begins, "Well, um, I, um, have this problem." Suddenly both his parents are all ears. In school the other day one of Colin's friends was trying to keep the other boys from playing with Colin. He didn't know why, but today no one would play with him. "What am I going to do?" Colin asks.

Colin's dad suggests that he talk with his friend and find out what is going on. Colin nods his head, but he's not so sure. If this boy is telling everyone that Colin is a dork, why would this boy want to talk with him about it? What do you think he should do?

Should Colin . . .

A. Get a second opinion from his mom?
B. Try and solve the situation himself by offering a dollar to every boy who plays with him?
C. Try his dad's advice and see what happens?

 Check out Proverbs 4:1-2 for help in knowing what Colin should do.
Ask your mom or dad to share a time when they received some advice from a parent about a problem they were having. Did they follow the advice? What were the results?

The correct answer is C.

Take It from Me

Lynne sits down at the computer and gets ready to type the report for her science project. Lynne feels quite grown up. For the first time she is going to do her whole report on the computer by herself. She took a computer class over the summer and learned a lot about writing reports. As she is working, her older brother wanders into the family room. "What's up, squirt?" he asks. Lynne shows him how she is setting up her report.

"You know, it might be a bit easier if you do it this way. It also will look better than what you are going to do. Here, let me sit down and show you," he says. Lynne doesn't care if her brother can make it look better. She wants to do this report on her own. What do you think Lynne should do?

Should Lynne . . .

   A. Let her brother show her another way to do the report, then decide the best way to do it?
   B. Tell her brother to take a hike because she wants to do it her way?
   C. Let her brother show her another way but hit the delete button as soon as he leaves?

 To see how Lynne should handle her brother's advice, read Proverbs 10:8.
With your mom or dad, role-play a similar situation to the one above. What would you do if someone knew how to help you but you wanted to work on your own?

The correct answer is A.

You Believe That?

When Dalton gets to school, he knows something is up. All his friends are standing around, talking excitedly. "Hey, Dalton," one of his friends calls out. "Did you hear the news?" Dalton has no idea what is going on, but he soon finds out. "It's all around school that the principal is going to make us go to school an extra hour every day. Can you believe it? Now we won't be able to play kickball after school. It's a total bummer," his friend tells him. "I think we should tell the principal we're not going to stay an extra hour no matter what." Dalton's mom is on the PTA, and she didn't tell him anything about going to school an extra hour. What do you think Dalton ought to do?

Should Dalton . . .

A. Check out the information with his mom or another adult before going crazy?
B. Tell his family he will be coming home from school an hour later now?
C. Get his friends and go to the principal's office to tell her they will not stay in school the extra hour?

 Look up Proverbs 14:15 for help in knowing how Dalton should handle this "news."
Rumors have a way of spreading quickly, especially when they are not true. Talk with your family about ways to check out facts to see if they are true.

The correct answer is A.

The Shouting Match

Avi and his friend Rajeev are big fans of their city's baseball team. They have followed the team throughout the season and even got to attend one of the games. The season is almost over, and once again, their team hasn't done well. As they walk to school, Avi and Rajeev discuss what the team needs to make it a winner next year. "I think we should get better pitchers," Rajeev suggests. Avi has heard that the team really needs hitters. When he talks about that, Rajeev says, "No, that is totally wrong." Avi points out a few more facts he heard on the radio. Now Rajeev is really angry. He says, "I don't care what they said on that stupid radio program." What do you think Avi should say to his friend?

Should Avi . . .

A. Say, "It's no use talking with someone like you," and walk away?
B. Tell Rajeev that he's stupid and doesn't know anything about baseball?
C. Shrug and say, "We'll see what happens," and leave it at that?

 For help in knowing how Avi should handle this situation, read Ecclesiastes 9:17.
Think of a time when you and a friend got into a shouting match. How did it end up? Talk with your family about one or two ways to avoid that type of fight.

The correct answer is C.

The Sleepover

Mackenzie is sleeping over at Naomi's house, along with a few friends from school and Naomi's cousin, Lianne. Mackenzie has met Lianne before and doesn't feel comfortable around her. Lianne is older than the other girls and is on the hyper side. She takes control of the sleepover from the very beginning. When it's time to turn off the lights, Lianne waits until Naomi's mom leaves, then turns the lights on again and brings out her collection of *Young Teen* magazines. She starts reading some of the articles about dating, boyfriends, and other things that are off-limits to Mackenzie and her friends. Mackenzie wonders how to handle this situation. She needs help *now!* What do you think she should do?

Should Mackenzie . . .

A. Ask if she can use a telephone to call home and ask her mom what to do?
B. Put her pillow over her head and try not to listen to Lianne?
C. Say a quiet prayer and ask God how to handle the situation?

 Take a look at James 1:5 to see where Mackenzie can get some wisdom right away.
Talk with your mom or dad about how important it is to pray when you don't know what to do. When you need an answer right away, remember who to call!

Correct Me If I'm Wrong

Dakota and his friends have been back in school for only a month, but Dakota already knows he is in for a very long year. His teacher, Mrs. Andrews, is nice enough, but boy, does she make the class work hard! So far, Dakota has turned in about a dozen homework papers, and every one of them has come back covered with red marks. He's gotten some of the answers wrong, but mostly it's picky stuff—like forgetting to cross the *t* in his name, or forgetting to write in the date or the subject. Every time Dakota gets a red mark, he corrects that mistake the next time, but Mrs. Andrews always finds something else to mark with her red pen. Dakota has even stayed after school to go over a red-marked paper. He is beginning to feel like he'll never get it right. What do you think Dakota should do?

Should Dakota . . .

- A. Keep on trying?
- B. Sneak in after school and take Mrs. Andrews' red pen—at least the corrections will be in another color?
- C. Wave the red, er, white flag, and give up?

 Check out Proverbs 12:1 for help in knowing what Dakota should do.
Think of something that was hard for you to learn how to do. When you were learning, what made you want to give up? What made you want to keep trying? What possibly could help in Dakota's situation?

The correct answer is A.

The Gymnast

Jasmine is a very talented gymnast. She has been taking gymnastics since she was four, and she does well on the balance beam and the tumbling routines. She is so good that she has been asked to work out with the high school gymnastic team to get ready for state competition. The local newspaper did a story about her practicing at the high school, and a big color picture of her is on the front page. Everywhere Jasmine goes, other kids—and even adults—call out, "Hey, I saw your picture in the newspaper." It's quite an honor, but Jasmine is getting tired of it all. For about the hundredth time today one of her friends comes up to her and says, "Jasmine, I saw your picture in the paper. That is so cool! Congratulations!" What do you think Jasmine should do?

Should Jasmine . . .

- A. Say, "Oh it's nothing—I'm really not any good"?
- B. Wear dark sunglasses from now on so no one will know who she is?
- C. Say, "Thanks—it's a lot of fun to practice with the older girls"?

 Take a look at Colossians 2:18 to see what the Bible says about people who claim to be humble but really are not. Talk with your mom or dad about the difference between being truly humble (understanding who you are in God's eyes) and just acting as if you're humble (saying bad things about yourself so others will think you are great).

The correct answer is C.

Plan Ahead

Lisette's dance class is starting to rehearse *The Nutcracker.* Lisette is really excited because she has several special parts. At dance class tonight Lisette gets her schedule for the next two months. From the looks of it, Lisette is going to be a very busy girl. When she gets home, she and her mom put all the dates on the calendar so they don't miss one. At school the next day Lisette's teacher hands out a list of dates when the monthly book reports are due. Each month the students are supposed to read and report on a different type of book—mystery, biography, sports, humor, and so on. Lisette sees that one of those book reports is due the same week that she has a dress practice and two programs. What do you think Lisette should do?

Should Lisette . . .

    A. Ask her teacher if she can turn in the book report after that week is over?

    B. Don't worry, be happy—it's a good ten weeks away?

    C. Begin planning a way to get the report done before that week?

 Read Genesis 41:33-40 to see how one wise leader in the Bible planned ahead.
Think of a big project you or your family must do in the next month or so. With your mom or dad make a plan of how you will get the work done.

The Whiz Kid

To help the class get ready for their big social studies test, Kelsey's teacher has a social studies bee. Each student has a chance to answer a question. If a student misses a question, he or she has to sit down. The first few rounds are easy, and most of Kelsey's class keeps standing. As the questions get harder, more and more students sit down. Finally, it's down to Kelsey and Noel. After several rounds of questions, Kelsey comes out as the winner. Her teacher gives her a candy bar and a blue ribbon for being the "Social Studies Whiz Kid of the Month." Kelsey is still excited when she leaves school. She catches up to some of her friends who didn't do well in the bee and are worrying about the test. What do you think Kelsey should say?

Should Kelsey . . .

A. Tell them no one can help them better than she can because she is the "Social Studies Whiz Kid"?
B. Wave her blue ribbon in their faces and say, "I'm not worried—that test is going to be easy"?
C. Ask if there is anything she can do to help?

 Check out Proverbs 12:23 to see what Kelsey should do. What subject or sport do you do well in? Have your mom or dad help you think of several ways you can use what you know to help others.

The correct answer is C.

Hey, What's the Big (New) Idea?

Simon's class just read a book about Colonial times. Now their teacher has put them in several groups to gather more information about Colonial life. They are to present what they learn to the class. Simon invites his group over to his house to work on the project. After much discussion, the group decides to do a presentation on the kinds of games children played in Colonial times. Simon suggests that the group make posters about the games and write a short paragraph explaining what each one is. Simon's older brother is in the next room and hears the plans. He tells Simon, "You know, when I was in third grade we made some Colonial games and *showed* the class how to play them." Simon hates to admit it, but his brother has a good idea. Still, Simon is in control here. What do you think he should do?

Should Simon . . .

    A. Ask the group what they think of his brother's idea?
    B. Roll his eyes and say, "Hey, who asked you?"
    C. Politely say, "Thanks for the idea," but ignore his brother's advice?

 To find out what Simon should do, check out Proverbs 18:15.
Think of a project you have done for school. How would you have reacted if someone offered you a new idea on how to do it?
Reminder: Don't forget to work on your memory verse for October. (You'll find it on the page just before October 1.)

The correct answer is A.

The Wise Way

Denzel's dad greets him as he walks in the door. "I've got some great news for you," he says. Denzel knows this can only mean trouble. His dad goes on, "A couple of the parents in the neighborhood are going to have an after-school Bible club every Thursday. We've got all sorts of great lessons and crafts to do. It's going to be a blast. What do you think about coming along with your younger brother and sister?" Denzel doesn't think much of the idea. He would rather play video games after school. And he is sure that none of his friends will want to listen to Bible lessons. His dad, as if reading his mind, adds, "A couple of the high school kids are coming to help teach. You may just learn something." What do you think Denzel should do?

Should Denzel . . .

    A. Tell his dad he'll take a pass on the Bible club?
    B. Ask if he can tell his friends about it—maybe some of them will want to come too?
    C. Explain to his dad that he gets all the Bible teaching he needs at church?

 Look up Hosea 14:9 and see what Hosea has to say about listening and learning from God's Word.
With your mom or dad, come up with a list of ways you can listen and learn from God's Word throughout the week.

The correct answer is B.

Take My Advice

Liliana is planning on making her own gifts for Christmas this year. She spends an afternoon looking through a number of her parents' craft books and selects a special gift to make for each of her four family members, her five friends, and her teacher. She figures if she gets started now she will have enough time to finish the ten gifts before Christmas. Liliana goes through each of the crafts and writes down everything she'll need to make each one. When she is done she is surprised to see that her list is nearly three pages long! *Maybe I'm trying to do more than I can handle,* she begins to think. But she doesn't want to spoil the surprise by discussing it with her parents or her older sister. What do you think she should do?

Should Liliana . . .

- A. Go ahead with her plans and keep her fingers crossed?
- B. Ask another adult, like her grandma or a craft store worker, for some advice?
- C. Give it up and buy everyone something?

 Take a look at Proverbs 15:22 for help in knowing what Liliana should do.
Ask your mom or dad to share a time when it was hard for them to ask for advice, or when they didn't ask for advice. What happened as a result?

The Computer Crash

Sterling's family just bought one of the new computer programs for making greeting cards. His dad showed him how to use the program and how to put in fancy graphics and lettering. Now Sterling is ready to go! He is designing the invitations for his birthday party on the computer. Sterling has worked about an hour on the invitations when he stops to take a break. His "ten-minute break" lasts about an hour. When Sterling comes back, he discovers that his invitations (and all that work) are gone because he forgot to save his work! While Sterling was on break, his mom came in, saw no one using the computer, and turned it off. Sterling is mad at himself and mad at his mom; but most of all he is mad at the computer! What do you think Sterling should do?

Should Sterling . . .

    A. Give the computer a swift kick for losing his work?
    B. Yell at his mother and make her redo the invitation?
    C. Take a deep breath, count to ten, and start all over?

 Look up Proverbs 29:11 for help in knowing what Sterling should do.
Discuss with your family three wise ways you can handle the times when you are so mad you are about to explode!

God's Wisdom

There is a big difference between the world's wisdom and wisdom that comes from God. Color in the dotted spaces to see two words that tell what God's wisdom is like. (You can find more words about wisdom in James 3:17.)

The wisdom that comes from heaven is first of all pure.
It is also peace loving, gentle at all times,
and willing to yield to others.

James 3:17

The Car Wash

16

October

Ellis begs his parents to let him wash the car for ten dollars to earn money for the upcoming fall carnival. Ellis has helped them before, and he is sure that he can do it by himself. Finally his parents give in. Ellis gets out the buckets, the hose, and all the other car wash stuff. As he hoses down the car, Ellis hopes one of his friends will ride by and see him washing the car. He's in the middle of soaping up the car when his older brother rides up on his bike. "Hey, you're doing it all wrong. If you don't rinse off the soap right away, it's going to get all streaky. And I betcha Mom and Dad won't even pay you if you mess up," his brother says. Ellis thinks he *is* doing it the right way and he *is* doing a good job. He is upset with his brother for bothering him. But what if his brother is right? What do you think Ellis should do?

Should Ellis . . .

    A. Ask his brother to show him the right way?
    B. Start yelling, "I am *too* doing it right!" and then ignore his brother?
    C. Give his brother a deluxe wash and hose him down?

 For help in knowing what Ellis should do, read Proverbs 13:10. Saying "I was wrong" or "I need help" is hard—especially when you feel you know what you are doing. Think of a time when you had to say that. How hard was that for you to say?

I've Got a Deal for You

Ethan watches as his friend Phillip swings into his driveway riding a really cool 18-speed bike. "Hey, when did your parents buy you that?" Ethan asks.

"They didn't! This is my cousin's bike—isn't it awesome?" The bike is just like the one Ethan wants someday. Phillip's cousin is selling the bike. Phillip and his twin brother want to buy it, but they are twenty dollars short. They ask if Ethan would like to own a piece of it. Ethan has twenty dollars in his room, so he gives it to Phillip. Now he is the proud part owner of an 18-speed bike. Later, though, Ethan thinks this isn't such a good deal. When does he get to ride the bike? Where will they keep it? Ethan wants to get his money back, but he doesn't want to let his friend down or look like a wimp. What do you think Ethan should do?

Should Ethan . . .

    A. Come up with a detailed schedule of when he will get to ride the bike, and have Phillip and his brother sign it?
    B. Report Phillip and his brother to the Better Business Bureau?
    C. Tell the brothers he made a mistake and wants his $20 back?

 Read Proverbs 6:1-4 for help in knowing what Ethan should do. Ask your mom or dad to tell you if they ever made an unwise purchase or loan and had to go back and get out of it. What was the hardest part about doing that? What advice can they give you?

The correct answer is C.

The Play Date

Stephanie lives in a very nice neighborhood. The houses are bigger than most, and the yards are all neatly trimmed and mowed every week. Through church Stephanie has gotten to know Catherine. She lives on the other side of town, where the houses are not so big and the yards are often filled with rusty cars and used tires. As the girls get to know each other, they find that they really enjoy each other's company. Today Catherine is coming over for the afternoon. Before she comes, Stephanie gets a call from her friend next door, who wants to play. Stephanie invites the girl to play with Catherine and her. "Catherine Ross, who lives across town? Why are you playing with her? You can count me out if she is going to be there," the girl next door says. Stephanie is surprised. What do you think Stephanie should do?

Should Stephanie . . .

A. Cancel with Catherine because she doesn't want to upset her friend next door?
B. Tell the girl next door that she is sorry, but she and Catherine have already made plans?
C. Tell her neighbor to get a life—Catherine is a really cool girl?

 Read Psalm 113:5-8 to see how God feels about people who don't have so much.
Talk with your mom or dad about three things you can do to show that you care about all people, for they are special in God's eyes.

The correct answer is B.

I'll Do It Myself

Fourth and fifth graders get special privileges at Ned's school. They can ride their bikes to school. They can eat with anyone they want at lunch—they aren't told where they have to sit. And best of all, they have the second-floor classrooms. (Everyone else is on the first floor!) Not only all that, but last summer Ned also got to fly in an airplane alone and spend a week with his grandparents! Ned is feeling pretty proud of himself these days. This morning Ned's mom is helping his sister gather all her school supplies together. She offers to help Ned when she's done with his sister. Ned really doesn't have a clue where all his stuff is, but he doesn't want to look like he needs as much help as his sister! What do you think Ned should do?

Should Ned . . .

    A. Accept his mom's help and get his act together?
    B. Tell his mom he doesn't need any help—he can do it himself?
    C. Say no, but when his sister goes in the other room, ask his
       mom to help him out?

 For help in knowing what Ned should do, look up Jeremiah 49:16.
Being proud can make you feel as if you don't need anyone's help, even God's help. Ask your mom or dad to let you know if you ever act too proud. Ask God to help you always look for his help.

The correct answer is A.

Just Admit It

Grant has put together a mobile of the solar system using different kinds of fruit. He thinks his teacher will love it. Before Grant is ready to leave for school, his mom suggests that he take his mobile apart and carry it in a paper bag. Once he gets to school, she says, he can put it together again. Grant, however, insists on carrying the project as it is. As Grant is walking to school, he hears the first bell ring. He starts to run and doesn't see the bump in the sidewalk. He goes sprawling. His mobile goes sprawling, too, and Jupiter (a grapefruit) lies squashed beneath him. His project is destroyed. When he gets home, his mom asks how his teacher liked his science project. What do you think Grant should say?

Should Grant . . .

    A. Tell his mom it was a real smash?
    B. Grunt and say, "Just fine"?
    C. Tell his mom what happened and admit that he should have listened to her?

 Check out Isaiah 57:15 to see the kind of attitude that pleases God.
Does this situation sound familiar? You and your mom or dad can share a time when it would have been better to listen. Talk about how you acted afterward.
Reminder: Don't forget to say your memory verse for October. (You'll find it on the page just before October 1.)

The correct answer is C.

Best Seat in the House

Debbie folds the last program and puts it in a big box with the others. She is helping her dad get ready for the week of special services at church. Debbie and her father have folded nearly five hundred programs! Several well-known speakers and singers will be leading the services, so the church is expecting a big crowd. Debbie is very excited about seeing one of the singers who will be at the church tonight. He has recorded many of her favorite songs, and she listens to him all the time! The only trouble is that good seats are hard to come by. Debbie really wants a good seat. Looking at the dark church, Debbie thinks it might be good to go inside now and save a few seats for her family and her. What do you think Debbie should do?

Should Debbie . . .

A. Suggest that her family go and get some fast food so they can get back to church early and beat out everyone else?
B. Go ahead and put some programs on a few seats front and center?
C. Take whatever seat she gets because everyone else wants to see too?

 Read Matthew 23:12 to see what Jesus has to say about grabbing the best for yourself.
In what ways do you see the people around you "exalt" themselves, or act important? In what ways might you try to exalt yourself during the day? Plan one way you can exalt or build up someone else.

The correct answer is C.

The MVP

Last night Rudy's basketball team won the city championship for boys ten and under. Tonight they are celebrating their winning season. The coach always names an MVP, the most valuable player to the team. Rudy doesn't tell anyone, but he thinks he will get the award. He has been to all the practices, he has never missed a game, and last night he made the winning shot. Not only that, but he also has been the player with the most steals on the team. At the celebration the coach stands and holds up the trophy. "This year's MVP award goes to a player who has worked very hard this year and who got better with each game—Jackson Branch." Rudy almost spits out his milk. Jackson is the shortest and newest player on the team. He did get better during the year, but he was terrible to begin with. What do you think Rudy should do?

Should Rudy . . .

A. Go up to the coach after the dinner and say there must be a big mistake?
B. Congratulate Jackson on having a great season?
C. Take the trophy when Jackson is not looking and chalk up another steal?

 Look up Proverbs 25:27 to see how Rudy should act.
With your mom or dad, think of three ways to keep you from thinking about all the honors you think you deserve.

The correct answer is B.

Grandmotherly Advice

Kiana's grandmother is spending the week with Kiana's family. Kiana always looks forward to being with her grandmother, who has traveled all over the world and has lots of interesting stories to tell. Her grandmother also always brings a suitcase full of gifts for Kiana and her sister! After dinner Kiana says to her mom, "I need to read a book for school about the pioneers. Do you think we have anything like that around?"

Before Kiana's mom can answer, her grandmother says, "Oh, Kiana, I know just the books for you. I read them when I was in school and they are wonderful." Kiana's grandmother goes on talking about the author and how much fun she had reading those books. Kiana has never heard of these books or the author. What do you think Kiana should tell her grandmother?

Should Kiana . . .

A. Politely tell her grandmother that she really wants to pick out her own book?
B. Go to the local library and see if the books are even available—it's been a long time since her grandmother was a little girl?
C. Ask her grandmother to tell her more about these books?

 Check out 1 Peter 5:5-6 to see how Kiana should handle this situation.
Think of one or two things you can ask your own grandparents or other older people you know.

Starry Night

Greg and his family pitched their tent last night and got up when the birds began to sing this morning. They have had a wonderful day. They fished earlier in the morning and caught four big trout to cook for dinner. Then they went on a hike and saw three different types of snakes along the trail. Dinner was terrific. The fresh trout were really good. After dinner they roast some marshmallows, and Greg's dad gets out his guitar to play a few songs. Greg begins to yawn. It has been a tiring day, and he is ready to hit the sleeping bag. Just as he is about to nod off, his dad calls to him, "Greg, take a look at this." Greg's dad is looking up at the stars shining brightly in the clear night sky. "Isn't that amazing?" What do you think Greg should do?

Should Greg . . .

> A. Look with awe at God's beautiful creation?
> B. Yawn and say, "Sure, Dad," and go back to sleep?
> C. Say, "Hey, that reminds me—I'd love a Milky Way"?

 Look up Psalm 8:3-4 to see how David felt when he saw the wonder of God's creation.
Together with your mom or dad, share a place where you have been that reminds you of God's love and greatness.
Together read all of Psalm 8 aloud. Does this make you feel humble? Why?

The correct answer is A.

Bath Time

It's Saturday night and time for everyone to clean up for church on Sunday. Mom comes into the family room where Mackenzie and her brother Samuel are watching a video. "Okay, you two. Time for your showers," she tells them. Mackenzie jumps up right away. "I'm going first," she says. "I want to use the new shampoo I got."

Samuel begins to complain right away. "Aw, Mom, if she gets in there with her new shampoo, I'll never get a chance. It'll be Sunday morning before I can get in the bathroom."

Mackenzie's mom agrees with Samuel. "Why don't you let your brother go first? He doesn't take as long, and he's looking pretty tired." What do you think Mackenzie should do?

Should Mackenzie . . .

    A. Race her brother upstairs and do her best to get to the bathroom first?

    B. Let her brother have the bathroom first and use the time to read over her Sunday school homework?

    C. Flip a coin with her brother: "Heads you lose, tails I win." Winner gets dibs?

 Take a look at Philippians 2:3-4 to see how you are to respond to the interests of others.
Discuss with your mom or dad what it means not to be selfish but to be interested in what others are doing. How can you do that at home? With your friends?

Best of Show

Marco's school is having an art fair. All students are welcome to enter something they did either at school or at home. Marco has been working on a clay piece to enter in the fair. He got the idea by reading one of the craft magazines his mom has lying around the house. When Marco finished it, even he was surprised. It really turned out well. But still Marco doesn't expect what he sees when he comes into school today. His piece is one of five that have won Best of Show. When his art teacher sees him in the hall, she pulls him aside. "Marco, that was a wonderful piece you did. So creative, and what great use of color. You did an outstanding job," she says. Marco doesn't know what to say. How do you think he should respond?

Should Marco . . .

A. Quietly thank his teacher?
B. Tell his teacher, "You think that's good? Wait until you see my next work of art. It will be perfect"?
C. Say nothing, but wear his Best of Show ribbon for the next several weeks?

 Read 1 Samuel 18:14-18 to see how David acted even when the whole country was proud of him.

It's easy to get a big head when everyone is praising you and telling you how great you are. Talk with your mom and dad about how important it is to keep your head just the right size!

The correct answer is A.

Tryouts

Nisha and her best friend Kavita are both in the children's choir at their church. Both girls want to try out for the solo part in the Christmas musical they are starting to practice. For the past several weeks they have spent hours with each other going over the songs. Finally it's tryout day. The girls go together, but Kavita is called up first. Nisha listens as her friend sings the songs. Kavita mixes up some of the words and doesn't sing the right notes in a couple of places. When Kavita finishes, it's Nisha's turn. She does a wonderful job. She doesn't mix up any of the words, and she doesn't get any of the notes wrong. When she leaves the room, she sees Kavita waiting for her. "So how did you do?" Kavita asks. What do you think Nisha should say?

Should Nisha . . .

  A. Say, "I did great! I didn't miss a note. I think I have a good shot at getting the solo part"?
  B. Say, "Well, I think I did better than you did"?
  C. Say, "I think I did pretty well. We'll have to see what Mrs. Strong thinks"?

 Read Proverbs 27:2 for help in knowing what Nisha should do.
Role-play the situation (or a similar one). Pretend you are Kavita, Nisha's friend. How would you feel if she were to answer either *A* or *B*? How do you act toward someone who likes to brag about himself or herself?

The correct answer is C.

The Carpool

Tami is in a carpool for soccer practice with two other families. Most of the time it works out okay, but every once in a while there's a problem. Like last week. Tami had to stay after school to get some extra help in reading, so she was late getting home. Her ride was already at the door when she still was eating her snack. They all were late, and the coach was not happy. Today it's her mom's turn to drive, and Tami wants to get in some extra practice time before the game begins. As her mom pulls into the first driveway, there is no sign of the Thomas girls. Tami and her mom wait five minutes and still see no sign of them. Tami is beginning to get upset. She'll never get to practice at this rate. What do you think Tami should do?

Should Tami . . .

A. Go ring the doorbell and tell the girls that they are now eight minutes late?
B. Remember that she has been late a few times herself and give the girls a break?
C. When the girls get in the car say, "Thanks a lot. Now I missed my practice time"?

 Look up Romans 2:1 for some help in knowing what Tami should do.
Sometimes it's easy to blame others for things they have done and not know that we have been doing the same thing. Talk with one of your parents about whether that has ever happened to one of you.

The correct answer is B.

And the Biggest . . .

Vince heads over to Seth's house to play. When he arrives he discovers Seth and another friend are shouting at each other. "Well, you're wrong, and that's that. My house is bigger than yours," Seth is saying.

"How can you say that? We've got a family room *and* a computer room. Our house is bigger," Niles says.

Vince is about to turn around and leave his two friends when they see him. "Vince, tell Seth he's wrong," Niles pleads.

Seth jumps in, "Vince, you've been in both our houses. Tell us which of us has the biggest house."

Vince *has* been in both houses, and he knows that *his* house is bigger than either of their homes. What do you think Vince should say?

Should Vince . . .

A. Point out that his house is actually the biggest?
B. Tell his friends that he'll come back after they have stopped shouting at each other?
C. Say it doesn't matter who has the biggest house—they each have a great house to live in?

 Check out what Jesus had to say about wanting to be great in Matthew 18:1-4.
Jesus had to correct his disciples when they began to fight about who would be the greatest in heaven. Read the Bible verses aloud. How does Jesus say you can have the right attitude?

On Thin Ice

Joshua just got a pair of the coolest hockey skates for his birthday. He lives in the Canadian Rockies, where the thermometer
has been dipping below the freezing mark for some time.
This morning he and his friend Aaron decide to check out the
ice. The town always puts out a green flag if the ice is okay
for skating, but there's no flag out yet. Still, the ice *looks* thick
enough. In fact, it looks great—clear and smooth, just like a
mirror. The boys tap at the edge with their skates. It *feels* okay
from the shoreline. Aaron says, "Let's go. We'll be the first ones
to try out the ice." Joshua points out that the flag is not out
yet. "Oh, that's because we're here so early," Aaron answers.
"I'm sure they'll be around soon. Don't you want to try your
skates?" What do you think Joshua should do?

Should Joshua . . .

    A. Take a quick spin on the ice, but don't go out too far?
    B. Come back later to see if a flag has been posted?
    C. Be brave and daring, and go for it?

 Look up Proverbs 14:16 for help in knowing what Joshua
should do.
Ask your mom or dad to share a time when they might have
gone ahead and done something dangerous instead of being
careful. When are you tempted to "go for it"?

The correct answer is B.

Review Time!

List three things you learned about wisdom this month.

1.

2.

3.

Bonus

List three ways you can become wise, according to the Bible.

1.

2.

3.

Say your memory verse to someone you think is wise.

The Christian Character

You've probably seen the bracelets and key chains with the letters *WWJD—What Would Jesus Do?* Maybe you have some of them. The initials remind you all day to think about how Jesus would act or think if he were there with you. When we talk about developing a Christian character, or growing in our faith, we are talking about the same thing—having the same attitudes, actions, and thoughts as Jesus.

Being a Christian is more than just saying we believe in Jesus. That's just where we start. Once we say we are followers of Jesus, he wants us to grow and become more and more like him every day! How do we do this? Reading the Bible, going to church and Sunday school, having daily devotions, praying—these are all ways we can learn how God wants us to live.

Is this easy? Not at all! Paul talks about living like Jesus as running a race or training for a sports event. It takes a lot of energy and effort. It also means making mistakes and failing at times. Problems might come up as we run this race. But God uses all these things to help shape our character until we become more and more like his Son, Jesus.

As you work through this month's *Sticky Situations,* remember that you are a Christian in training, just like your mom, your dad, or anyone else who calls Jesus Lord!

Memory Verse: I am still not all I should be, but I am focusing all my energies on this one thing: Forgetting the past and looking forward to what lies ahead, I strain to reach the end of the race and receive the prize for which God, through Christ Jesus, is calling us up to heaven. Philippians 3:13-14

Down Memory Lane

Jillian loves being outdoors. It doesn't matter what she's doing—riding her bike, Rollerblading, or playing tag with a group of neighborhood kids—as soon as Jillian is done with her homework, she's out the door. Jillian also enjoys sports activities, like soccer or basketball—the more running around the better! So when her mom signs her up for the church school's Scripture memory program, Jillian is not happy. All this means is more time inside, sitting around trying to cram Bible verses into her head—verses that don't mean that much to her. Besides that, it's hard for Jillian to memorize things. She'd rather be moving than sitting still trying to remember something. What do you think Jillian should do?

Should Jillian . . .

    A. Come up with a way to memorize Bible verses while playing soccer?
    B. Toss the Scripture memory verses under her bed and tell her mom she has forgotten where they are?
    C. Give it her best effort because spiritual exercise is as important as physical exercise?

 Read 1 Timothy 4:7-10 for help in knowing what Jillian should do.
With your mom or dad, come up with three different ways you can get in shape spiritually. Pick one of the ways to try out for the next month.

The correct answer is C.

The Pity Party

About two weeks ago, Carmen fell off her bike and broke her leg. It turned out to be a rather bad break, and Carmen will be in her cast for at least six weeks. Her leg doesn't hurt much anymore, but being in a cast and having to walk on crutches is a real pain. At first all her friends came to see her and write their names on her cast. Now, though, not as many friends stop by to see her, unless it's to drop off schoolwork for her. Carmen misses her friends, and she hates to admit it, but she misses school, too. It turns out that while her leg is healing, she will miss the class trip to the science museum and a camping trip with her scout troop. Carmen is tired of watching TV and playing video games. What do you think she should do?

Should Carmen . . .

- A. Complain loud and long enough that everyone in the house will be as upset as she is?
- B. Make an effort to find out what she can learn from her situation and be thankful that she will be able to walk and run again soon?
- C. Get angry with her friends for leaving her alone and demand that they come see her?

 Take a look at Job 10:1 for how Job acted at first when bad things happened to him.
When something bad happens, you might first ask, "*Why me?*" But God wants us to learn from troubles. (See what Job said in Job 42:1-6.) Ask your mom or dad to share what they have learned from troubles.

The correct answer is B.

The Big Church

Beginning this fall, Quentin's parents want him to come to the church service with them besides going to his Sunday school class. This means that the family will be at church for two and a half hours every Sunday. Not only that, but Quentin will have to sit quietly in church for a whole hour or more! At least in Sunday school, he can move around and talk. Quentin is not happy about this change in plans. He has been to church with his parents before. The music part is okay, but when the pastor begins to preach, it's nap time! Totally boring! Quentin can't see how he could sit through a whole sermon. What do you think he should do?

Should Quentin . . .

    A. Try listening to the pastor and see if he learns anything?
    B. Make paper airplanes and fly them around the church to keep from going to sleep?
    C. Bring in his personal CD player and listen to his favorite Christian rock singers while the pastor is preaching?

 Take some advice from Deuteronomy 5:1 on what Quentin should do.
Talk with your mom or dad about the parts of the church service you enjoy. Think of two things you could do to help you learn more from the church service.

The correct answer is A.

The Prayer Chain

Gia likes the kids' choir at church because the members pray for each other after every practice. They even have a prayer chain. If something comes up during the week, anyone can call the director and start the prayer chain. As choir members receive a prayer request by phone, they pass it along by calling another member. Tonight Gia receives a call. One girl is asking the group to pray for her mom, who was just taken to the hospital. Gia writes down the request and calls the next choir member. She puts the prayer request inside her notebook, planning to pray after she finishes her homework. But Gia forgets. The next morning Gia sees the girl at school and remembers right away that she forgot to pray for the girl's mom! What do you think Gia should do?

Should Gia . . .

   A. Send up a quick prayer right now?
   B. Ask the girl how her mom is doing and promise to pray for her?
   C. Decide to set aside a special time each day that she can spend praying?

Read Matthew 14:23 to see the example Jesus gives us for spending time alone with God.
Jesus was very busy, but he found time each day to be alone with his Father in prayer. Talk with your mom or dad about ways to make prayer a part of your daily routine. If you already have a quiet time each day, talk about why that time is important to you.

The correct answers are A, B, and C.

No Church

David has decided to go on a church strike. He has been going to church ever since he was a baby, and he has heard the same stories in Sunday school year in, year out. He has heard about Creation a zillion times, Noah and the ark probably a zillion and a half times, and the Christmas and Easter stories—well, he knows both of them from beginning to end! David could teach the class if they would let him. What David doesn't understand is why his parents still go to church every Sunday. They must hear the same stories too. Aren't they bored? Why can't he stay at home and listen to Christian music on Sundays while he reads his Bible for a few minutes? Isn't that good enough? What do you think David should do?

Should David . . .

A. Make a list of suggestions as to how Sunday school can be more interesting?
B. Promise his parents he'll take out the garbage for a whole year if he doesn't have to go to church?
C. Wake up and discover that he can learn a lot at church from other Christians and from the Bible stories he knows so well?

 Look up Isaiah 27:11 to see how the Bible describes people who turn away from God.
Make a list with your mom or dad of ways you can stay connected to God during the week and at church so that you can grow and not be a "dead branch."

The correct answer is C.

Give Up or Get Going?

Last summer Carrie went to an overnight church camp with her older sister. She had a wonderful time and came back really wanting to live for Jesus. To do that Carrie knew she had to stop talking about other kids behind their backs. But for the last several months Carrie has been gossiping about the girl down the street! This morning Carrie has hardly gotten in the front door of the school when she finds one of her friends and starts telling her, "Did you see Treva's haircut? It is so tacky. I can't believe she got her hair cut that short." All of a sudden Carrie begins to think about her time at camp last summer, and she knows she should not be gossiping. Carrie almost starts to cry. She didn't think living for Jesus was going to be so hard. What do you think Carrie should do?

Should Carrie . . .

A. Realize that it is just too hard to be perfect and go back to acting the way she always does?
B. Keep on praying and keep on trying to live like Jesus?
C. Put tape over her mouth so she can't possibly gossip anymore?

Read what Paul has to say in Philippians 3:12-14 about living the Christian life. (Note that your memory passage for this month is from verses 13 and 14.)
Do you think we can ever be perfect in the way we live for Jesus? Read the Bible passage aloud. Talk with your mom or dad about what you think Paul means when he talks about reaching for the end of the race.

The correct answer is B.

It's Greek to Me

Trent's Sunday school teacher, Mr. Henry, is talking to the class about how important it is to study the Bible. Each week the class will get a question, and students will have to use their Bibles to answer it. Trent takes his Bible home and opens it. He really has never actually *read* his Bible before. (Sure, he looked at all the cool pictures when he first got it, but that took five minutes.) Trent turns the pages. To him it looks like it is written in another language. The type is small, and it has funny-looking numbers and words. Trent also wonders how he is supposed to learn something from a book that was written so many years ago. What do you think Trent should do?

Should Trent . . .

    A. Get some help from his mom or dad in learning how to use his Bible?
    B. Call up his teacher and say, "Hey, this looks like Greek to me"?
    C. Put the Bible on a shelf and use it as a bookend?

 Read 2 Timothy 3:16 to find out what Paul has to say about the importance of reading the Bible.
If you don't have a plan already, work with your mom or dad to come up with a way to learn from the Bible each day. Try it out during this month.

Bible for Beginners

Last month Colleen asked one of her best friends from school to come to Sunday school with her. To Colleen's surprise, her friend Delaney really enjoys going to Sunday school now. She has missed only one class so far, and that was because her family went out of town. Colleen is happy that her friend is so excited, but one thing is bothering her. Everyone in the class can tell that Delaney has not been to church very much. She doesn't know anything about the Bible, has hardly heard any of the stories that the others have heard since they were four, and asks silly questions. Some of the boys in the class are starting to laugh every time Delaney raises her hand. Colleen feels bad for her friend but doesn't know what to do about it. What do you think she should do?

Should Colleen . . .

    A. Suggest to Delaney that she may want to join the class for four year olds?
    B. Tell Delaney to stop asking questions in class because she is making everyone think she is really dumb?
    C. Help her friend learn more about the Bible?

 Take a look at Romans 14:1 to see what Paul has to say about those who don't know as much about the Christian faith as you do.

Think of one or two ways that you could help someone you know who is weaker in his or her faith than you. (Maybe you could help a younger brother or sister, or a friend who is new to Sunday school.)

The correct answer is C.

The Perfect Role Model?

Brett's next-door neighbor is one of the coolest kids Brett knows. Christopher is a star football player at the high school. He is in the school service club, and he teaches Sunday school at Brett's church. But what Brett really likes about Christopher is that he always takes time to talk with Brett. Once Christopher even spent an afternoon showing Brett how to throw a football. Brett really looks up to Christopher. It comes as a shock, then, when Brett finds out that Christopher was arrested the other day for speeding and for having beer bottles in his car. Brett can't believe the news. He is very upset and feels let down. What do you think Brett should do?

Should Brett . . .

A. Tell Christopher the next time he sees him what a no-good guy Christopher really is?
B. Pray for Christopher and realize that the only perfect role model is God, who shows us what he is like through his Son, Jesus?
C. Forget about Christopher and look the other way whenever he sees him?

 Look up Ephesians 5:1 to see who should be Brett's role model—and yours.
Ask your parents to tell about a time when someone they looked up to let them down. How did they feel? How did they handle the situation?

The correct answer is B.

Is This Yours?

Brooke has been going to an after-school Bible club led by a teacher at her school. About a dozen kids go, and Brooke has enjoyed getting to know some of the other kids from school who are also Christians. They usually sing a few songs, have a Bible lesson, and do a neat craft. Brooke is learning a lot. She's even thinking about asking a couple of friends to join her. Brooke is a bit late going to the Bible club today. As she hurries through the hall, she drops her books and her Bible goes sliding across the floor. A couple of older boys are passing by at the time. One of them picks up the Bible and says, "Hey, what dork lost the Bible?" The boys start laughing and making jokes. Brooke feels her face getting red and hot. What do you think she should do?

Should Brooke . . .

    A. Ask the boys for her Bible back and continue on?
    B. Pick up the Bible and tell the boys she'll find out who it belongs to?
    C. Look around and say, "Beats me. I never saw it before"?

Read Romans 1:16-17 for help in knowing what Brooke should do.
Role-play the situation above with your mom or dad. What else might be good for Brooke to say to the boys?
Reminder: Don't forget to work on your memory verse for November. (You'll find it on the page just before November 1.)

The correct answer is A.

Changes

Damon has been hanging out with Noel, a boy he knows from church. Damon really didn't know Noel very well before. He is one of the quieter boys in the class and always has the answer to whatever the Sunday school teacher asks. Damon thought Noel was too "churchy" to play with, but he really has enjoyed Noel's company. Damon has discovered a true friend. Since hanging around with Noel, Damon has changed how he feels about the things he used to enjoy doing with some of his wilder friends. This afternoon Damon gets a call from one of those buddies. His friend begins by saying, "Hey, you've got to come by. You won't believe the stuff I've found on the Internet." Damon can just imagine! What do you think he should do?

Should Damon . . .

    A. Ask his old friend to join Noel and him for an afternoon game of hockey?

    B. Tell his friend that surfing the Net makes him seasick?

    C. Tell his old buddy that he will come over when no one else is around to find out what he is doing?

 Check out Colossians 3:8-10 to see what Damon should do. As a Christian you may find yourself changing as you grow in your faith. With your mom or dad, talk about ways you can handle situations like the one above as your attitudes and ideas change because you are growing to be more like Jesus.

The correct answer is A.

Don't Forget Us!

April looks at the ceiling. Although she has been in bed for nearly an hour, she can't fall asleep. She can't stop thinking about her little sister, who is in the hospital with all sorts of tubes connected to her. About a month ago her sister began complaining about pain in her legs that wouldn't go away. After many appointments the doctors discovered that her sister has leukemia. Her grandmother is now living with them to help April's mom and dad. Yesterday her sister began chemotherapy treatment. As April left the hospital today her mom whispered, "Don't forget to pray for your sister." The trouble is that April thinks God has forgotten about them. Why else would these terrible things happen to her sister and her family? What do you think April should do?

Should April . . .

    A. Forget about praying—it's just a waste of time?
    B. Remember that God does love her and her family and will
       take care of them?
    C. Let her parents know how she feels?

 For help in knowing how April should respond, read Hebrews 10:35-36.
When you go through difficult times or when someone you love is in trouble, it's easy to think that God is not around or doesn't care. But read the Bible verse aloud. What is the confidence that we can have in Jesus?

Just One More

The latest craze to hit Hailey's school is the Beanie Weenies—tiny beanbag toys that come in a variety of dogs. Each Beanie Weenie costs about four dollars, and as soon as the newest ones come out, the old ones are gone. Hailey's parents have bought a few of these beanbags for Hailey and her sisters, but now they won't buy any more. "You have enough, and the ones you do have are just lying in your closet!" her mom says every time the girls ask for one. At school today one of Hailey's friends brings in the latest Beanie Weenie. It is an adorable Dalmatian dog. Her friend says that the store had only a few left. If she goes right after school she may still be able to get one. Hailey really, really wants one! What do you think she should do?

Should Hailey . . .

    A. Promise her parents that this will be the last Beanie Weenie she'll ever ask for?
    B. Enjoy her friend's Beanie Weenie and go on with her day?
    C. Hold her breath until her parents give in and buy her one more?

 Look at what John has to say in 1 John 2:15-17 about wanting more things.
Together with your mom or dad, make a list of the "crazes" that have gone through your school in the past year or so. Can your parents remember the fads from when they were in school? Where is all that stuff you collected? Has it been fading away?

The correct answer is B.

The New Girl

The new girl in Kari's class this fall is very unfriendly. Kari's teacher asked Kari to show Mollie around school on the first day. Kari did her best to make Mollie feel at home, but Mollie hardly said a word to her. Mollie never smiles. She never sits with the other girls at lunch, even when they ask her. And she walks by without ever saying hi. Since the beginning of school Kari has really tried to get to know this girl. She always says hello when she sees Mollie. Kari invites her every day to have lunch with her and her friends. But Mollie either says no or just looks the other way. Kari doesn't understand and is hurt by the girl's behavior. She is ready to give up trying to be friendly. What do you think Kari should do?

Should Kari . . .

A. Keep smiling and continue to invite Mollie to have lunch—who knows, someday Mollie just may join Kari and the other girls?
B. Ignore Mollie and see how Mollie likes it?
C. Talk to her teacher about the situation and see if her teacher has some suggestions?

 Read Hebrews 6:11-12 for some help in knowing what Kari should do.
Is there a person like Mollie at your school or at church? Can you think of some reasons why someone might act unfriendly? Role-play with your mom or dad what you might say to someone like that.

The correct answers are A and C.

The Prize

Living as a Christian and growing in faith takes a lot of hard work, practice, and training. In fact, Paul often compares living as a Christian to training as a sports player. In Philippians 3:14 Paul says his goal in life is to keep going until he reaches the prize that Jesus has for him in heaven.

In this maze, help the runner reach the prize. And remember, Jesus has a prize for you, too, in heaven!

I strain to reach the end of the race and receive the prize for which God, through Christ Jesus, is calling us up to heaven.

Philippians 3:14

The Eyewitness

A rumor is going around school that several of the fifth-grade boys are picking on the younger students and taking away their milk money. Devin knows that sometimes these rumors get started and are totally untrue. But today he finds out differently. As he is walking across the playground to school, he sees an older boy talking to a younger boy. He can't see the older boy's face, but he can see the face of the younger boy, and he looks scared! Devin starts walking toward the two boys when he sees the younger boy hand something over to the older boy and then run away as fast as he can. Just then the bell rings, and Devin has to hurry to class. Devin thinks he ought to do something, but he doesn't know what it is. What do you think Devin should do?

Should Devin . . .

> A. Report to his teacher right away what he saw happen?
> B. Figure the younger boy's parents ought to take care of the situation?
> C. Get everyone excited by going around and telling everyone that the rumors are true?

 Read Ephesians 5:12 for some good advice on what Devin should do.
Read the Bible verse aloud. Name two or three things you should do when you see something wrong going on.

The correct answer is A.

17

November

Saturday Plans

Daniel and his friends are planning to get together over the weekend, but they're not sure what to do! One friend suggests they play touch football in the park, but the only football they have among them is flat. Another suggests a game of tag, but most aren't interested. Daniel suggests that they go ice fishing on the pond. That gets a big response from everyone except Calvin. "My mom won't let me go near the pond. She's afraid I'll get out on thin ice," Calvin says.

Justin jumps in, "You don't have to tell her. We'll be back before she even misses you. We'll test the ice to see if it's thick enough."

Calvin is Daniel's best friend, and Daniel doesn't want Calvin to get into trouble because of his idea. What do you think Daniel should do?

Should Daniel . . .

    A. Let Calvin decide what he wants to do?
    B. Suggest that the guys do something else that Calvin can do?
    C. Go plead with Calvin's mom to let him go fishing with the guys?

 Look up 1 Corinthians 10:23-24 for help in knowing what Daniel should do.
In the Bible verse above, Paul tells us to be thoughtful of others. Have your mom or dad help you think of ways to be thoughtful of your friends.

The correct answer is B.

Can I Play?

Clark and his friends are getting together to play basketball at the school playground. Clark and another boy are picked as team captains, and they choose teams. Clark is short one player, but he also has some of the better players on his team. He figures even with one less player they ought to beat the other team. The boys are in the middle of a tight game when they decide to take a breather. As they are resting, a boy who has been watching the game comes up to Clark. "Hey, can I play? You're down one player; I can help you guys out," the boy says. Clark looks the boy over. He's wearing glasses, is on the short side, and doesn't look very athletic. Clark is not sure he wants the boy on his team. What do you think he should do?

Should Clark . . .

    A. Arrange for a trade with the other team and let the boy play for the other guys?
    B. Give the boy a tryout; if he can make three baskets in a row, he's on?
    C. Let the boy play on his team?

 Read 1 Samuel 16:7 to see what God has to say about judging people based on the way they look.
Discuss with your mom or dad what might happen if you judge someone based on the way that person looks. What kinds of things about that person might you not be able to see?

The correct answer is C.

No One Likes Me

Cassie is bored. She has finished all her homework and wants to go outside and play for a while. She calls her best friend to see if she can come over, but her friend is already over at someone else's house. Cassie calls another friend, but that friend can't make it because she has piano lessons. Cassie goes through her whole list of friends but can't find one friend who can play. Even Cassie's brother (the one she plays with only when she can't find anyone else) has a friend over and doesn't want her to play with them! Cassie can't get the dog to come out and play either. The more she thinks about her problem, the more lonely and sad she feels. Cassie is beginning to think that no one likes her anymore. What do you think she should do?

Should Cassie . . .

  A. Go eat some worms because no one likes her?
  B. Think about all the good things she does have going for her?
  C. Try to figure out why it seems like all her friends don't like her anymore?

 Read Psalm 42:5 to see how Cassie should respond to her situation.
Think about a time when you were sad or felt as if no one liked you. What made you feel more sad? What made you feel better?
Reminder: Don't forget to say your memory verse for November. (You'll find it on the page just before November 1.)

The correct answer is B.

The Protection Plan

Conan really needs help—big time. Some boys at school think it's fun to pick on him. Whenever they see Conan, they make fun of him and toss his backpack around. Conan knows he ought to tell his teacher or his parents, but he doesn't like to talk about it. The boys start at it again while Conan is walking home. Suddenly they take off. Conan looks around and sees Kyle coming up behind him. Kyle is big and tough, and no one messes around with Kyle. "Are those guys giving you a hard time?" Kyle asks. "Why don't you let me and my friends take care of them for you? They won't bother you after we get through with them." Conan is not so sure he wants to know what Kyle means by "taking care of them." What do you think Conan should do?

Should Conan . . .

   A. Tell Kyle no thanks, then talk to his parents about what's happening and pray together about it?
   B. Tell Kyle that if he wants to "take care of" the mean guys, he can go ahead, but ask Kyle not to tell him about it?
   C. Hire Kyle as his bodyguard?

 Check out Psalm 146:3 for help in knowing what Conan should do.
What is wrong with wanting someone bigger than you, or smarter than you, to take care of a problem for you? Where can you go for help when you have a problem?

The correct answer is A.

Too Tough for God?

It's the Thanksgiving season, but Claudia feels anything but thankful. Her parents just got a divorce, so Claudia lives with her mom and sister in a small townhouse. Claudia is in a new school. She misses her old friends and her old school. She misses her dad, too. On Thanksgiving Day, when all her friends' families will be *together,* her family will be celebrating in two different places. She is having dinner with her dad and his family, and dessert with her mom and her family. More than anything Claudia wants her family to be like they once were. The only person Claudia feels she can talk to is Mr. Lazor, her Sunday school teacher, but he just tells Claudia to pray about her problem. Claudia doesn't think even God can fix the mess her family is in. What do you think she should do?

Should Claudia . . .

A. Remember that God is powerful and can be trusted to take care of her and her family, too?
B. Tell her mom and her dad that she is skipping Thanksgiving this year because she is not feeling too thankful?
C. Accept that she will be unhappy the rest of her life?

 Check out Matthew 8:23-27 to see the awesome power of God, who is in control of the storms of nature and of our lives.
What situations in your life do you tend to think are too tough for God? Share them with your mom or dad. Then come up with a list of things that God has done that show his love and power.

The correct answer is A.

Try, Try Again

For her birthday last summer Joy received a brand new pair of Rollerblades. She really wanted a pair so she could Rollerblade to the park with her friends. Summer is long gone, and Joy's Rollerblades have been sitting in the box for some time. The last time she had them on Joy went rolling down the driveway, across the street, and right into a big bush! Joy's knees healed quickly, but now it is several months later and Joy still is afraid to try Rollerblading again. On a warm, sunny Saturday her mom suggests that Joy give the Rollerblades one more try. "You can ride a bike, and you can ice skate. There's no reason why you can't do this," her mom tells her. Joy really wants to go Rollerblading, but she is afraid of falling again and looking dumb. What do you think she should do?

Should Joy . . .

A. Tell her mom it's no use, so she might as well give the Rollerblades away?
B. Wear a mask so no one will recognize her if she falls down again?
C. Ask a friend who is really good at Rollerblading to help her, and try again?

 Look up Joshua 7:1-5 and Joshua 8:1 to see what Joshua did after failing the first time.
When you fail at something, what makes you afraid to try again? Talk with your mom or dad about ways to overcome those fears.

The correct answer is C.

The Experiment

Melanie loves science. She loves learning about why the world operates the way it does. And she likes to do experiments to see how things work. Melanie has a beginner's chemistry set. She has done a few experiments that were in the kit. Now Melanie wants to come up with her own experiment. Her dad offers to help her come up with an idea, but Melanie thinks she can do this on her own. Melanie is down in the basement working on her experiment. She puts one chemical into a dish with another one, and a huge cloud of stinky smoke fills the room. What do you think Melanie should do?

Should Melanie . . .

   A. Figure that this is a good time to get her dad's help?
   B. Start a fan and try to blow the smoke out the basement door?
   C. Tell herself she doesn't need to worry about the smoke—this is part of her experiment?

 Look up Proverbs 28:26 to see what Melanie should do. Think of a time when you tried to do something on your own without getting any advice or help from your mom or dad. What happened? What advice would you give to Melanie (or yourself)? How does that apply to listening to God?

The correct answer is A.

Stolen Sweets

Gina's teacher hands out candies as rewards. Students can earn candies for turning in their homework on time, for helping out another classmate with something, or for good behavior. Everyone loves getting candies. Today, though, Gina's teacher looks very upset. After school yesterday someone took some candy from Mr. Shaw's desk. No more rewards will be given until someone admits to taking the candy. At lunch Gina and her friends are talking about who could have taken the candy. They decide it must be the janitor. Later Gina's friend Marlee grabs her. "Look," she says. "You'll never guess what I have— and you can have some if you don't tell that I took it." Inside Marlee's backpack is a bunch of candy like the kind Mr. Shaw hands out. What do you think Gina should do?

Should Gina . . .

    A. Gently but firmly tell Marlee that she has to return the candy?
    B. Scream, "Candy thief!" and get someone to lock the doors so Marlee can't get away?
    C. Go to a quiet corner and eat some candy with Marlee, looking around often to be sure no one sees her?

 For help in knowing what Gina should do, read Galatians 6:1.
Role-play the situation above with your mom or dad. What would you tell Marlee to do?

Dive In

Ever since Rod began to walk, he has been going to his sisters' swim meets. When he was little he mostly ate candy and played with some other younger kids. He never really watched to see what his sisters were doing. Now Rod is old enough to join the swim team himself. His dad brings it up at dinner tonight. "So, Rod, are you going to join your sisters on the team this year? I think you're ready!"

One of his sisters says, "You'll love it. It's a lot of fun." Rod is not so sure. He only knows how to do the freestyle, and he's never swum the entire length of the pool. What if he can't make it across? Besides, everyone talks about how hard you have to work to be on the team. The more Rod thinks about it, the less he thinks it's a good idea. What do you think he should do?

Should Rod . . .

    A. Come up with a list of twenty reasons why he should not join the swim team?
    B. Tell his dad swimming is not his thing?
    C. Talk about his fears, but try it and see for himself what swim team is really all about?

 Read Numbers 13:25-28, 30 to see how most of the Israelites looked at the bad things that could happen instead of the good things.
When you try something for the first time, are you more like the Israelites (and Rod), or are you more like Caleb? Talk with your mom or dad about some times when you should ask God to help you be more like Caleb.

The correct answer is C.

The Math Problem

Judah's teacher this year expects a lot more from the kids than last year's teacher did. Judah did okay in math last year, but this year he is getting very poor grades. Today a letter from Judah's teacher arrives explaining to his parents that he will need a math tutor to get the math grades he was getting last year. It will mean working harder than he has before. And Judah will get extra homework each night. It definitely will not be as easy. Judah's parents ask him if he will work with a tutor. They won't give him this opportunity unless he promises to do the work needed to bring his grades back up. What do you think Judah should do?

Should Judah . . .

A. Take the easy way and not worry about getting good grades in math?
B. Go for it, and do the best he can?
C. Try it—if he doesn't like the tutor, drop out?

 Look up Romans 5:3-5 for some help in knowing how to handle the difficulties and trials we encounter in our lives. Rejoice when you run into problems or trials? Sounds strange, doesn't it? Read the Bible verses aloud, then discuss what there is to rejoice about when you have problems.

The correct answer is B.

Grow Up—Now!

Roxanne has an older brother and an older sister, both of whom are in high school. She thinks they are way cool, much cooler than any of her friends. She sees her brother drive his friends to the drive-thru for burgers. She watches her sister get dressed up and go to parties. And she sees that they both get to stay up much later than she does. Roxanne thinks it is so dumb to hang out with totally uncool kids who are her age. She can hardly wait until she can drive and go out with her friends and wear perfume and do all that great stuff. More than anything Roxanne wants to be as cool as her brother and sister are. Some days Roxanne thinks she can't stand one more day in elementary school. What do you think she should do?

Should Roxanne . . .

A. Put on her sister's clothes and makeup so at least she can look cool?
B. Hang out only with her sister and brother (if they let her)?
C. Accept her age, knowing in time she will be just as grown up as her brother and sister are now?

 Read some wise words from Solomon by looking up Ecclesiastes 3:1.
With your mom or dad, make a list of three things that you think will be cool about growing up. Now make a list of three things that are cool about being your own age. Celebrate your age!

The Fear Fighter

Madison's parents are going out for the evening, but that's okay because one of her favorite baby-sitters is coming over. Madison loves having Keely come because they always play all sorts of games, and Keely tells good stories. Tonight as the girls are finishing their dinner, they hear thunder. A few seconds later a big flash of lightning lights up the backyard. A minute later the sky lets loose with buckets of rain. The girls huddle together, and Keely begins to tell Madison about the time it rained for a day and a half. Streets and basements were flooded. The power went out. And no one could get anywhere in town. Madison doesn't want to admit it, but Keely's stories are scaring her. It sure is raining hard, and it sure doesn't seem like it's going to stop. What do you think Madison should do?

Should Madison . . .

A. Run out the door yelling, "Flood warning, flood warning"?
B. Find her swimsuit—she needs to be ready for a flood?
C. Remember who can help her fight her fears?

 Check out Psalm 56:3-4 for help in knowing what Madison should do.
Share with your mom or dad (and let them share too) the things that frighten you. Print this part of Psalm 56:4 on poster board and hang it up as a reminder of who can help you fight your fears: "I trust in God, so why should I be afraid?"

The correct answer is C.

Split Personality

André has two sets of friends—his friends at church and the group of kids he hangs out with in the neighborhood. When he's with his church friends, he always has a good time and he feels good about being with them. André loves the Wednesday night gatherings and Sunday school. He has no trouble talking about God or his faith with his church friends. When he's with his friends from the neighborhood, however, he never mentions that he even goes to church. Today he is over at Peyton's house. A bunch of guys are sitting around Peyton's room when Peyton turns on the radio and says, "Hey, listen to this." André knows right away that this is the D.J. who likes to shock his listeners with bad words and gross jokes. André also knows that this is not the type of radio program he should be listening to. What do you think he should do?

Should André . . .

A. Start coughing and say he's getting a cold and has to go home?
B. Say he doesn't want to listen to this guy, so could they please do something else?
C. Figure it won't hurt him to listen this once?

 Read Hosea 7:8 and listen to the strong warning God gives us about hanging out with the wrong crowd.

30

Review Time!

List three things you learned this month about growing as a Christian.

1.

2.

3.

Bonus

Make a list of three things you plan to do in the next year to help you grow in your faith.

1.

2.

3.

Say your memory verse to an older Christian you know.

Thankfulness & Contentment

For what are you thankful? A loving family and friends? A comfortable house, plenty to eat, and clothes to wear? Your pets? School? How about troubles, or suffering? It's easy to be thankful when things are going your way. But how about when things get hard, or when you or a family member get sick?

Paul teaches us in 1 Thessalonians 5:18, "No matter what happens, always be thankful, for this is God's will for you who belong to Christ Jesus." This doesn't mean that we need to thank God for all the bad things that happen to us. But we can thank God that he is with us in *everything* that happens to us. We can be thankful that God will see us through the bad times and that he will accomplish good in everything.

Part of developing a thankful attitude is learning to be content— to be satisfied with what God has given us and whom he has created us to be. We aren't all the same, but we can be thankful and content for the special gifts and abilities that God has given to each of us. We can learn to be content in any situation when we keep our focus on God and his gifts and not on our circumstances and what we don't have.

As you work through this month's *Sticky Situations,* think about everything you have to be thankful for. Think of how you can learn how to get along happily whether you have a little or a lot.

Memory Verse: No matter what happens, always be thankful, for this is God's will for you who belong to Christ Jesus.
1 Thessalonians 5:18

Got to Have It!

Melinda has been flipping through all the Christmas ads to see what's in this year. She and her friends decide that they each absolutely have to have one of the new neon-colored fleece vests. But they can't wait until Christmas. They want to get their vests this weekend. Melinda talks to her mom after dinner about going out to get a vest. "Melinda, I don't think you *need* a fleece vest right now," her mom tells her. "Maybe later—that might be one of your Christmas presents." Melinda stomps away. She just *has* to have a fleece vest before next Monday. What do you think Melinda should do?

Should Melinda . . .

A. Keep nagging her mom for a fleece vest until her mom gives in?
B. Tell her mom that if her mom really loves her she'll buy the vest for her?
C. Cool down and realize that she'll get along without the fleece vest?

 Find out what Melinda should do by reading 1 Timothy 6:6-8.
Make a list with your mom or dad of the things that you really *need* to be content. Talk about how *needs* differ from *wants*.

Saving Up

Pablo's parents have been teaching him how important it is to save his money and not run right out to spend it. He has saved all the money he's been getting for his birthday and other occasions. Now he wants to buy himself a new computer. It's the first time Pablo has saved his money for anything, and he is being very careful about spending it. Yesterday his Sunday school teacher explained that the church is raising money for a family who lost everything in a terrible fire. Pablo knows the family and the kids, and he really wants to help out. But if he gives some of his money to the family, he might not have enough left to buy the computer he wants. What do you think Pablo should do?

Should Pablo . . .

- A. Be happy to give a nice gift of money to help out the family and buy a new computer later?
- B. Give some money to the family after he has saved enough for the computer because then he'll know he has enough?
- C. Scrape up a few old toys and some clothes he doesn't need anymore and give them to the family?

 Read 2 Corinthians 9:7-10 for help in knowing what Pablo should do.
Think of what you have to share (not just money). What happens when you try to keep those things for yourself and not share with others? What happens when you do share?

The Brand-New Bike

Jacob's best friend just got a brand-new twenty-one-speed bike. It is one of the coolest bikes Jacob has ever seen. His friend brings it over and lets Jacob take it for a spin. It is even better than Jacob imagined. He can almost fly down the street with all the gears he has to use. It's not at all like the clunker Jacob has to ride. That old thing (a hand-me-down from his older brother) has only three gears and one hand brake, and it's rusting in certain spots. Sure, the bike gets him where he wants to go, but it doesn't get him there fast. And Jacob doesn't look as cool riding it as his friend does riding his shiny new bike. After his friend leaves, Jacob looks at his old rusty bike. It looks so . . . old and so . . . rusty. What do you think Jacob should do?

Should Jacob . . .

A. Get some paint and try to make everyone think his bike is newer than it is?
B. Be content with the bike he has?
C. Give his bike a kick and decide he's walking from now on so he doesn't have to be seen on that old thing?

 Check out Hebrews 13:5 to see what Jacob's attitude should be toward what he has.
Think of a time when a friend got something new and you didn't. How did it make you feel? Talk with your family about some ways to fight those "got-to-have-it" feelings.

The correct answer is B.

The Class Helper

Every week Courtney's teacher selects one student to be her helper for the week. The helper gets to run errands for the teacher, take the attendance, pass out all the papers, and do anything extra the teacher needs done. *Everyone* wants to be the helper. The teacher usually picks a student who has worked hard, has a good attitude, and has been helpful to other class-mates. Courtney really has tried to do all those things this past week. Okay, so she could have helped others out a bit more, but she feels she has a good chance of being named the helper this week. She is really upset when she finds out that a shy girl named Eva is selected. Courtney has never seen Eva helping anyone out. What do you think Courtney should do?

Should Courtney . . .

- A. Quietly point out to the teacher that Eva really didn't help anyone during the last week?
- B. Every time Eva does something, say loudly, "I can do that better than her"?
- C. Be content with waiting for her turn to be the class helper and be glad for Eva?

 Look up James 3:16 to see what Courtney should do. Ask your mom or dad to tell about a time when they were passed over for a position they wanted. How did they handle that situation?

The Unwanted Present

Jorie can hardly wait! Her neighbor, Ms. Alexandra, went to a big discount art and craft store today. She promised to bring Jorie a new art set. Jorie told Ms. Alexandra just which one she wants. She saw it in a catalogue. It has tubes of oil paints, several brushes, a dozen light-colored chalks, and thirty-six colored pencils. She pointed it out to Ms. Alexandra so Ms. Alexandra would know how to find the right set. Jorie rushes her family through dinner and then the grand moment arrives. She hears a knock on the door. It's Ms. Alexandra with a box under her arm! She hands it to Jorie with a smile. Jorie opens it and sees an art set—but not the one she wants. It only has watercolor paints, one brush, eight light-colored chalks, and twenty-four colored pencils. What do you think Jorie should do?

Should Jorie . . .

A. Let Ms. Alexandra know that this is not the art set she wants?
B. Be thankful for the gift Ms. Alexandra gave her?
C. Grumble and ask, "How can I color anything with only twenty-four colored pencils?"

 Take a look at Numbers 11:4-6 to learn about some other people who were unhappy about what they got.
Why were the Israelites complaining? The Bible tells us that Moses was upset with the people. God was too. Why should they have been thankful?

The correct answer is B.

Good Enough for Me

Glenn lives in a nice, comfortable house in one of the older sections in his town. It's not the biggest house in the area. In fact, most of his friends live in another, newer neighborhood where the houses are all bigger, with three-car garages and fancy front entrances. He shares a room with his brother, which is okay at times, and sometimes it's not. He doesn't have his own personal computer in his room like many of his friends, and he doesn't have the latest video game equipment. His family doesn't have a big-screen TV, and he doubts if they ever will get one. His friends can't seem to understand how he can live without all those "necessary" things. In fact, they feel sorry for "poor" Glenn. How do you think he should respond?

Should Glenn . . .

    A. Tell his friends that he has everything he needs—and more?
    B. Start complaining to his parents about their lack of stuff?
    C. Tell his friends that he may be poor, but at least he isn't a snob?

 For help in knowing how Glenn should respond, read 2 Peter 1:3-4.
Is your situation like Glenn's or like his friends'? Who gives you what you need? How should that make you feel?
Talk with your mom or dad about some of the wonderful promises that you have in Jesus.

The correct answer is A.

Soccer Camp

Noah and his friend Terry have been on the same soccer team since first grade. Both boys have become very good soccer players, especially Noah. The two have been invited to attend a special camp that prepares them for more competitive play. After practice Terry asks Noah if he plans to go to the camp. Noah tells Terry that he and his parents have decided against it this year. Terry can't believe it. "What do you mean you're not going? If you don't go to the camp, you probably won't make the junior traveling team next year. And if you don't make that, forget about playing in high school. Everyone on the high school team goes to that camp," Terry explains. "You are making a big mistake." What do you think Noah should say?

Should Noah . . .

A. Run home and tell his parents they are making a big mistake?
B. Not worry about what Terry and the others do—everyone doesn't need to have the same goals?
C. Tell Terry he plans to practice twice as hard as the boys at camp so he can keep up with everyone?

 For help in knowing what Noah should do, read Psalm 131. Read this psalm aloud. According to the writer, should we spend all our time trying to become better than everyone else? Or should we not be so proud? Should we trust in ourselves or in the Lord?

The correct answer is B.

The Family Party

Tomorrow is the Norton family's Christmas gathering. They have it early every year so Owen's grandparents can leave for Florida. This year it is at Owen's house. About thirty of his aunts, uncles, cousins, and, of course, his grandparents will be coming. Owen knows just what's going to happen. His great-aunt will pinch both his cheeks and say how big he has grown. His younger cousins will race down to the basement and tear apart every game he owns. (Owen also will have to clean it up later.) His grandparents will tell the same old stories he has heard every year. Then, at the end of the day, Owen will have to give up his bed and sleep with his older brother, who snores. Sound like fun? Not to Owen. What do you think he should do?

Should Owen . . .

    A. Be thankful for the time his family has together and enjoy it?
    B. Hide all his games so his cousins can't play with them?
    C. Go up to his great-aunt and pinch her cheeks and say, "My, how big you've grown"?

 Look up Ecclesiastes 5:18-20 to see what Owen's attitude should be.
Even though Christmas is a wonderful time, are there some family activities you would rather skip? What chores would you rather not do? Take some advice from wise Solomon and see if it doesn't help change your attitude!

The New Teacher

Sonia and her best friend, Faye, are both in Mrs. Hamilton's class. She is the best teacher Sonia and Faye have ever had. But many new families have been moving into the neighborhood. It seems as if they all have kids in third grade! The class has become so big that the school is going to bring in an extra teacher. There will now be two third grades. Today the class lists will be posted at the school. A large crowd has gathered by the front doors. It's hard for Sonia to see, but she and Faye manage to squeeze up front. Faye shouts happily, "I'm staying with Mrs. Hamilton!" Sonia looks at the lists and sees that her name is on the list for the new class with Miss Fish! Sonia has never heard of the new teacher before. And what kind of name is Fish? What do you think Sonia should do?

Should Sonia . . .

A. Tell the principal there's been a mistake because her name is not on the right list?
B. Make the best of her school year and give Miss Fish a chance?
C. Come to school wearing swim flippers to make Miss Fish feel at home?

Read Philippians 4:12-13 for help in knowing what Sonia should do.
When things don't go your way, how do you respond? According to the Bible verse, what do you think is the secret of getting along in any situation? Discuss with your mom or dad ways you can do that.

The correct answer is B.

Picture Perfect

Jaimee's next-door neighbor is, in two words, picture perfect. She has shoulder-length wavy hair, not too curly, not too straight. She has a beautiful smile and a cute little nose. Every morning she leaves the house looking as though she just walked out of a fashion magazine. Everything she wears matches, including her socks! Jaimee, on the other hand, has hair that does its own thing every morning. Jaimee likes to roll around and play with the dog before school. So when she leaves the house, her clothes have dog hair all over them and she looks like, well, like she's been rolling around on the floor with the dog. Jaimee knows she'll never be "picture perfect" like her neighbor. What do you think Jaimee should do?

Should Jaimee . . .

  A. Let the dog out each morning to "say hello" to her neighbor?
  B. Realize she doesn't have to be picture perfect?
  C. Ask her neighbor if she'll give her a few fashion tips?

 For help in knowing how Jaimee should respond, read Exodus 20:17.
Coveting goes beyond wishing you had what others have. It also includes envy—being upset about what you don't have. Share with your mom or dad some things your friends or family members have that you are envious of. Talk about ways to fight envy with thankfulness for who you are and what you have.

The correct answer is B.

Sick Days

Erica was in the hospital for nearly a month. At first the doctors weren't sure what was wrong with her. They finally learned that she had picked up an unusual virus. Erica was very sick, but she is better now. While she was in the hospital, Erica received cards from her friends at school and at church. Her room was filled with flowers and stuffed animals that people had sent to cheer her up. Most of all, Erica knew that many, many people at her church were praying for her to get better. Today she is finally going home. When her dad turns in to the driveway and she is finally home, her heart jumps. She gets out of the car and breathes in deeply. What do you think Erica should do first?

Should Erica . . .

    A. Get on the phone and call her friends to catch up on the news?
    B. Unpack her suitcase and arrange all her new stuffed animals?
    C. Say a quiet prayer of thanks to God for healing her?

 Take a look at Numbers 31:48-50 to see what the Israelite military officers did first after realizing they had not lost one soldier in battle.
Think of a time when God helped you or one of your family members through a difficult time. Say a prayer of thanks right now to God for being with you and your family.
Reminder: Don't forget to work on your memory verse for December. (You'll find it on the page just before December 1.)

Rock 'n Roll Church

Gabriel has been wanting Ross to come to his church for some time. "You're going to love it," Gabriel says. "We've got a worship band that really rocks." Ross is used to a more quiet church service with an organ, a choir, and old hymns. He likes his service just fine, but he agrees to go with Gabriel just this once. Ross is not sure what to expect, but he doesn't really like the band. It's loud, and like Gabriel told him, it's really rockin'. In fact, the whole church is rockin'. The people are clapping and moving to the music. Gabriel tells Ross to "get into the music." Ross feels a bit silly. He's never clapped his hands in a church service before. What do you think Ross should do?

Should Ross . . .

    A. Worship in whatever way feels right to him and be thankful for the many different ways people worship God?
    B. Tell Gabriel, "Sorry, but this isn't a real church"?
    C. Just sit still and stare at the woman in front of him who really looks weird?

 Read 1 Chronicles 15:28-29 to see how King David worshiped God—and what his wife, Michal, thought about it.
With your mom or dad, think of all the different ways to worship God and show thankfulness to him. Talk about what should be the focus of worship. Is it *how* we worship or *who* we worship that's important?

Worship Time

This is one of those days when it just feels good to be alive. The sky is a brilliant blue, the sun is shining, and it's not too cold. Christmas is coming, and smiles cover people's faces as they get ready for the holidays. Lydia is walking home from her friend's house and feeling very happy. Her mom recently had a baby, and he's been a lot of fun—even though he seems to need new diapers all the time! Her grandparents have moved into a house close by, so they get to see each other more. Lydia really likes school this year. And she is beginning to take piano lessons, which she loves. Even her older brother has been nice to her lately. Lydia feels she is going to burst with joy. What she really wants to do is shout, "Thank you, God!" What do you think she should do?

Should Lydia . . .

A. Store up all those feelings and save them for church on Sunday?
B. Go ahead and shout—it's good to thank God anytime and anyplace?
C. Wait until she gets to her room and write down a prayer of thanks to God for all he has done?

 Read Psalm 92:1-4 to see how one psalm writer thanked God.
With your mom or dad, write down or draw pictures of some things for which you are thankful. Remember that you can say thanks to God at any time, not just on Sunday.

The correct answers are B and C.

Thanks!

The local science center is featuring a terrific new bug exhibit. Raisa's best friend, Griffin, and his family ask Raisa to go with them to see the exhibit. The kids have a great time. There are a lot of cool bugs to check out. The kids even get to hold one of the biggest millipedes they have ever seen! It's totally gross and totally awesome. The kids spend a couple of hours at the museum taking in everything. Afterward Griffin's parents take them to get some ice cream—the perfect ending to a great day. Griffin's parents drop off Raisa at her home. Raisa really has enjoyed herself this afternoon, but she doesn't know how to let Griffin and his family know. She doesn't know how to thank them. What do you think she should do?

Should Raisa . . .

> A. Jump out of the car, run to her front door, and yell, "See ya later"?
> B. Offer to take Griffin to the movies the following afternoon?
> C. Just tell Griffin's family, "Thank you for the great afternoon"?

 For help in knowing what Raisa should do, read Luke 17:11-16.
God doesn't *order* us to thank him. People who do things for us don't do that either. But God is pleased (and so are others) when we do remember! Who do you need to thank today? Do it now!

Praise Him

Read Psalm 145 aloud with your mom or dad. Then unscramble some qualities of God that are worthy of our praise and thanksgiving. Remember to say thanks to God today!

Great is the Lord! He is most worthy of praise!
His greatness is beyond discovery!

Psalm 145:3

Word Bank

compassion   goodness   greatness   kindness   power

1. S T N S A G E R E _ _ _ _ _ _ _ _ _
(verse 3)

2. N O D S E O G S _ _ _ _ _ _ _ _
(verse 7)

3. S O A N I P S M O C _ _ _ _ _ _ _ _ _ _
(verse 9)

4. W E P R O _ _ _ _ _
(verse 6 (NIV) or 11 (NLT))

5. N E S D N I K S _ _ _ _ _ _ _ _
(verse 17)

The Piano Players

December

Isabella and Rosie both take piano lessons from their choir director at church. Rosie has her lesson right after Isabella, so she gets to hear Isabella play every week. It's clear that Isabella is going to be a very good piano player. She already has passed Rosie in their music book and is playing more difficult pieces than Rosie can play. Rosie still struggles just to make sure her fingers are on the right keys and going in the right direction! It's no surprise when the choir director asks Isabella to play a song for the Sunday school Christmas program. As Isabella plays her song, one of Rosie's friends leans over to her and says, "Boy, she is really good." How do you think Rosie should respond?

Should Rosie . . .

A. Say, "Oh, she's okay"?
B. Say, "I'm going to play as well as she does someday—we take from the same teacher"?
C. Agree with her friend and thank Isabella later for sharing her gift of music?

 Check out Romans 12:6-8 for help in knowing how Rosie should respond.
God has given each one of us different gifts to use for him. When you see someone using his or her gift well, remember to say thanks! Tell God thank you for the different gifts he has given you and your friends.

The correct answer is C.

The Big Help

Mikhail is not very good at school. He doesn't do well in reading, and he struggles in math. Mikhail dreads going to school, except for one thing—art. Mikhail has a real talent for drawing and a good eye for color. His art teacher, Mrs. Wood, is helping Mikhail develop that talent. She has helped him to try other art forms, like computer graphics. By doing the things Mrs. Wood suggests, Mikhail has really become more sure of himself. He is even starting to work hard in his other subjects and is having a good time doing it. Mikhail owes a lot to Mrs. Wood, but he doesn't know just how to tell her thank you without looking dopey. What do you think he should do?

Should Mikhail . . .

A. Assume that Mrs. Wood must know how glad he is for her help?
B. Create a piece of art for Mrs. Wood and give it to her as his way of saying thanks?
C. Run by the art room and shout, "Thank you!" as he goes by?

 Read 1 Thessalonians 5:12-13 to see the importance of honoring those who work so hard for us.
How can you honor the leaders in your life—your teachers, pastors, Sunday school teachers, parents? One way is to tell them thanks. Another way is to show them thanks by doing something for them. Thank one today!

The Right Attitude

Hannah loves to make things from clay. She is very excited because her school just bought a kiln for the art room, so now the art classes can do ceramics. To give the children experience with ceramics, the school is planning to offer a beginners' class during the after-school program. The class will start at the beginning of the new year. The art teacher knows that a large number of students will want to sign up for the class, so she tells her students to get their names in early. Hannah waits just a day to get her form in. But it is one day too long. Hannah doesn't get in the ceramics class. In fact, she doesn't even get her second choice. She gets her third choice, "Book Cooks," which her mom made her sign up for just in case. What do you think Hannah should do?

Should Hannah . . .

    A. Tell her mom the only program she wants to do is ceramics—
       and that's her final answer?
    B. Go to Book Cooks—with a bad attitude?
    C. Adjust her attitude and have fun?

 Read Proverbs 15:15 for some hints on making an attitude adjustment.
You can't always choose what happens to you, but you can choose your attitude! With your family, tell about times when you've had good attitudes and times when you've had bad attitudes. Are you happiest when you have a bad attitude or when you're thankful for everything?

The correct answer is C.

Thanks, Friend!

A while before Christmas, Gary gets very sick with the flu. He has to be out of school for about two weeks. Several of his friends come to visit him once Gary has gotten over the worst of the flu, but one friend keeps coming and spending a lot of time with him. Julian comes every day and spends at least an hour telling Gary what's going on in school. He brings Gary his schoolwork each day, and when the class has its Christmas party, Julian saves Gary some of the cookies the class made. Julian really has helped Gary keep his mind off all the things he is missing and has helped cheer Gary up. Gary feels he ought to do something for Julian. But he has no idea what it should be. What do you think he should do?

Should Gary . . .

    A. Send Julian a card, thanking him for being a good friend?
    B. Next time he sees Julian in school, give him a punch on the arm and say, "Hey, bud"?
    C. Say nothing to Julian—he must know that Gary is thankful?

 Look up 1 Thessalonians 3:9 for some help in knowing how Gary should respond.
How do you let your friends know that you appreciate them? Do you thank God for your friends? If not, tell God thank you right now for the friends that you have.

Making a List

Cassie can't believe what her friends expect to get for Christmas. One girl says she collects all the Christmas catalogues that come into the house and circles everything she wants. That way, she says, there are no mistakes and no unwanted surprises on Christmas. Another friend pulls out a three-page list of "gift suggestions" listed alphabetically. (Her secret? Her mother's secretary types it up for her every Christmas.) The girls look at Cassie. "So, how do you do your list?" the girls want to know. Cassie doesn't know what to tell them. At her house, gift giving is not a big deal. No one at her house even makes lists! Everyone usually pulls a name from a bag and gets that person several small presents. What do you think Cassie should say?

Should Cassie . . .

A. Tell her friends that she thinks list-making is greedy?
B. Say she likes surprises?
C. Nicely explain to her friends that Christmas is not just about getting but also about giving?

 For help in knowing what Cassie should do, take a look at Proverbs 30:8-9 to read about a proper attitude about getting more stuff.
Talk with your mom or dad about why having a lot of stuff is not necessarily a good thing. Try to include on your list of people to buy gifts for, someone who can't give a gift back to you.

The correct answers are B and C.

Christmas Break

Today is the last day of school before Christmas break. Everyone is excited about getting out of school and about getting ready for Christmas. But Bella seems more excited than anyone. At lunch Addy asks her what is going on. "I can't wait to show you. My parents gave us our Christmas present early. Our entire family is going on a cruise! We leave tomorrow and will spend Christmas on the boat. Look at these pictures!" Bella shows Addy what the ship looks like, the three different pools it has, and all the activities available for kids. Addy and her family are staying home and doing what they do every Christmas—going to their grandma's house to eat turkey. What do you think Addy should say?

Should Addy . . .

    A. Say, "Well, next year we're going to the beach for two weeks, and it's going to be just great"?

    B. Say, "I could never go on a cruise—I get seasick just looking at these pictures"?

    C. Tell Bella what an awesome time she'll have and ask her to send a postcard?

Take a look at Luke 1:42-43 to see what Elizabeth said when she learned that Mary's son would be greater than her own child.

How do you handle it when you have a hard time being happy for someone else? Talk with your mom or dad about someone you can be happy for this Christmas season.

The correct answer is C.

What Now?

Lina finally understands God's gift to her! Throughout the year, Lina's Sunday school teacher has been talking about the gift of salvation. She has explained that God sent Jesus, his only Son, to come to earth as a baby, to grow up, and to die on the cross. He took the blame for our sins so that all who believe in him will be forgiven and live with him in heaven forever. The other day, with her mom's help, Lina asked Jesus to be her Lord and Savior. Lina couldn't wait until Sunday to tell her teacher. When she sees Mrs. McCall, she runs up and tells her the good news. "Lina, that is wonderful!" Mrs. McCall exclaims. "So what do you plan to do now?" Lina looks at her Sunday school teacher in surprise. What does she mean? Lina didn't know she needed to do something *more*. What do you think she should do?

Should Lina . . .

   A. Show her thankfulness for what God has done for her by helping others?
   B. Run right out and tell someone the Good News about Jesus?
   C. Keep her faith locked inside and not talk about it so she won't lose it?

Take a look at Ephesians 2:8-10 for help in knowing what Lina should do.

Salvation is a gift—it is not something we can earn. But when someone gives you a gift, what do you usually say? Think of ways to thank God for the great gift of his Son, Jesus.

Reminder: Don't forget to say your memory verse for December. (You'll find it on the page just before December 1.)

The correct answers are A and B.

Storm Clouds

Ron and his family have been extra busy before Christmas. There have been shopping trips, days set aside for baking, Christmas programs, and parties. Now Ron and his family are getting ready to leave for their grandparents' house. As they pack, the first snowflakes begin to fall. Soon the snow is so heavy that they can't even see across the street. It becomes very clear that they won't be leaving soon. Then they hear the weather forecast— heavy snow for the next three days! Since they didn't plan on being here for Christmas, Ron and his family didn't even decorate or get a tree! As Ron walks into the family room, he sees his mom getting out the Christmas decorations. "If we're going to be here a few days, let's get into the Christmas spirit," his mom says. How do you think Ron should respond?

Should Ron . . .

    A. Grumble and say, "Nice try, Mom"?
    B. Tell his mom that he lost his Christmas spirit?
    C. Pitch in and start decorating the house, and be thankful that he can be safe and warm in the house with his family?

 Read 1 Thessalonians 5:18 to see what Ron should do. Together with your mom or dad, think of a time when it was hard for your family to be thankful. Talk about one or two ways you could be thankful in that situation.

The correct answer is C.

"'Twas the Night Before . . ."

When no one is looking, Reilly quietly makes his way into the living room. On Christmas Eve the living room is off-limits to the children because Reilly's mom and dad lay out all the presents under the Christmas tree before church. Reilly doesn't plan to open any of the presents. He just wants to look around and see what's there. As he does that, he sees that his younger brother has several more packages than he does. And his older sister, as usual, has the largest present under the tree. Reilly doesn't do an actual count, but it appears from a first look that he has fewer and smaller presents than either his sister or brother. What do you think Reilly should do?

Should Reilly . . .

A. Switch a few name tags to even out the number of gifts for each person?
B. Be thankful for the gifts he will receive?
C. Talk to his parents about being more fair in the future when it comes to gift giving?

 Read Psalm 16:6 and check out the attitude of David toward what was given to him.
Think of a time when a family member received a bigger or better gift than you did. How did you feel about it? What did you do? Pray for a thankful heart this Christmas, and you'll find yourself happy with all your gifts—big and small!

The correct answer is B.

The Real Gift

Christmas morning is finally here! The long weeks of waiting are nearly over. Kristen and her brother run downstairs and race each other to be the first to see the Christmas tree. It is loaded with glittering ornaments, and beneath it are piles of beautifully wrapped presents. Kristen beats her brother by a few steps and gasps in delight! There appear to be a jillion presents underneath the tree this year. She already can see several with her name on them. One box looks about the right size for holding the new basketball she has been asking for. What do you think she should do?

Should Kristen . . .

A. Jump right in and start tearing open those presents?
B. Shout for her mom and dad to hurry up so she and her brother can start opening the gifts?
C. Take a few moments to remember the true gift of Christmas—Jesus, God's own Son?

 Look up 2 Corinthians 9:15 and read it aloud!
With your family, read the Christmas story found in Luke 2:1-20. Name one gift from God that you are thankful for. Then name one gift you plan to give to God. You could sing a song to him to show how thankful you are, or you could help others. When you do things like this, you're giving gifts to God.

The correct answer is C.

Look What I Got!

It's not quite nine o'clock, and the doorbell is already ringing. Emma, who is still in her pajamas, can guess who it is—her neighbor down the street, Adrienne. Almost every year on the day after Christmas, Adrienne is at their door early. She can't wait to tell Emma about every present she got. Sure enough, Adrienne is at the door, and this time she even has a few presents with her. Emma opens the door and is about to say, "Come in," when Adrienne breezes right past her. "Wait until you see this, Emma. This is the coolest laptop computer for kids you ever saw. Wait till you see what it can do." Adrienne proceeds to relate in great detail every gift she received, who gave it to her, and how much it probably cost. Emma has just about had it. What do you think she should do?

Should Emma . . .

   A. Yawn very loudly and say, "Hey, it's time for my nap"?
   B. Listen politely and change the subject as soon as possible?
   C. Start screaming, "I've heard enough already"?

 For help in knowing what Emma should do, read Galatians 5:26.
Do you know someone like Adrienne? Role-play with your mom or dad what you would say to keep your cool and not get upset with that kind of person.

The Big Snow

Last night it snowed about ten inches. Ben and his brother, Reed, can't wait to hit the sled hill. First, though, their mom says they need to go across the street and shovel the driveway and front walk for old Mrs. Walker. The boys put on their snow gear and hurry over there. Maybe they'll each earn a few dollars from Mrs. Walker for shoveling. The boys work hard and get the job done. They are about to leave when Mrs. Walker comes to the door and calls out, "Come on in, boys!" Inside the house Mrs. Walker has two steaming cups of hot chocolate and some homemade cookies waiting for them. She says, "I thought you boys would like something to warm you up after all that hard work." She mentions nothing about money. What do you think Ben and Reed should do?

Should they . . .

    A. Send Mrs. Walker a bill for their work?
    B. Thank Mrs. Walker for the hot chocolate?
    C. Tell each other they will never work for hot chocolate again?

 Read Luke 3:14 to see what John the Baptist had to say about the pay you receive for work you do.
If you don't already have one, talk with your mom or dad about allowances. What do you consider fair? What does your mom or dad think is fair? What chores are expected of you in exchange for an allowance? How can you show thankfulness for the pay you get?

The correct answer is B.

You Promised!

Quinn's mom has promised to take him downtown to see the new dinosaur exhibit with computerized, life-size dinosaurs. Tomorrow is the day. His mom lines up a baby-sitter for his baby sister. The day does not start well, however. First the baby-sitter calls and says she has the flu. Quinn's mom says they'll take the baby with them. When they get there, Quinn's mom has to feed her right away. Then, because the exhibit area is dark and crowded, Quinn's sister starts to howl. Finally his mom says, "Let's go home and try again when I can get a baby-sitter." They leave the exhibit without ever seeing the computerized dinosaurs. Later that night Quinn's mother comes into his room and says, "I'm really sorry about today, Quinn." What do you think he should say?

Should Quinn . . .

A. Thank his mom for trying?
B. Not say anything and let his mom feel bad because he still does?
C. Complain about his baby sister, who messes up everything?

 For help in knowing what Quinn should do, read Philippians 4:4-5.
With your mom or dad helping you, see how many times you can find the word *joy* in Philippians. Share what you think is the secret to being joyful when things don't go as planned. Does it have something to do with thankfulness?

The correct answer is A.

The Soda-Pop Machine

Gavin and his brother, Clint, are hanging out at the rec center this afternoon. They've been playing a friendly but hard game of floor hockey. The boys have to go home in about ten minutes, so they stop to turn in their floor hockey sticks. Both boys are hot and really thirsty. They don't have any money for the soda machine, and the water fountain is broken. Gavin sits down to wait for his mother when his brother comes up smiling broadly, holding a soda can. "Where did you get that?" Gavin asks. Clint explains that there is a boy standing by the soda machine who knows exactly where to hit it to get a free soda. What do you think Gavin should do?

Should Gavin . . .

    A. Get in line so he can get a free soda too?
    B. Tell the rec center manager that the soda machine is broken?
    C. Tell everyone that there are free sodas, compliments of the rec center?

Check out Psalm 37:16 to see what Gavin should do. Have you ever been tempted to cheat a little to get something because you saw someone else do it? What does God have to say about that? Can you be thankful even when you don't have very much?

The correct answer is B.

The Right Kind of Friend?

Zandrah's next-door neighbor Dominique is in the same grade, but Zandrah does not really count her as one of her friends. Dominique is bossy, and she gets mad when things don't go her way. Zandrah doesn't enjoy being with Dominique, but lately Dominique has been coming over and wanting to play with Zandrah. Zandrah thinks it's because she's the only person in her class who is halfway nice to Dominique. Zandrah isn't sure what she should do. She knows from her Sunday school lessons that she ought to be nice to Dominique. But she can't believe that God would want her to be friends with this type of person. What do you think Zandrah should do?

Should Zandrah . . .

    A. Continue to be polite whenever Dominique is around but not go out of her way to be friendly?
    B. Ask God to help her be a good example for Dominique?
    C. Tell Dominique to go away?

 Read 1 Corinthians 7:17 to see how Zandrah should approach this situation.
Ask your mom or dad to tell about a time when they had to learn to accept whatever situation the Lord had put them in. Pray for God's help to show you how to handle every *Sticky Situation* you will face in the year ahead.

Review Time!

This is a good time, before a new year begins, to remember how God has blessed you and your family this year. List three things that you are especially thankful for.

1.

2.

3.

Bonus

Write a thank-you note to God for these things.

Repeat your memory verse to someone who is wearing red.

January
John 13:34

February
Matthew 6:19-21

March
Luke 16:10

April
James 3:5-6

May
1 John 2:5-6

June
Matthew 20:26-27

July
Ephesians 5:1-2

August
Ephesians 4:32

September
Colossians 3:23

October
Proverbs 1:7

November
Philippians 3:13-14

December
1 Thessalonians 5:18

Index of Monthly Memory Verses

Old Testament

Betsy Schmitt lives with her husband, Don, and their three children, Allison, Dana, and Kevin, in Naperville, Illinois. The family recently added a dog, Nikki, to their ranks. She has presented all sorts of new sticky situations!

Over the years, Betsy has been involved with children in a number of different ways—as a Scout leader, classroom volunteer, book discussion leader, Sunday school teacher, and recently as assistant director for Children's Ministries at her church in Naperville. All of these experiences, combined with a great deal of input from her own children, have helped Betsy write first *Sticky Situations*, and now *Sticky Situations 2*.

Currently Betsy is Project Editor for Youth and Children's Products at Livingstone Corporation in Carol Stream, Illinois. A graduate of Northwestern University in Evanston, Illinois, Betsy has worked on many children's activity books, devotionals, CD-ROMs, and kids' Bibles for a variety of Christian publishers.

About the Author